AF855458

EMPATH

A PRACTICAL GUIDE FOR SENSITIVE PEOPLE TO OVERCOME ANXIETY, HEAL AFTER A RELATIONSHIP WITH A NARCISSIST, DEVELOP THEIR EMOTIONAL INTELLIGENCE AND SENSE OF SELF, AND CONTROL THEIR EMOTIONS.

JUDITH HEAL

THIS BOOK INCLUDES

© Copyright 2020 - All rights reserved.

The content contained within this book may not be reproduced, duplicated or transmitted without direct written permission from the author or the publisher.

Under no circumstances will any blame or legal responsibility be held against the publisher, or author, for any damages, reparation, or monetary loss due to the information contained within this book. Either directly or indirectly.

Legal Notice: This book is copyright protected. This book is only for personal use. You cannot amend, distribute, sell, use, quote or paraphrase any part, or the content within this book, without the consent of the author or publisher.

Disclaimer Notice: Please note the information contained within this document is for educational and entertainment purposes only. All effort has been executed to present accurate, up to date, and reliable, complete information. No warranties of any kind are declared or implied. Readers acknowledge that the author is not engaging in the rendering of legal, financial, medical or professional advice. The content within this book has been derived from various sources. Please consult a licensed professional before attempting any techniques outlined in this book.

By reading this document, the reader agrees that under no circumstances is the author responsible for any losses, direct or indirect, which are incurred as a result of the use of information contained within this document, including, but not limited to, — errors, omissions, or inaccuracies.

EMPATH HEALING:

A GUIDE TO CONTROL YOUR EMOTIONS, GETTING RID OF FEAR AND ANXIETY AND RELEASE NEGATIVE ENERGY.

JUDITH HEAL

Table Of Contents

Introduction

Without empathy, people would go about their lives without considering the feelings and thoughts of other people. Every person has differing perspectives on life; therefore, if we did not have something that made us accommodate each other, life would be very complicated. We all experience moods, joy, sadness, pain hurt et cetera, and if we focus only on the things happening in our lives, we will limit our capabilities. It is easy to jump into conclusions if we do not take a moment to truly understand what the other people stand for. Lack of empathy normally leads to bad feelings, misunderstandings, poor morale, conflict, and even divorce.

When one uses empathy in real life to understand why a person is angry, or a child is throwing a tantrum, he/she might learn about things in their lives that trigger the behavior. For example, one might find that something happened at home, thus pushing the angry person to act out or that the child did not have a meal in the morning thus they are not okay.

Empathy enables one to ask questions about the situation or behavior of another person before taking a defensive stance or reacting to some emotions. There may still be the need for disciplinary action, but one should use empathy first. Empathy makes a person feel valued and understood even if they are punished for the wrong deeds, and as such, they will accept responsibility for their action. Empathy is currently the missing link in schools, families, workplaces, and the world at large.

There are a few misunderstandings that arise when one is applying empathy in real life. Some people believe that being empathetic involves agreeing with the opinion of everybody else. That is wrong and will only lead to exhaustion. Understand the perceptions of the other person, acknowledge them but you do not have to sing along every tune.

Other people believe that being empathetic involves doing what everyone else wants or doing anything to make others happy. That is wrong. You are not obligated to please everyone; you do not have to cooperate in every other situation. Just because you fail to accommodate every other matter does not mean that you are evil. The world is complicated; therefore, use empathy but do not agree with everything.

Empathy does not mean being there for someone for a lifetime. After listening to a person and offering a solution, you do not have to always be there for them, you have other tasks to accomplish and if you feel that the person is just using you, walk away. Empathy does not mean you should have no ego or intention. Once you assist someone, allow your ego to help you walk away or change the discussion.

Applying empathy in real life can be challenging therefore, there are investments that one needs to make, and they include time, patience and proactivity.

1. Time

It takes some time for one to listen to others, pay attention and not jump into conclusions. Coming up with good solutions also takes time. In most cases, we want to arrive at an answer very first without taking the time to understand; this only leads to more problems. Empathy is like watching sand draining in an hourglass; it takes time, but not that much time, and it is very satisfying.

2. Patience

Empathy does not only take time; it requires a lot of patience. Paying attention to someone, listening to everything they are saying, and selecting a comprehensive solution takes a lot more than just jumping into conclusions, listing arguments and repeating an opinion. Normally people fail to give the patience and attention required when making conversations; therefore, it becomes harder than it should be.

3. It takes proactivity

Some people think that empathy should only be given when both parties have something to gain. In the real sense, we should show empathy even to people who show no sign of understanding our perspectives and opinions. This can be very frustrating, and one might find it very unfair, but empathy begins with you. It will not work if both of you wait on each other to start the conversation.

4. Be the role model, set the example, be a good listener and do not talk until the other person is done. Understand the opinions of other people but remember you do not have to agree with them. Being empathetic can be a tough challenge but still, there are many people that practice it. Apply empathy every day and enjoy the benefits.

Of all of the talents an Empath possesses, listening may be one of the most notable. Listening skills are effective in any situation and are what help us to engage more fully with the world around us. When you can hear what is going on, you can participate more closely and provide a keener sense of understanding. You can also hear things on another level- things that are unspoken but nevertheless still communicating to us through body language, gestures, facial expressions, and energy.

For the Empath, listening comes naturally and so does absorbing energy from the person you are talking to. This can mean that you end up taking on a lot of negativity, anger, frustration, and other uncomfortable emotions. As you start to feel the effects of these feelings, it can make it harder to listen well and comfortably. The ability to listen can get upset by the emotional energy of the people around you and can distort your emotional state as well.

Finding your tactics for listening from the heart can be helpful, and with a little practice, you can learn how to compliment being a heartfelt listener while still protecting and shielding your energy from being disrupted from the negativity involved. As an Empath myself, I have tried a variety of techniques and models to help me find the best approach to being a better empathic listener without feeling drained by other people's emotions.

You can use one or all of these methods to help you better explore the best ways to provide you with grounding and centeredness while taking in, and not taking on, the feelings of the people in your life. As you read, try to keep in mind that some of these techniques will work better in some situations than in others. Use your intuition and your best judgment to decide.

CHAPTER 1:

What Is Empathy?

What is Empathy?

Empathy is a word rooted in Greek. Broken down, you have two components: "em- "meaning "in," and "pathos," meaning feeling. Effectively, then, empathy is "in feeling" and that makes a lot of sense when you think about it. Empathy is the feeling that you get for other people. It is the absorption or understanding of someone else's emotions, or in some cases, both the absorption and understanding.

Empathy itself, if you were to break it down to the bare minimum, is the awareness of the emotions of other people. It is being able to feel what other people are feeling, what they need, and what concerns them. When you look at someone else and are able to identify what is going on with them on an intimate level, recognizing that they have thoughts and feelings of their own and becoming well-acquainted with those thoughts and feelings, you are likely to be empathizing with them.

Typically, the empathy that you feel is entirely automatic—while you can, to some degree, cognitively empathize with someone else at will, the sort of emotional, compassionate empathy that we are talking about right now is usually immediate or instinctive. It happens whether you want it to or not, and this is exactly why that sort of assumption that, as an empath, you can simply stop feeling what you are feeling is false. Empathy is not something that can be turned off.

Empathy is believed to be the work of mirror neurons—neurons within your brain that are meant to trigger an understanding of what is happening with someone else. These effectively allow you to read and display emotional body language as you interact with the world around you. These mirror neurons activate, for example, when you are having an interaction with someone else.

It is believed that in empaths, these mirror neurons respond stronger than they would in someone else. Instead of being able to read someone else's body language, then they become entirely absorbed in it. The empath takes on the emotional states that someone would usually only read and feels them much more intensely. Empaths, then, usually experience empathy much more thoroughly than those around them. It is their ability to feel the emotions of someone else without really understanding why. It is effectively walking in someone else's shoes, so to speak. It is being innately aware of how someone feels and what they need—usually, because you are feeling it yourself.

Empathy, then, acts as a sort of method in which you can communicate with others. When you understand how someone else is feeling, it can greatly change how you interact with them. For example, imagine that you are talking to your child. Your child did something that probably should not have been done—perhaps he was not following rules and, in the process, broke something that was precious to you. You immediately get angry—as anyone would. Your prized item, perhaps something left behind by your late mother, has been ruined and there is no getting it back. You begin to yell, but immediately see that look on your child's face. You see that he is guilty, sad, and scared, and then it clicks for you—you begin to feel that same guilt in the pit of your stomach with the grief of losing the item. You realize that if someone several times larger than you were yelling at you, you would be scared, and it would be worse if that person were your parent, who you loved dearly. That realization starts to slow you down. It stops you from yelling and you are able to apologize because you recognize how you were impacting your child.

This is what empathy does—it allows you to communicate better. You were able to self-regulate because you recognized those feelings in your child. When you can self-regulate, you better relationships.

The only problem, however, is that empaths typically are empathetic in situations where others would not be. Sometimes, empathy is quite beneficial. Other times, however, it can be harmful. It is harmful to empathize with someone who is furious if you do not know how to distance yourself from this to some degree- you need to be able to stop and tell yourself that you are unwilling or unable to allow that anger to rule you.

Forms of Empathy

Empathy is typically thought of in three specific forms. It can be cognitive empathy, emotional empathy, or compassionate empathy. For most empaths, they live in a constant state of compassionate empathy. They constantly feel that they need to empathize with other people all around them and cannot help that they do. Within this part, we will look at all three forms and the purposes that they serve.

Cognitive Empathy

Cognitive empathy is the ability to know how someone else is feeling. You may also know how someone is thinking as well. It is usually described as perspective-taking—it is the ability to recognize and check in with others to really be confident that you do understand someone else. It is all about thought, and that is not a bad thing.

Think about looking at someone and thinking, "Oh, he looks sad," but not actually feeling anything about it. You may not feel sad yourself or feel motivated to do anything at all. You simply acknowledge that he looks sad and move on with your day. This is cognitively empathizing with someone else. Generally speaking, this form of empathy is great in situations where emotions themselves can be clouding for the mind. For example, you would not want your doctor to be swayed by your fear if your doctor is going to be operating on your heart—you want your doctor to focus on the operation. Your doctor being aware of that fear, cognitively empathizing, allows him to understand that you are afraid and therefore make sure that he behaves in a way that will be soothing or reassuring for you. The best doctors are experts at this.

Emotional Empathy

Emotional empathy is a bit different. It is the sensation of physically feeling someone else's emotions as if they were your own, or as if they were contagious. This is the feeling that you have when you see someone that is grieving after the loss of a loved one, and you feel sadness as well. This is common in the empaths in particular—it is that absorption of the emotions of everyone around you, whether you want them or not.

This is particularly important within relationships—it can allow you to understand those that you are close to properly, and that can help relationships. It can help you, and the other person feel closer to each other, particularly because you are sharing the same feelings. This is the way that you bond with other people—it is showing the deep connection and that sort of emotional intimacy can be great when you need to strengthen a relationship.

Compassionate Empathy

Finally, compassionate empathy exists somewhere between the two. It requires skills from both cognitive empathy and emotional empathy to work properly. You must be aware of the other person's needs, understanding the situation that they are in, and what they are feeling. That understanding and awareness of someone else is then related to emotionally. You feel what someone else is feeling as well, recognizing that you are doing this. This then becomes motivational—you try to help if you can if it is needed. You try to ensure that you can meet the needs of others.

This is what you should strive for. As an empath, this is the best form of empathy that you can have. This is recognizing the emotions belong to someone else while also being able to feel them. That understanding of what someone else is feeling means that you are spurred to help. It means that you are motivated to be a problem solver and ensure that other people have their needs met on a regular basis. By making sure that you are aware of the emotions of the other party, you ensure that you are able to avoid losing yourself in their emotions. Think about it this way—if the biggest problem with empathy is that you risk being unable to identify that the feelings that you have are not your own, but rather are your empathetic response to those around you, then being able to be cognitively aware of the emotions of someone else could help mitigate this.

Empathy and the Empath

Despite the similarities in names, empath and empathy are not the exact same. Just because you empathize with someone else does not mean that you are an empath. Think of the idea that a square is a rectangle, but a rectangle is not a square—this is the kind of relationship the two have. You can have empathy without being an empath, but you cannot be an empath without empathy.

Empaths take empathy further—instead of just recognizing the emotions of someone else, they live them. The empath always takes it further. They are able to pick up on feelings that are not spoken. They are able to feel the energy of the room, so to speak. They can tell when those around them. Those feelings and that energy in other people become the energy of the empath. It is not just feeling excited for your friend because your friend just announced major news—it is literally feeling your friend's excitement as if it were your own.

Practical Test:

1. What is Empathy?

2.What are the forms of Empathy?

3. What is believed to be the work of mirror neurons?

CHAPTER 2:

Practical Exercises to Protect Against Empathy

The most important thing we can do in our lives as human beings is to connect with other people. Strange how this looks so normal for children, while many adults still fail to understand it. Empathy goes far beyond the simple decision to be nice and kind to people. It means volunteering to "put yourself in the shoes" of another person, especially when this is the last place you would like to be. Only when we try to indirectly enter another person's reality are, we able to understand it at a much deeper level.

Renowned human relations researcher Brene Brown says:

There are no instructions for empathy. There is no right and wrong way to do it. You just have to listen, to fill the space, without judgment. Connecting emotionally with the other person and communicating the incredibly healing message: “You're not alone!” That's why empathy is such a difficult and important thing. It is a skill and a choice to be connected. Even if it's difficult. And truly, empathy is the best thing the human race has to offer.

So how can we teach our children empathy?

First, be the example. Trying to see the world through the eyes of your child, your partner, even through the eyes of your dog, is the best way to teach your child to do so. Kids find it easier to follow habits than you say.

Accept all emotion.

We tend to praise the positive and to ignore and downplay the negative emotions. Because it makes us feel better as parents, when the child is in a good mood, then we do our job well. It's easy to be happy and share feelings when our child is in a good mood. Accordingly, we accept poorly the negative emotional manifestations of the few. This is wrong. We need to show children that these emotions are normal and teach them how to overcome them. You can always say something very simple and easy to show your child that you see his or her pain: "I'm very sorry you're sad" or "I know it's annoying to wait." Otherwise, the child will do anything to be heard and seen, and to recognize his or her right to feel bad sometimes.

Talk about other people with understanding.

When you talk to a third person in a conversation and the child is around, the likelihood of hearing words of disapproval and condemnation is very high. Naturally, it teaches them instantly. Consequence will treat people in their environment that way. The first thing to look out for if you want your child to build the ability to empathize is how you perceive yourself and your human behavior—with acceptance and understanding, or with rejection and condemnation. And the easiest way to train your child's empathy is by asking him or her questions related to other people's feelings and asking him or her to put them in their place: "How do you think Maria felt when she fell?" "Why do you think that Nicky cries?" "What can improve your mood when you're sad?"

Talk about feeling, hypothetically.

Talk to your child about the existence of people who live in different cultures, with different values and traditions. The world of the child is limited to what he or she knows immediately. Show your child that there are many different socio-cultural options in the world. This will broaden the outlook, the understanding that people are different, and develop the ability to accept the "other." Introduce the child to the serious problems in the world and reduce them to simple concepts. "How would I feel if I didn't have a home" or "How can we help people who don't have enough food?" Encourage your child to think locally as well as globally.

Help your child recognize emotions.

Emotions such as shame, frustration, and jealousy are scary when we are unable to identify them. Imagine how awful it is to have such feelings without even knowing what to call them, let alone what they are due to. By calling them by their names and explaining their origins and meanings, it will be much easier for your child to confront them.

Apologize when you are wrong.

Show them that this is completely human. By seeing your weaknesses, children will learn that imperfection is universal. Parents have the same rights to experience emotions, whether negative or positive, just like children. Learn to control them and deal with them in the best possible way, then teach your children the same. Teach them to act with humility and to understand that parents are human beings, too.

Don’t ignore others’ feelings

We often see manifestations of child anger, sadness, or disappointment as small and insignificant. Sometimes they even look pretty stupid to us. We tell them, "Well, if I were your age, I'd have your problems." Don't dismiss your child's feelings just because he or she is small because they are completely correlated with the child’s size and development. This will teach children to never diminish the feelings of others.

Practical Test:

1.How to accept all emotions?

2. Will you apologize when you’re wrong?

3. How to Understand people?

CHAPTER 3:

How to Manage Empathic Sensibility

You can't change the way that you are an empath. This is the means by which you are made at soul level and you can't change this otherworldly blessing. A few people talk about turning on and off being and empath, this is somewhat deceptive in light of the fact that it is beyond the realm of imagination to expect to kill this capacity on and freely. What you can do is turned out to be mindful. Being an empath is the sort of person you are, and you are here to figure out how to utilize your empathic blessing as an amazing asset for sign and self-change.

How about we plunge into my most helpful otherworldly clearing methods that I use myself as an empath and that I prescribe to my customers:

1. Cutting the Cords

This is a significant undertaking that empaths need to turn out to be dexterous at. Since you are so great at connections and individuals cherish you, they likewise remove your vitality from you on the grounds that your vitality feels so great, recuperating and adoring. This happens in light of the fact that you permitted it without knowing.

At various times associations or etheric ropes with relatives, companions, and sweethearts can in any case be available even after the relationship is finished. It's a great opportunity to cut the strings!

To cut lines, just think about the individual with which you have had a relationship and imagine the string being cut. Favor the individual and state the accompanying: "I presently discharge you in affection and light"

There are further developed systems on the best way to cut ropes, however this basic technique is as compelling. My conclusion is that the more we need to confound things, the more things get convoluted. It's up to you! My recommendation is to make it straightforward and make it simple. Be that as it may, do it and do it as frequently as you feel the need.

For instance, before nodding off every night, ask yourself: "Do I have any connections or lines with anybody that I met today?" If you discover something, discharge it and favor it.

Return a couple of days after the fact to ensure that the rope has been discharged. In the event that you don't know or feel that the string is still there, get proficient assistance. I regularly discover ropes associated with one of the chakras or appended to the vitality field.

2. Clearing Your Aura from Negative Thought-Forms

Your psychological body is always communicating with the psychological assortment of others, so you get adverse musings from other individuals.

You likewise make your own considerations and huge numbers of them may not be in arrangement with your most noteworthy great. Know about the accompanying kind of considerations:

•Negative

•Redundant

•Repetitive

•Automatic

On the off chance that you need to find out about your reasoning examples convey a journal with you and record every one of the musings that you have inside a 24-hour time span. You will be shocked on the fact that it is so difficult to monitor your musings!

At the point when your musings are certain you adjust to positive vibrations and you make recuperating, equalization and concordance. When they are negative, they make obstruction and blockages.

Negative idea structures can be sustained for a considerable length of time, particularly when associated with a horrendous encounter.

These negative idea structures are made by negative understanding and desires. The more vitality you give them, the more vitality they obtain and the more grounded their impact on your condition of equalization.

They can be founded on supposition and desires for other individuals. In any case, they can stall out in your brain and happen again and again undetected, until you begin to focus and effectively choose to watch your idea patters.

Contemplations who are made out of dread, sadness, dread, fault and outrage they stay appended to your vitality field and cause you to vibrate increasingly more in arrangement with these sorts of energies. After some time, they cause you to draw in these very encounters throughout your life.

These idea structures vibrate inside you so that they catalyze a fell response at all the degrees of your vitality bodies: profound, mental, enthusiastic and physical. They cause you to pull in individuals, circumstances and experience that are in vibrational arrangement with them. It resembles a greeting for low energies to connect to your vitality field.

To clear this example, take a gander at your life and check whether you are pulling in circumstances you don't care for. On the off chance that you do, you are by one way or another vibrating in arrangement with them without your cognizant mindfulness.

Your undertaking is to check in with your vitality field a few times during the day, particularly in the event that you feel worn out and discouraged, to check whether you have get or made any negative idea structure and intentionally let it go.

3. Adjusting Your Chakras

Chakra adjusting for empaths is an absolute necessity and it's a day by day practice. Two times per day, morning and night times, you have to take a couple of minutes to wash down your chakras.

4. Make A Sacred Space

This is so significant for everybody, except particularly on the off chance that you are an empath. A consecrated space can be any area in your home where you can be independent from anyone else and see a spot as completely self-communicated.

This could be your craft room, your contemplation room or just your office. This spot must be yours and yours alone. Try not to impart this space to other people (indeed, you children and pets can come in and out!). It doesn't need to be inside; it very well may be outside.

Be inventive with this, however, locate an uncommon spot for you to go at any rate once every day. On the off chance that it is outlandish for you to make a genuine space, make one up in your psyche and go there. You will be astounded what you can make in your psyche.

A few people wind up in the wide open, others along the coastline, a desert island, a recuperating sanctuary; others see themselves on different planets, out in space, or a spaceship made totally of light vitality.

5. Smearing Yourself and Your Environment

I cherish this part and it is an absolute necessity, particularly when you feel down, pitiful, or restless. Smearing your vitality field and the earth truly transmutes negative energies from your vitality field.

Do this regularly, particularly on the off chance that you have been in circumstances that made you feel out of synchrony with your passionate, mental and physical body. Utilize white sage. Additionally, remember to smirch your home normally to keep the vitality of your living space crisp and clean.

6. Interface with Nature

For anyone who feels overpowered by passionate pressure and mental anguish, nature gives the best type of vitality recuperating accessible. It is my conviction that empaths are here right now to help the vigorous frequencies important to clean the planet.

Most negative considerations and negative feelings are conveyed by people. In this way, on the off chance that you are an empath proceed to invest energy in nature alone in any event once every day to energize, you will enable nature to purge you. Contacting a tree can enable you to ground and wipe out undesirable energies from your body.

Associating with creatures, blossoms, floods of water and normal scenes is the most relieving vitality recuperating treatment you can get. What's more, it's free!

7. Utilize Protective Stones

I don't accept that we should be always worried about security since I accept that we are the main expert in our life. Accepting that we need steady assurance can draw in the negative contemplations of debilitation, dread and victimhood.

So as to ensure your vitality field, you should know about your vitality.

I do accept that empaths need to discover approaches to keep themselves grounded and purified constantly. This is, as I would like to think, the best type of insurance.

After the Heart-Wall clearing, it's essential to put a shield of insurance around the hear so as to keep the heart totally protected and ensured structure negative energies and consistently in arrangement with positive energies. When you have cleared your Heart-Wall and put a shield of insurance, you should simply enact your shield.

When I work with individuals, I instruct essentially vitality methods that they can use to ensure their auric field, yet I don't advance the requirement for insurance as much as the requirement for vitality mindfulness.

When we are intentionally mindful of our vitality, we can't fall casualties of others except if we permit it. Your energies should be always moving in doing what we are here to do as empaths: process, transmute and intensify vitality. In the event that you are not doing this throughout the day, you will feel dormant vitality. Frequently time this is the motivation behind why you fallback into the negative part of your blessing and feel the requirement for insurance.

In this way, working with gems and stone encourages you remain focused and mindful of what's happening in your life. This isn't anything but difficult to do when you are out there in reality making your background. Be that as it may, you need not to free core interest. Be over your vitality!

8. Use Journaling, Art and Drawing

Empaths will in general be extremely imaginative and love communicating their own ability when they feel incredible. When they don't feel extraordinary, they will in general oppose their imaginative capacities since craftsmanship necessitates that they work with their sentiments and this can regularly cause torment.

I welcome you to think about utilizing workmanship as a type of recuperating and enthusiastic discharge to help you when you feel stuck and out of equalization.

9. Cry as A Form of Emotional Release

Empaths have a very refined enthusiastic body and they have to cry when they want to do as such. Crying has such a large number of mending benefits. The vibration of crying fills in as purging system for your emanation. Kids do this constantly.

Doing Yoga, Tai Chi or different types of vitality development can be exceptionally valuable to help discharge pressure, let go undesirable negative energies, purge the emanation and realign the body and chakra framework.

Likewise, doing vitality work is the most ideal approach to keep your air washed down and in congruity with your spirit's way.

10. Ocean Salt Baths

Ocean salt has stunning purifying capacities. Ocean salt coaxes vitality out. Having a hot shower containing ocean salt when you feel vigorously overpowered can truly have a tremendous effect in the manner you feel. You can utilize ordinary ocean salt, Himalayan salt, Epsom salt, or other.

You can likewise include a couple of drops of fundamental oil to the water. On the off chance that you have sensitivities, make a point to test them first. The best basic oils to use for purifying the emanation are rosemary, citronella, and eucalyptus.

Practical Test:

1. Is Cutting the chords significant?

2. How to Utilize a Positive stone?

3. Is an absolute necessity and it's a day by day practice. What is it?

CHAPTER 4:

How Not to Absorb the Negative Energies of Others

Empaths and intuitive are like sponges in water. A sponge can't help but absorb what it's put into. If it's dropped into clear, clean water, it can be used to make the environment around it clean as well. If it's dipped into water that has bacteria like salmonella, however, it is no longer useful, but dangerous until it's been fully sterilized.

Even though it's impossible to guard against being in any negative situation ever, there are steps we can take to filter out negative energies trying to drain us.

Chances are, you've experienced a toxic relationship in which you're required to interact with that person. These can be extremely stressful, especially if they're work or family relationships. A mother separated from an emotionally abusive husband is court-ordered to work out custody arrangements on a regular basis. A law associate not only has the stress of his job, but he has to deal with a boss who can never be satisfied and constantly threatens him with his job. Both the mother and the associate can build up their resistance against the negativity and thrive. It just takes intention and patience with themselves.

Visualization

This sounds a bit "out there," but if practiced before stepping into a potentially negative environment, it can serve you in fantastic ways. Take time when you're alone to sit or stand quietly and envision a protective sphere around your whole body. Imagine anything that's bothering you as particles floating around in your safe space, then imagine them moving out of it. Once your safe space is clear, focus on your breathing: six seconds to inhale, six seconds to exhale. Do this for a minute several times a day. Your own energy will begin to shield you from negative external influences. When you've got this weapon in your arsenal, you can take it and use it anywhere.

Tokens

A token is a physical object that you can keep on your person and touch to help you remember to be present in your body and maintain your energy. In the film Inception, Leonardo DiCaprio's character Cobb keeps a top that he would spin to determine if he was awake or still dreaming. Other tokens, or totems as they are called in the film, were a weighted red die, and a golden bishop chess piece that is hollowed out to feel different than others. A token for an empath could be a rosary, a scarf, a foreign coin, a crystal, or a piece of jewelry.

Move Something

If you are assaulted by negative energy in a certain place, say your office at work, it can help to rearrange things drastically. If you usually reach up to your left to get a piece of tape, put the tape dispenser on top of the cabinet to your right. If small items are cluttering the top of your desk, get an attractive container to corral those things and put the container somewhere new. The act of reaching in a different way should act as a prompt for you to remember that your office isn't what's different, but your mind is. Use it as a reminder that you are making new, better decisions for yourself.

Declutter

Because empaths tend to spend a lot of time in their own heads, clutter tends to take over their workspaces. Take time to declutter those places. At home, the kitchen counter and sink may fill up with dirty dishes and foodstuffs. Your bedroom may not collect dirty laundry, but it may collect clean, unfolded clothing just the same. Taking the time to find homes for all of your belongings and creating clean surfaces will go a long way for your ability to deal with intangible problems.

Tap into Marie Kondo's wisdom and lovingly let go of things you don't have active use for or don't spark joy. For many empaths, hanging on too tightly to clothes and objects is intertwined with guilt. We feel ungrateful for giving away unwanted gifts. We feel selfish if we don't like a perfectly good sweater. We feel foolish for having bought something that broke too soon, and not either getting it replaced or fixed quickly enough. The best way to free up that emotional space is to take the time to downsize.

Recognize Threats

If a person walks into a convenience store brandishing a gun, they don't have to issue threats for the store's customers and employees to recognize a threat. People without special training to handle this sort of situation are likely to freeze up and want to get as far away from the threat as possible.

If a man is walking through the forest in the deep South and happens across a large snake in his path, he won't just continue walking. He will pause and assess the situation. What kind of snake is it? What are his routes of escape? Is there a better way to continue to his destination? He may weigh his odds and consider stepping over it. He may recognize it to be a non-venomous breed and feel comfortable either moving it or crossing over it.

The difficulty with most threats in an empath's daily life is that they're not easily identified. When it comes to toxic people, here are some things to look out for:

- After most encounters with the person, you feel drained of life.
- You experience signs of stress when their name is mentioned.

□ When in a public place like a restaurant, you feel the need to check the door every time someone new comes in to be sure it isn't that particular person.

□ You realize you're giving more than you're being given. Such a dynamic is not unhealthy if it's a parent caring for a child or an aging adult, but not in a friendship or romantic partner.

□ You feel like you're walking through a field of land mines: you never know what's going to set the person off.

□ When you have begun drawing away from mutual friends because you worry that they may report back to your toxic acquaintance.

□ You often feel like you're being set up to fail with them.

□ They employ triangulation, which is a tactic to keep you from someone else you enjoy being around. This can include the abuser telling lies to each party, so they think the other is the abuser.

□ Gaslighting becomes common. They take your history with them and change facts, usually so well that you think there's something wrong with your own mind and memory.

□ You feel as though you're literally bruised after an encounter with them, even if they didn't lay a finger on you.

□ If they show no interest whatsoever in what's going on in your life.

□ If you ask for help and they repeatedly drop the ball.

□ They shift blame to you when you address an inappropriate behavior or action.

□ Every encounter brings a new criticism, even if it's played off as "constructive criticism."

□ If you make progress on a project or toward a goal, such as weight loss, they don't congratulate you but instead undermine you. "If you just cut out sugar, it would come off faster." Or, "You can't expect to lose all that weight if you're not working out."

□ If they're the victim or hero of every story they tell.

□ They feel the need to be the center of attention when around other people. As the adage goes, "The bride at every wedding and the corpse at every funeral," as they say.

□ If, when the attention or positive talk turns to anyone else, they seem to sour.

□ Last minute change of plans with no good reason at a clear inconvenience to you. For example, they ask you to pick them up at the airport an hour away. You agree and when the day comes, are there with a few minutes to spare. You wait a while, sending a few texts to let them know you're there and where you're waiting, with no responses from them. You check their flight and see it landed twenty minutes ago. Finally, you call them. They answer and when you tell them you're there, they laugh. "Oh, I decided to have my sister come and get me. I thought you'd talk to her."

□ They move goalposts: that is, they'll tell you they need one thing from you but once you give them that, they want something completely different and you never seem able to appease them.

□ You become the joke at social events, as they love to tell stories about your failures without your consent.

□ You go out of your way to look a certain way in hopes of avoiding a comment about your appearance.

□ You catch them in small – or large! – lies on a regular basis.

□ Your friends seem to pull away with you less now that you're associating with a certain person. Sometimes the people who love you see things you can't, even though you're an empath.

□ You are afraid to miss any messages from them because you know you'll get an earful about how you're difficult.

□ They can't keep a job for long. Their story about each employer focuses on everyone else's failing and it's never their fault.

□ Everything must be on their terms and in their timing. If you ask them to call you at noon, they'll call earlier or significantly later. If you tell them you'll call at noon, they won't answer. If you say you'll help them with their project on Tuesday morning and not Tuesday afternoon, they get short with you and likely make a passive-aggressive comment about how it must not be important to you, so never mind.

Practical Test:

1. What is declutter?

2. How to Recognize Threats?

3. Is Token a good thing?

CHAPTER 5:

Meditation Practices

It is difficult for a non-empath to grasp the concept of feeling people's emotions. Imagine feeling happy, sad, anxious and fearful all at the same time. And these are just some of the emotions that could be going on through an empath at any given time.

Meditation is recommended for anyone but highly recommended for empaths. Your ability to absorb foreign emotions and energies make you susceptible to anxiety and stress, which make your life difficult.

Meditation seeks to quieten the mind for a moment and give it a break from the dozen competing emotions seeking to occupy it. Empathy is a gift that can make things easier at the workplace, but it can also make things difficult. If you cannot control the dozens of emotions, you are dealing with, you will be overwhelmed, and your work performance will suffer. That moment of silence and calm clears your mind, so you can go through your day without being overcome by emotions. These are just some of the many ways in which meditation will enhance your day:

1. Improve concentration

You achieve more when you focus on one task at a time as opposed to multitasking. Sounds like an irony, right? Shouldn't attending multiple tasks at a time get more work done? In making this assumption, we assume that the brain can focus on multiple things at a time. However, research shows that the brain cannot multitask. It only rapidly switches back and forth between the tasks, losing details in the process.

Our affinity for multitasking can be seen on the way we work on the computer. How many tabs do you open at a time? Some have as many as 10 tabs, sometimes even more. You are answering emails, working on a report, downloading a song, watching a sport rerun, listening to a podcast and so on; all at once. Or rather switching rapidly from one to the other. Try to open one tab at a time. You can only open another one if the content is directly related to the first one. For instance, you may open an email that has data that you need for your report. Basically, attend to one task at a time. After the report is done, you can then proceed to answer emails. Tick as you go along. Check out how much you manage to get done by the end of the day, compared to when multitasking. The difference is clear; single tasking achieves more.

Enhance working relationships

Meditation makes you a happier, more positive person, and this reflects in your relationship with others. At the workplace, positive interactions with colleagues lead to higher productivity. In companies where employees participate in meditation training, the teamwork improves significantly.

The manner in which colleagues relate to each other plays a significant part in the efficiency of the entire company. Work issues aside, think of each of those workers as a separate individual, with their personal issues ranging from family, relationships, finances, health and so on. They come to work on the backdrop of these issues. Add to these the dynamics of the job. You have a lot that is potentially fatigued and stressed.

With such emotions, the relationships suffer. Arguments, disagreements, and frustrations will be common. Eventually, you have a batch of disgruntled workers and declining productivity. Here, meditation comes in handy both at an individual and institutional level. When people meditate, they are calmer and more grounded. They respond to the issues of their lives more positively. At work, they interact well with their colleagues and form a strong, efficient team, boosting productivity.

3. Reduce stress

Stress originates from your body's reaction to threats and demands. The danger here may be real or imagined. Your mind goes into overdrive; the common 'fight or flight' response. Meditation may not affect the issues causing you stress, but it will change your reaction towards them.

Meditation helps you achieve moments of total peace and relaxation. Some will describe it as that moment when you think about nothing. Your mind is blank, and pleasantly so. You actually deflect all thoughts so that your mind is quiet for a moment.

Whether your stress is coming from work-related issues or from personal ones, it is bound to affect your productivity. A stressed mind has a horde of thoughts constantly going in and out, trying to find a solution. If your mind has a sound, you would be hearing multiple voices shouting back and forth at no particular order. The thoughts keep you from focusing on any particular task. You will have your mind racing all day, yet nothing productive to show for it.

Meditation teaches your mind to be silent. Every time the thoughts seem to overwhelm you, you can quieten your mind and regain clarity. It only takes a few minutes, and the positive effects will be felt for hours.

Meditation does not mean that you ignore the issues stressing you. It means that you do not allow these thoughts to cloud your entire day and disrupt your focus. By meditating often, you can remain productive even as you seek out solutions.

The meditation processes

Can you train your mind to be quiet? Can you calm your mind enough to concentrate only on the present moment and nothing else? Can you block out your emotions? As an empath, you are probably so accustomed to multiple emotions that the idea of having a clear mind seems unattainable.

Think about it; how many things are on your mind at any given time? Let us say you are sitting at your desk at work editing a document. You have multiple tabs open. The first one is your email, so you can check out any new one that comes in. Remember they are also those you are yet to reply to. On a different tab, you are antagonizing over some sports rerun, noticing how badly your team is doing. You are also half-listening to a conversation your colleagues are having about that finance meeting last week. Oh, you also have your eye on the clock. Is it lunchtime yet? You have to check out that restaurant in the new mall two blocks away. Oh, and there's a gym there too. You need to stay in shape.

All these items fighting for space in your mind. How many are these; like 7? Sounds like such a high number when you stop to count, yet this is nothing unusual. Our minds are constantly burdened with information going in and out. No wonder fatigue and anxiety have become the order of the day. Unfortunately, even with all this activity on your mind, you are hardly productive. You are like the proverbial rocking chair, activity without much progress.

Every person deals with such thoughts, but as an empath, you have to include the emotions as well. As if your own emotions are not enough, you have to deal with the emotions of those around you. The numerous emotions exhaust you and drain your energy.

Meditation seeks to give your mind a break from the stresses and anxieties of such thoughts and emotions. You can clear your mind and heart. You can focus on this moment and this moment only. Here you can experience the calm and relaxation of a clear mind.

If you are just starting out, you begin by learning how to concentrate. Here you focus on breathing naturally, and probably repeating a phrase. Sounds pretty easy, right? How hard can breathing get, don't we do it every second of our lives? That is until you give it a try. The point here is not the breathing but concentrating on the breathing. Most beginners will only achieve a couple of conscious breaths before their mind wanders to something else.

It may not feel relaxing at first. In fact, in the beginning, you may struggle with the entire concept. The mind takes about 20 minutes or so before it settles, and longer for others. Do not dwell on the difficulty. Do not stop trying. Meditation is a skill; you get better with time.

10-minute meditation plan

a) Sit quietly in a calm place with no distractions. Most people prefer to sit with their legs crossed and arms stretched out, like the basic yoga pose. However, you can sit in any position that you find comfortable.

b) Focus on your breathing. You can add an encouraging or affirming mantra to the meditation. Repeat words such as 'I am healthy and whole' over and over again. Let the thoughts come and go without giving them much attention.

c) Pay attention to the parts of your body in turns. Listen out for tightness, tingling or itching in every part of your body. Start from one point, such as the feet, and proceed all the way up to the head. Focus your mind on that particular sensation and allow your mind to feel it fully.

d) Should your mind wander, don't stress about it. Simply notice it and guide your mind back to the breathing.

e) Once the 10-minute session is over, transition slowly. Don't just get up and leave. Open your eyes, look up and take some time to notice the difference in your body and mind. Don't you feel lighter?

If you still can't seem to get the hang of it, find company. Having someone beside you attempting the same technique will encourage you to keep trying. You can also listen to guided audio meditation clips. These ones tell you exactly what to do; you simply follow instructions. Aim for just 5 minutes a day in the beginning. Some even start with as little as 1 minute. Fair enough; every second count. Should your mind keep wandering, that does not mean that the meditation was not successful? You can still reap the benefits from the sheer seconds that you manage.

Eventually, a 30-minute undistracted meditation period will be easily achievable. You will also be able to get into meditation right away. In the beginning, you may sit there with your eyes closed for minutes, yet your mind continues to wander. It could take up to 20 minutes to guide your mind to your breathing. With practice, you'll learn to start meditating as soon as your eyes are shut. Keep practicing; it only gets better with time.

You can have brief meditation stints in the course of the day when the emotions build up. If the environment allows it, such as in the office, you can simply close your eyes and meditate. If you're in a crowd, one of the most grueling tests for an empath, you can step away. You can go sit in the car, or in an isolated corner, and meditate.

Most importantly, schedule a meditation session at the end of each day. Here you're at home, you can sit comfortably in your designated spot and let go of all those emotions that you had to deal with throughout the day. You can even meditate as you soak in the bathtub. That double rejuvenation: for body and mind. Those moments that you spend in meditation will help you sleep better, and more importantly wake up refreshed and ready to face another day.

Practical Test:

1.What is Meditation?

2. When to Transition Slowly?

3. Where to Meditate?

CHAPTER 6:

Have Solutions for Nervous People

Simple Meditation

Step 1: find the perfect place

Meditation, like all other types of meditation, must be done in a quiet place. First, find a quiet place. The meditation process must take between 10 minutes and 1 hour. Depending on the length of your session, make sure your quiet location stays calm for a long time. You do not want intruders to enter when you are at your meditation center.

Step 2: gather all the basics

During meditation, you need a few basic things. For mindfulness meditation, the only important consideration is the meditation mat or chair. If you choose a chair, make sure your back is straight.

Step 3: Position yourself

When you are ready to begin your meditation, position yourself accordingly. Attention is needed when practitioners sit upright. You can sit on the bed with your legs and arms crossed or sit upright in a chair. Make sure you are comfortable and can breathe freely.

Step 4: Close your eyes and focus on your breath

Now focus on your breathing with your eyes closed. Feel the airflow in and out without trying to control it. Let your mind focus on your breath only until you gain full concentration. It takes around 5 minutes to concentrate on your mind. If you find that your mind is still wandering, try refocusing your mind. It takes more than 5 minutes for beginners to focus their minds.

Step 5: Focus on a specific part of the body

Once you have mastered the art of meditation and focused on your breath, you must be ready to take your attention to the next level. Don't try to reach this level until you are sure that you can meditate by focusing on your breath. During the first few days, you have to focus on your breath. Concentrate on other parts of your body as you develop. At an advanced level, you can focus on your body shape. Visualize your body shape, your weight, and the overall harmony of your body in your head. This way you can know what you like and what you don't like in your body. You can also focus on your mind. Meditation allows you to see your deepest desires. You can see your thoughts, what you think about life and what you think about love. All of these aspects help you understand who you are and why you make the decisions that you make in everyday life, why mindfulness meditation is important for anxious and panicked patients.

Patients with fear and panic

I) Mindfulness is practiced in a nonjudgmental space: the first rule for anyone who wants to practice Mindfulness is that you must be nonjudgmental. As we have seen, Mindfulness will reveal the dirtiest secret of your desires. If you practice Mindfulness, you will see many bad things about yourself that you may not want to show the world. The only way to practice Mindfulness and stay happy is to live a life without judgment. People who suffer from anxiety and panic attacks are usually mindful. They are difficult for you and others. Patients with anxiety judge others based on their appearance, race, or gender. They quickly crucify people and describe them as dangerous or harmful. However, if you practice vigilance, you will learn criminal punishment.

- Practitioners who care about self-awareness: Another reason people get anxiety and panic attacks is that they don't know what they feel or want. If you don't know your feelings or desires, events around you can easily provoke you. However, Mindfulness allows you to know yourself in detail. You will know your preferences and desires in detail. If you practice Mindfulness, nothing will surprise you. You know people to avoid and how to deal with your triggers.

- Mindfulness promotes self-acceptance: When you practice Mindfulness, you learn to accept your strengths and weaknesses. This is a very important aspect for patients with anxiety and panic. Most people who suffer from panic attacks don't know how to make love. They suffer from low self-esteem and see themselves as weak beings. When you practice mindfulness meditation, you will learn your strength and ability to fight all your enemies.

- Peaceful and Loving Meditation: Peaceful and loving meditation is another technique that you can use to deal with anxiety and panic attacks. Peaceful and loving meditation is very different from Mindfulness. Every aspect of your mind consciously revolves around your feelings and existence. In peace and love meditation, you are a source of peace and love for the world. You must think of yourself as a central part of the world where love transcends the whole world. In this type of meditation, you focus on making the whole world happy. If you are the center of peace and love, see yourself as someone who has the responsibility to make people happy. In peace and love meditation, you give love and calm even to your enemies. Teleport yourself to a beautiful world where everyone must smile for your love.

Ways to practice peace and love meditation.

Step 1: Find your location and prepare the area

If you want to practice peace and love meditation, you need to prepare a room as we do with mindfulness meditation. Make sure you choose a quiet place. You can use a chair or mat as in mindfulness meditation.

Step 2: Position and focus your mind

You must also stand on a mat or chair, as you do with careful technique. Make sure you stand on your bed or chair. Now close your eyes and focus on your breath. This will help you focus on your mind. Breathe normally in about 5 minutes with your mind focused on your breath. After 5 minutes, change your focus from breathing to dark. With your eyes closed, there should be a dark cloud in front of you. Just close your eyes and focus on the dark. Think about anything except darkness for about 5 minutes.

Step 3: Focus on your enemies and give them love

In this step, you need to choose the people you consider your enemy. Focus on that person and choose to give them love. Visualize yourself as a source of happiness for your enemy. Talk to your enemies as completely as possible in your head. Think about your enemies and even give them gifts. You must think of yourself as the center if you like. Be the one who pours love into the world and teaches them how to love. Just visit your enemies with a smile and show them that life is beautiful.

You can do this with everyone in your life, one at a time. You don't have to imagine loving everyone on the same day. If you have a lot of enemies, preview every day. When you are done with your enemy, spread the love of the poor and the weak. Extend your visualization to the homeless on the streets. One hour of peace and love meditation a day can completely reverse your mindset. If you always see the world as a place of violence, this meditation will help you see it as a place of peace.

After practicing peace and love meditation, you must go ahead and practice everything. Begin to show love and kindness to the people around you. You can visit the orphanage and show love to the child. If you feel someone needs your love, go there and show them that love, and kindness remain in the world. Be someone who gives love without expecting much.

Why meditation for peace and love is important for patients with fear and panic.

I) Extend Forgiveness: Most people who suffer from anxiety and panic are only people who choose to stick with experienced painful cases. If you choose to endure the pain of experience of the past, you will think that people are out to hurt you. This type of meditation allows you to see the beauty of forgiveness. It helps you realize that life can be beautiful if you choose to forgive your enemies and live in love.

II) It promotes love and trust: There is no love without trust. This type of meditation teaches you to love and trust the people around you. It also helps you learn that love and trust do not come from being loved. It teaches you that you can love and trust others even if you are not in love. You can choose to love and trust the people around you, including your enemies. If you show kindness and love to the world, you will eventually enjoy the happiness of life that results from loving and trusting the people around you.

III) Practical: If you suffer from anxiety and panic attacks, you need something practical to help you see the beauty of this world. Peaceful and loving meditation goes beyond visualization. After the meditation process, you have to go out and ask for your friends' love. You have to go out and visit the children on the road. You must visit your enemies and show them some kindness. This movement will help you realize that many people in the world want love and those who want to give love. When you see all the love in the world, you must learn to trust others. Those who live with a negative mentality only focus on negative aspects of life. Life has negative and positive aspects. If you want to see the negative, you may never see the positive. You decide which aspects of life you want to see. Ending and showing love for the world is one way to see and see the beauty of the world. If you manage to see all the beauty of the world, you will stop hating people and begin to appreciate the love you have in your life. You will find that many people want to have the love you already have. Only by interacting with other groups in your community will you realize that you have enjoyed a great love and begin to appreciate the love you have in your life.

Behavioral Therapy

Behavior therapy is another way to deal with anxiety and panic attacks. If you suffer from anxiety, you should check your lifestyle. Your life pattern determines the way you think. You can change your perspective of life by changing your daily patterns.

Behavioral therapy focuses on changing mindsets by changing lifestyles. This is a proven scientific fact that when the body is made to behave in a certain way, the human brain can be changed to think in a certain way. Because of this, people can adapt to the new environment. Finally, if you are forced to eat only once a day, your body adapts to one meal a day. This is because the human body can adapt to everything. This is based on the theory of elasticity of the human brain. In this theory, the human brain is considered resilient, with the ability to expand and contract. The brain can adapt to whatever new information you provide. It can expand and receive excessive information on orders.

Practical Test:

1. How to position and focus your mind?

2. Is being calm helpful?

3. What is behavioral therapy?

CHAPTER 7:

How Empathic People Can Have and Deal with Relationships.

In your own life, you have a lot more power than you think. The relationships in your life have been placed there on purpose—either to help you grow, to help you learn more about yourself, or to help you feel nurtured and supported. Chances are, you will find that each relationship in your life serves as a "test" of sorts, so you must be able to understand what those relationships are about and how they are currently impacting your life.

If you have relationships in your life that feel as though they are meant to help you grow or learn more about yourself, you may find that these are either positive or negative. In some cases, you may have these friendships with other empaths who teach you about who you are and what is possible for you and who encourage you to grow into your gifts and become stronger with them in general.

In other cases, you might find yourself in negative relationships where the purpose is to learn about your weaknesses and where you may not presently be taking care of yourself with stronger boundaries. In these cases, you should consider these relationships as an opportunity to understand how you are allowing others to take advantage of you and harm you. Take the opportunity to know how you can eliminate that by being more present and available for yourself. As you learn to navigate these negative relationships and set boundaries for yourself, you may find that some naturally grow into healthier relationships, and they become more enjoyable and safer for you to navigate. On the other hand, some may become even more toxic, and you may find yourself with the need to eliminate your relationship with that person so that you are no longer being entrapped by that relationship and all of its toxic elements. Sometimes, learning to let go and give yourself space to decline toxic relationships is an important lesson for an empath.

In relationships that are meant to help you feel supported and allow you to feel safe to be yourself, these are naturally healthy and positive relationships that you should continue to nurture in your life. These are the ones that are meant to support you with understanding the value of strong relationships and the value of who you are. Typically, nothing needs to be done in these relationships aside from possibly asserting some of your new boundaries more clearly if you find that some of them are not being respected. Often, you will find that in these relationships, the boundaries were not being respected, not because the other person is not respectful, but because the other person had no idea they existed. Once you begin to assert your new boundaries, these individuals will often shift their behaviors immediately and celebrate you by choosing to honor yourself in a deeper way.

While we may agree that being in love requires vulnerability, the experience can be heightened when one or both partners are sensitive. In discussing this, we must remember that relationships are not necessarily a happy place for highly sensitive people—mainly because they are more aware of their surroundings and of the people they are relating with. As such, they are more likely to become unsettled by their partners' behaviors or the possible outcomes of such behaviors. Generally, an HSP will often feel more stressed and will need more downtime—a combination that can strain and bring down any relationship.

In spite of the challenges involved, many people are attracted to HSPs and their sensitivity. They like them for their openness, compassion, empathy, and concern for other people. The tendency of HSPs to foster deep, meaningful relationships and their distaste for superficial stuff makes them even more likable. Their authenticity in their dealings in life is a breath of fresh air.

Unsurprisingly, highly sensitive people tend to be attracted to people who need their help, but sometimes, this attraction can be deceptive. Sometimes, they fall into the arms of others who never give a thought to taking advantage of the caring and giving nature for their benefit. Because of these characters, highly sensitive people become the doormats of their circles and end up in the therapists' office.

The lack of acceptance and appreciation for the sensitivity of HSPs causes sensitive persons to suffer from low self-esteem and self-doubt. When it comes to establishing a romantic relationship, the HSPs tend to become more helpful, empathetic, compassionate, and sensitive to the needs and feelings of other people trying to gain love and acceptance from them. In particular, HSPs have a distinct characteristic called mate sensitivity, which is the ability to quickly decipher a spouse's needs and making an effort to resolve the problem so that they may be happy again. HSPs do this all the time, and sometimes make it their daily goal.

As you would expect, there are bound to be problems when one party is giving too much. The reality is that the more you give, the more your partner takes. When you focus more on giving without receiving anything in return, at the end of the day, your own needs will be unmet, and you end up feeling unhappy, resentful, and exhausted. Unfortunately, when this happens, you begin to blame yourself again but remain unfulfilled.

How HSPs Can Achieve More Satisfaction in Relationships

Relationships can be quite a challenge to a highly sensitive person. However, the following tips can help HSPs derive more satisfaction from relationships. They include:

1. Set Aside Some Alone Time

Among the significant needs of an HSP are the desire for a meaningful connection and the desire for some downtime, but the secret is in finding a perfect balance between the two. You need to strike a balance between the time you spend with your wife and the time you withdraw to your spot for some personal time. If you fail to balance and you fail to spend some time alone, you will end up feeling overstimulated, which leads to anxiety, illness, anger, and burnout, among other struggles. However, the way to work out a balance is to develop a consistent routine that allows you to have a little of both worlds.

2. Be More Direct

To ensure that your needs are met in the same measure as you respond to the needs of others, you're going to have to be more direct. You ought to realize that while your intuition and perception allow you to anticipate the needs of other people easily, others do not have the same ability.

Naturally, you anticipate receiving the same level of care and concern as you give to others, but the reality is that the non-HSP partners may not even come near to meet your desires in light of the fact that their minds are not wired to be as keen. When your partner is not responding to your call for a connection repeatedly, resentment and disconnection are bound to build. For this reason, you need to voice your wishes. If the volume of your voice has not been loud, make it louder (not harsh). Express your needs directly.

3. Take Some Time Off During a Conflict

Conflicts are a sticky situation for highly sensitive persons because they quickly are overstimulated and shift into the fight or flight mode. Whenever this happens, both partners begin to express anger on each other or will have an urge to leave during the conflict. This is the fight or flight reaction.

A conflict situation brings about a high physical and emotional degree of discomfort, and when this happens, the HSPs start to retreat to their shells, understating their needs, and opting to initiate a truce. Although burying the conflict can bring about some temporary solution, it does not keep the conflict from recurring; it only opens the door for some more resentment and conflict.

Instead of burying the conflict, take a breather, and allow the heated emotions to thaw. Once you are relaxed, with your partner, come up with a plan on how to manage the conflict moments. Come up with the rules that you will be following when you want to speak to each other, when you should be taking breaks, and how you will be communicating with your partner to have your needs heard, especially when emotions come flooding. Having set the rules of engagement, it will now be easier for you and your partner, HSP or non-HSP, to navigate any conflict or uncomfortable situation with ease.

4. Allow There to Be Some Differences

Differences between couples are the primary source of conflict, added to the fact that people have different empathy capacities, sensitivity, and emotional responsiveness. Our humanity causes us to weigh situations based on our experiences, and sadly, the people we deal with have not had the same experiences, yet we expect them to have learned the lessons and rhythms we learned through our experiences. It does not matter if both partners are highly sensitive or not; they must remember that they have differences in sensitivity and preferences.

5. Create Intentional Connections by Sharing Experiences

HSPs are easily put off by the lack of connection, the misunderstandings, and the conflicts that occur in relationships that lack proper communication. The situation is aggravated by the myriads of things happening these days, the kind that takes your attention away, causing them to feel as though they are taken for granted. For example, these days, people are so committed to finding ways to make money that it's all they think about all day. When doing this, we assume that once we have money, the rest, including the relationship, will iron out and maintain themselves. Conditions like these are the perfect breeding ground for emotional distress with your partner, friends, family, and other relations.

Without actively connecting with those around us, the bond we have with them weakens quickly before the eventual break, and this makes both parties in the relationship susceptible to stress and conflict.

As an HSP, you should set clear priorities of what is of most importance to you based on your limited capacity to create connections with other people. Perhaps you and your partner could set aside some time to sit down and engage with each other either through communication, playing a game, or some other fun activity, without interruptions.

Take this time to know your partner at a deeper level. What are his likes, dislikes, joys, hopes, worries, and goals? Ask him what he or she is most grateful for, the things he or she has been up to, the challenges encountered, and any such information. Talk about what has been happening in your area, in the country, and across the world. Get to know each other's opinions about different things in life; it is by learning about how a person's mind works, his outlook of life, the growth he has undergone, the new knowledge he has and other like information that you begin to understand the person and what he is about. You also get to share with him or her in-depth knowledge about yourself. In the process, you create an intimate relationship with the individual from which you can build a lasting relationship.

Practical test:

1. Is relationship necessarily a happy place?

2. Do you need to take a time off during conflict?

3. Is it important to be more direct?

CHAPTER 8:

Self-Healing

Empathic people sense and obtain other people's liveliness, which might be quite challenging. The senses of an empath might be enhanced, and the observation of life might be irresistible. A stroll into the park or hanging out with acquaintances might be strenuous. Generally, a range of aspects, comprising the surroundings and group you meet, influences the physical and psychological wellbeing. This assumption is not correct for everybody; however, it is an exceptional one for people with empathy and the over-sensitive ones.

When you are a compassionate person, you are attached to the hurting of other individuals, trying to hang on it as your own. Keep in mind that there is a lot someone might do to assist other individuals. Empathic people might attempt to assist and direct people as they can, however at the end the individual feeling the pain should be ready to assist him or herself for true healing to happen. Frequently, the caring character blind empaths, consequently people do not desire or are not ready to be assisted since they are happy in the protection of their depression.

There are several steps that empathic people can put into practice to enable them to start the journey of healing.

Disconnection

Detaching from close individuals is tough for empathic people; however, it is the best technique to begin the healing procedure. Move away from people who are closely associated with you for a short period.

Accept

Similarly, to handling tricky situations in life, it is vital that you acknowledge that you are an empathic person. Do not assume the power of acceptance as it is one of the key steps of making progress in troubling situations. There is nothing bad about being an empathic person; the fact is that you are exceptional. People with Empathy are remarkable; however, they have a tendency of thinking that there is something regarding them. People in the world have to take good care of empaths, not empaths taking of other them.

Hold on It

After an empath has accepted that they are empathic, they should make it an ingredient of who they are. Hold on your life and accept who you are. Satisfaction in your compassion is the only means to move from reacting like a casualty of it.

Deliberate

Nobody can highlight enough the significance of contemplation. There are several meditation methods accessible to learn and understand; however, you have to discover what suits you. For instance, white sound or a particular sort of music is the best meditation technique for some people. On the other hand, other people require silence as a means of meditation. It is good to understand what works well for your mind.

Adore It

Accommodating your empathic state and holding on it are vital; however, you have to adore it. You are exceptional because communities in your life are lucky to have you in the society. Being a person with empathy is a part of what forms you.

Create limitations

As an empath seeking to heal, it is significant to create limitations. Let persons in your life live on the other part of that contour, and when they go over it that makes easier for an empath to move them far. One of the toughest sections for people with empathy is booting individuals out of their activities and crossing limitations is an excellent reason.

Hygiene Rituals

Spend time alone on a daily basis

As an empath seeking to heal, you should have your time separately each day; however, if it is not possible to be alone regularly, create your time occasionally. When you can spend time unaccompanied without several communications with other individuals and no exterior interruption, you shall have more energy. In addition, being alone implies that not even being in a similar physical state with other individuals. Spending time alone is significant to an empath as it allows them to recharge their energy. Inform your relatives and acquaintances that spending some time alone is something you require. Assist them to recognize how significant this is for you. When you start spending time alone, you shall see the dissimilarity.

Take a salt and scrubs

It is not an undisclosed that salt attracts unhelpful energy, and from different practices, it helps. Several people prefer using sea and Epsom salt in their bathwater, pooled with indispensable oil of preference. In addition, people do it when they sense they require cleansing. On the other hand, people apply salt cleanse in the bathe to clean residue energy they sense on their bodies. You can make these for yourself, mixing marine salt with emerald or coconut oil. What an empath adores, combine it collectively, and include necessary oils of your preference. You shall feel the distinction. People who live closer to safe oceans can take time to swim because oceans are an ideal source of marine salt.

Refining clean up

Occasionally, water is a fantastic decontaminant. Subsequently, people prefer using it to clear their energy whilst cleaning their bodies. Empaths imagine water rinsing away the energy obtained from other people and the energy they no longer desire to keep. Empaths might also picture a color of their choice while trying to release unwanted energy. Several people prefer visualizing blue or white; however, finding something that works for you is vital during the healing process.

Spend time in the natural world

When you may, relax a tree, contemplate in the recreational area or stroll to rejuvenate. Trees have gorgeous energy that might assist you feel healthier and recharging is pure in a natural setting. Several people established that farming assists as well because you acquire the energy from the ground. Therefore, you are refining and getting fresh energy spontaneously.

Protecting

Empaths should never depart their homes without their energetic guard on. Particularly, if they use municipal means of transport or arrange to intermingle with other group people.

Marking

When applying smudging, empaths might embrace sage or exasperate sticks of preference. Several people use Nag, as they adore the smell and how it usually gives them confidence. If empaths feel, they have obtained a lot of unhelpful energy they require smudging themselves entirely. Occasionally, empaths should do it instinctively as they cannot be erroneous. On the other hand, empathic people should do vertical or spherical actions and function through their chairs.

Sweep

Picture you had a few dust on your top and you wish to sweep it down. This is precisely a similar action. Empathic people should get rid of unconstructive energy. You may feel remains on your arms after getting rid of negative energy, therefore, make sure to clean hands with freezing water after the sweeping procedure.

Visualize

Comparable to the hallucination in the bathing room, sit in contemplation and envisage golden colorless brightness coming from the peak of your skull and cleaning away anything that is trapped on you, transferring it down on the ground. The visualization procedure shall also assist with preparation, which is recommended to assist you feel reasonable.

Avoid the phone and internet

Switch off your telephone and avoid the internet frequently. An empath should read a book or settle down. Occasionally, getting a lot of notices and news from your phone or laptop might be strenuous. The best step is turning off your laptop and switching your phone off and witness your energy increase.

Breathing tasks

Several yoga practices and breathing techniques do wonders to empaths seeking to heal. When removing negative energy from their body, empathic people should use energizing breathing tasks. The breathing practices should be performed in a secure place with the eyes blocked and in small periods, as they are influential. Yoga and breathing practices clear empaths energy and rejuvenate them instantaneously. This practice is realistic and simple to perform anytime you require feeling good.

Daily Routines for Healing an Empath

Morning habit

An empath might get up nourishing his or her uncertainties, doubts, and distress, or he or she might wake up encouraging your happiness and tapping into uncontaminated, constructive energy.

If you are a person with empathy, make a functioning morning schedule. As part of a functioning morning routine, empaths should try offering themselves Reiki and meditation. Putting the above practices into a daily schedule boosts one's body with constructive energy and helps me feel balanced, grounded and in harmony. Generally, it makes the attitude for the entire day and makes an empath less responsive and premeditated. Subsequently, an empath must note a purpose for the day and inscribe it down in their periodical. On the other hand, there should be days when empaths insert extra activities to their morning schedule; however, the Reiki and contemplation are invariable. Generally, the first thing an individual does after waking up is vital, because it influences the outcome of the activities they undertake during the day. If you are an empath seeking to heal and you presently do not have a morning schedule, begin on a small note since little is better than doing nothing. Therapists meet several empaths who have no clue that there is a reference for their hypersensitivity. Empaths understand that they are destined to assist other people and do not know why they are exhausted each time and experience no happiness.

Midday schedule

When you desire to survive as an empowered person of empathy, you should offer yourself authorization to pause, reorganize, and rearrange at midday. Rearranging at dusk is not adequate for an empath seeking to heal. The amounts of energy people obtain from other people amass in their body. Fabricating a midday schedule plays a vital role in ensuring that the acquired energy is released from the body. Irrespective of the duration of refreshment, ensure that at least you go out to get some fresh air. You can take a swift stroll around the building. The air outside the building defuses the unconstructive energy you soak up from other people.

Evening schedule

Late afternoon is when a person desires to spend time contemplating the day's activities and planning for the day ahead. At this point, people have a tendency of awakening their powerhouse that comprises sensitivity, imagination, and instinct. Think of activities you like doing in your free time. Some people find pleasures in drawing while others in singing. If you love drawing, draw some of your favorite images in sand, in books, or on timber. Draw every evening and you shall notice some tremendous changes in your life.

Bedtime habits

Going to bed psychologically stimulated may lead to nervousness. Before retiring to bed, you wish to remove the unnecessary energy that pulls you behind, so your energy is sparkling, and your pulsation is excellent. Below are a number of thoughts for a bedtime schedule. People, who find writing enjoyable, make a periodical and release your feelings out on the manuscript. Take some minutes, around ten to twenty, working on yoga and Reiki to let go of the pressure from the mind and body. Use cold water to clean your face, rub the face, your arms, apply the whole body with a moisturizer, and comb your hair gently. Pay attention to calm, shooting songs, and say an appreciation. Say a short prayer to God because it is a spiritual way of staying positive.

Practical Test:

1. What are the daily routines for healing empaths?

2. What are the hygiene rituals?

3.Is it important to accept that you are an empathic person?

CHAPTER 9:

How to Protect Himself from Narcissists

Most sensitives have been around or come across energy vampires or narcissistic people at some point. Even after spending a few minutes in their company we often leave feeling violated and drained. In my experience, most emotional vampires are not aware of this trait within them but that doesn't help us not feel terrible in their company. Even though they may be oblivious to their own nature, most of them unconsciously recognize that being around an empath makes them feel better and more positive about themselves. For this reason, they can often cling to empaths because of the positive feelings they are able to gain from being in their presence. Due to an energy vampire overbearing personality, empaths often struggle against these types of energetic attacks because of their weak boundaries. Being around them can negatively impact their own ability to function well. After spending too much time with these people, our energy begins to diminish into negativity, whereas the energy vampire feels uplifted from taking positive energy from us. They essentially feed on others positivity. It is important to recognize if you feel depleted, stressed or drained around certain people as you're likely in the presence of a psychic vampire.

The Reasons Behind Vampirism & Narcissism

These people feel cut off from themselves and deep down feel unworthy of being loved which stops them from getting their own needs met. The only way they can get what they need is to take it from others. Due to their unconnectedness to themselves they are unable to find fulfillment within, so this void is then filled by stealing energy from other people. They prey on easy targets, i.e. those with weak boundaries who can easily be drained. Energy vampires are often singled out for being evil and harmful, but their actions are often unconscious. They don't know what they are doing. They are victims themselves, although this doesn't make it any easier on us. The paradox is that the energy vampire and the victim are similar on some level. They have been drawn together and that is why the vampire is able to attach to the victim through this identification. The opposites have attracted one another. Narcissists are often attracted to empaths and people in healing or spiritual circles as these people are the most open and loving. This makes them easy prey for an energy vampire. They will usually stay attached to these people for a long time, due to the victim's non-resistance. On the surface it will probably look like a positive friendship. It is also worth mentioning that while certain people are energy vampires per se, most people have some vampirism tendencies depending upon their mood. If someone you know, a friend perhaps, is going through a particularly tough time they may unconsciously reach out in an energy sucking way, as they seek an uplift in their mood. They probably won't realize they are doing this, but empaths should be on their guard against it. Telephone calls are one of the main way's friends can steal your energy. If a friend calls you regularly to talk about their problems, you may want to emotionally withdraw and detach consciously from the conversation. Be there to listen but not to take on their negative energy. Over time your friend will probably recognize they do not get a boost from unloading their problems onto you, so will probably stop sharing their personal issues as much. This doesn't mean your friendship with them will end but you are just setting a boundary between what is yours and what is theirs. Remember that healthy relationships are based on balance and an equal amount of giving and taking.

Energetic Cording

The primary way I have found to disconnect from these people is to cut them out of my life and stop communicating with them altogether. Not in a malicious way, but instead to essentially release them through love and forgiveness. This can be incredibly difficult to do however, especially if it is someone close such as a family member or a work colleague, we have to see each day. In these scenarios, we can disconnect from the other by cutting our energetic ties to them. 'Cording' refers to an energetic connection between two people. These connections are usually between certain chakras. For example, when a mother gives birth to a baby, they're energetically connected via the first charka (at the bottom of the torso). The root chakra from the mother connects to the root chakra to the baby. It would essentially look like a line of light from one to the other, this a healthy positive cord.

Healthy energetic cords can also form between people who are not related, such as spouses, close friends or anyone you feel a connection too. However, these cord connections can also be forced by one person onto another. This type of cording is unhealthy and draining to the recipient of such an act. For example, people often become attached to their ex-partners. Even after the relationship is over, we can sometimes still feel a connection to this person. It is possible that your ex-partner had created a cord into your system to remember and to stay in touch with you energetically. This enables them to experience a little bit of your energy. When your ex is thinking or remembering you, they are creating and reinforcing an energetic cord into one of your chakras, probably unconsciously. This is why, even after the relationship is over, we cannot stop thinking about the other person. They are connecting to us energetically. That's why it is important to heal your own energy to stop other people cording into you again.

Most energetic cording takes place on one of the torso-based charkas (1 to 4) these include the sacral (above the groin area), the solar plexus (mid-belly), the heart or the throat chakra. If you feel an ache or sensation in any of these areas when around a certain person, become aware that they may be draining your life force from you. You can block this by simply placing your hands directly over the affected chakra to help break the connection. Often in difficult social situations, people will cross their arms over their bodies (usually unconsciously), this helps us feel safer and defend our energy in this position.

The reason another person is able to cord you is because your chakras are not strong enough and must be healed. When the chakras are unhealthy or unhealed it leaves them open for others to attach to. Psychic vampires gain a strong feed of energy from the chakra points. For example, a person I used to know would attach to my solar plexus and I could physically feel the sensation of the connection. When the chakras and boundaries are healed, healthy and established, it becomes difficult for others to form this connection though cording your energy field. Energetic cords form when we still carry hurt or baggage with us from our pasts. These wounds leave our chakras open, so they become easily attachable. The low energy of this wound attracts the low energy of the vampire or narcissist. Empaths often feel a sensation in their solar plexus region. This chakra is the seat of our emotions. This is where the emotions of others are most deeply felt and where we are the most vulnerable to be corded and drained. Weakness in this area can cause digestive system and stomach problems.

Cord Cutting Exercise

Toxic draining relationships require what is often referred to as cord cutting. Once energetic cords are established it can be difficult to break them without conscious intention. If you feel drained from certain family members, ex-partners, work colleagues or anyone whom you have close regular contact with then it may be time to repair your connection to them. You might sense that this other person sends you negative, harmful thoughts and energy, even when you're not close to them.

If you feel you have been corded, then this cord cutting exercise will help release it.

1. Imagine the other person and envision a cord or tube connecting the two of you, from one of your chakras.

2. Next visualize a cutting tool (such as scissors or sword) slicing through and cutting the cord at your chakra point.

3. Ask for the other person's energy to be returned to them and yours to be returned to you. Visualize this in your mind.

4. Following this, ask yourself what negative belief you were holding which attracted this experience to you in the first place? With this realization, we begin to see that we are not innocent helpless victims but in fact we are attracting these experiences to us, for a chance to overcome and grow through them.

5. Realize your self-worth as an empath is not dependent on helping others. This is a common misconception which leads to us attracting the wrong relationships.

6. End the exercise by forgiving the other party and releasing them with love.

Meditation

If you have left an interaction with an energy vampire and feel drained, this is a great time to clear the connection. This can also be achieved through meditation.

1. Close your eyes and begin by making yourself comfortable.

2. Scan your body from the head down to the feet and pay attention to any attachments you feel. It shouldn't be too difficult to determine what part of the body you are being drained from.

3. Upon determining what part of the body you feel this connection too, look to see the shape or form of the connection. See a physical representation of this energetic attachment. To me, it looks like an energetic tube which sucks energy in.

4. Begin cutting the attachment away from you. Envision you have a sword made of light and see this sword cutting through these attachments which are then being released from your body.

5. Once the attachment or cord is removed. You must apply healing to the area by placing your hand over the chakra and send healing energy

to the area. See the open chakra begin to restore. Allow it to heal and repair itself.

6. As the chakra is healed visualize a new vibrancy and boost of energy within it.

7. Send the other person's energy and attachment back to them. There is no harm in this, it was their stuff in the first place.

8. Scan your whole body again noticing if there are any other attachments or sensations. If you do sense something carry out the same detaching for the new area.

9. Finally, envision a white light surrounding and protecting you. This bubble of protection will always remain with you unless you decide to release it.

You can practice this meditation almost anywhere. At work, on public transport or anywhere you are able to go within for a few moments.

The key to dealing with psychic attacks from unhealthy people is simply becoming more aware. Often energy vampires appear friendly, attractive and charismatic, which draws us in. The fact that they show us attention usually allows us to let them close to us

Practical Test:

1.What are the cutting cord exercise?

2. How to Meditate?

3. What is the Reasons Behind Narcissism

CHAPTER 10:

Techniques to Heal Negative Energies

Any negative feeling can come from a number of sources: everything you feel can be your own, it can be someone else's, or it can be a mix. Most people have empathy, but to some degree, everyone has the potential to be empathic, too–it may just take practice, and they can just feel the emotion in people they are close to, but it's something that anyone can practice!

If you're an empath, you appear to sense other feelings, emotions, and even physical suffering and sense it. You can also carry on this physical suffering without realizing it, depending on the degree of your empathic abilities. This is why energy perception and grounding are central elements of energy clearing and very critical components.

What are the types of empaths?

1. Emotional empaths: who takes on other people's feelings and sentiments

2. Physical empaths: takes on the body's energy

3. Geomantic empaths: environmentally friendly–pick up energy from another region

4. Plant empaths: who knows about the requirements of the plants.

5. Animal empaths: ones who know about the requirements of the animals

6. Intuitive empaths: which takes things up just being around individuals

7. Old Soul empath: who sees the positive in everyone, no matter what, and still tries to repair people.

8. Unaware empath: who don't realize that he is an empath

Ways of how empaths can release negative energies:

Sensitivity is a blessing. The fact that you can feel and absorb the energies of other people does not mean that you are frail or defective; it does mean you are free, positive, and different! It also means you have a real need to learn how to release negative or unnecessary energy, so you can feel lighter, healthier, and happier.

Meditation.

All empathy is required at some stage to absorb the frustration, negativity, and suffering of others. Another quick meditation for five minutes will help them release extra energy. Again, find a quiet, relaxed place to sit down, test posture, and start deep breathing to calm yourself down.

Cut the Strings

It is a very critical job for which an empath has to become very professional. Since you are so good at making friends and people love you, they also take away your happiness from you, because your happiness feels so good, soothing and caring. It occurs because you unknowingly permitted it.

Past and current ties may still be there with family members, relatives, and partners, long after the connection is over. It's time for cutting the cord! To cut ties, just imagine if the individual you had a relationship with and see the cord is broken.

They are clearing you the cloud of negative thought.

Your mental body is actively communicating with others ' mental body, and you pick up on other people's negative thoughts. You build your own thoughts as well, and many of them will not fit with your highest good. Be aware of the following kinds of thinking: Negative, Repetitive, Constant, and Automatic.

Your job is to check in several times during the day with your energy field, particularly if you feel anxious and stressed, see if you have picked up or produced some negative thought-form, and actively let go of it.

Using mind mapping, drawing, and painting

Empaths seem to be very creative and enjoy when they feel amazing, expressing their own talent. They prefer to suppress their artistic ability when they don't feel great because art requires them to deal with their emotions, and this can also cause pain. Try using art as a means of emotional release and healing to support you when you feel trapped and out of control.

Cry to release your emotions.

Empaths have an emotional body that is very refined, and they like to weep when they have the need to. Crying has many advantages in healing. The crying sensation acts as a soothing tool for your aura. This is what kids do all the time. Another way of keeping your aura healthy and in alignment with the course of your soul is to do the energy work.

Visualization to Shield

Shielding provides a simple way to secure yourself. Often empaths and emotional people rely on it to filter out negative energy while enabling positivity to flow freely.

The second you realize that you're uneasy with a person, location, or situation, secure yourself with a shield. Start by taking some long, deep breaths. Then imagine a stunning white or pink light shield that completely covers your body and stretches just a few inches beyond that. This shield will secure you from everything that is negative, stressful, harmful, or disruptive. Inside this shield's defense, feel centric, relaxed, and energized. This protection removes negativity so you can always hear what's good and love at the very same time.

Linking oneself to nature:

Nature is the best source of healing energy available for someone who feels overwhelmed by emotional tension and mental trauma. Humans bear the most pessimistic feelings and negative emotions. And if you're empathic, go and spend time alone in nature to refresh at least once a day. You'll let nature clean you up.

The most calming energy healing therapy you can get is communicating with plants, trees, streams of water, and natural landscapes. And it's completely free of charge!

Sit on the ground against the trunk of a tree with your back or walk around on your bare feet to draw positive energies from the earth. This technique is called earthing or grounding and will make you feel very good.

Massage.

There would be no full list of simple ways to release excess energy without relaxation, efficient stress relieving therapy. "Put away any thoughts that massage is either a nice way to treat yourself or pamper yourself. Massage may, on the contrary, be a powerful tool to support you take responsibility for your health and well-being, whether you have a serious health problem or are just looking for another stress reliever. It is also possible to learn how to do self-massage.

Salt.

Salt is one of the most time-tested and readily accessible methods of curing yourself of toxic energies. Though regular old table salt can do or use salt or sea salt from the Pink Himalayan.

Next to the sea, or a pit of saltwater? Take a bath and imagine the negative energy that washes away from you.

Another way to cleanse with salt is a neti pot, which is especially helpful in removing negative thoughts and memories. Because it scrubs the nose, mouth, sinus entries, and third eye, the utilization of a neti pot with salt assists with discharging recollections of deceptions spoken or carried on against you.

High Vibration Music.

On the off chance that they're rhythms, pop songs, or singing dishes, high vibration sounds are probably the simplest approaches to dispose of negative vitality. This passionate chemical will change the demeanor quickly in light of the natural capacity of the music to defeat the self-image.

Crystals.

Earth is filled with gems–as shown by Mother Earth's amazing storehouse of crystals. Some crystals are also excellent eliminators of toxic energy along with acting as decorative items and jewelry. Look for Black Obsidian, Rocket, Lava Rock, and Black Tourmaline when it comes to removing "evil vibes" from yourself or your house.

Often good for clearing are smokey quartz and selenite. Additionally, Green Calcite and Serpentine are recognized for their releasing effects.

Reiki.

Reiki is not a massage, but a religious practice. Reiki is a frequency of energy that eliminates emotional obstructions. Negative energy is always stuck (obstructed energy) when it comes into contact with Reiki, which releases it. With thousands of clinics, spas, and private practitioners now offering Reiki, localizing has also become easier.

Insomnia

Insomnia can be difficult because we are always thinking we need to learn to turn off our brains, as if it is easy! Also, since we do pick up on other people's energies and sleep next to someone each night, we may become overwhelmed if our partner is feeling stress, sadness, anger, or other emotions. We may not fall asleep until we know exactly what is causing them to feel the way they do, and that can be annoying to the partner; however, for us, it will allow us to fall asleep. It is a balancing act, and if you do live with someone, share a bedroom with someone, make it known that, if you are asking, you are seeking to find out what exactly is bothering them.

If your partner snores like a lumberjack, you have yet another obstacle to overcome. "In the event that you are resting close to somebody who wheezes or thrashes around a ton, clearly your own rest will be influenced. If someone is snoring next to you, empath or not, most people will not be able to sleep. Empaths may pick up on it more so, even in a deep sleep, because their brains are wired to care for others before themselves. Either way, the snoring lumberjack must be silenced (the safest way is by having them sleep on their side away from you), or you may choose to isolate yourself from being so close to someone in order to get a restful and peaceful night's sleep.

Exhaustion

Insomnia and exhaustion tend to go hand in hand. If you are up half of the night thinking or your snoring lumberjack has kept you awake, you will be extremely exhausted when you do wake up. Regardless of how many hours of sleep you may have gotten, if the quality of sleep is minimal, then you will still be tired.

If you are absorbing everyone's energy throughout the day, you may become exhausted. Some coping options that work for some include the following:

1. Taking a shower or bath
2. Using a mixture of honey and unrefined salt
3. Plugging in a Himalayan salt lamp

Find out what works for you to give you more energy. For some, a bath will help as it gives personal time to work out one's thoughts in peace.

Practical Test:

1. What are the types of Empaths?

2. Is it Important to cut the strings?

3. Is crying to release your emotion relevant?

CHAPTER 11:

How to Recover Positive Energies by Handling Negative Influence

When lots of people hear about the phrase negative influence, they assume it has to do with drugs, alcohol, or other social vices. However, the phrase negative influence is more than social vices. Negative influence implies those bad influences that push you into making bad decisions. For example, you can be influenced into thinking bad about yourself. This will lead to low self-esteem. You can also be affected to think a negative thought about your life or your job. This could lead to suicide if not curtailed fast. Negative influence doesn't stop at having negative thoughts or suggestions; it can lead to negative habits as well.

Getting rid of removing negative influence can be a daunting challenge. Your task removing negative influence can be made more difficult if people with negative habits surround you.

Furthermore, these individuals will remind you of your negative habits and forced to indulge in them even when you are trying to remove them. However, all hope is not lost. All you need is commitment and perseverance, and you will be able to remove negative influence, turn things around and begin to leave your life with more positivity.

Display a Positive Attitude with a Negative Person

However, to handle or diffuse their negativity, you should show them a positive response when they show their negative attitude. Recover your positive attitude by balancing out their negative displays with your positive one.

For example, when your negative friend says that no one cares about you, say that your friends or family love you very much. If they make a bad comment about something or someone, counter their statement by saying how vital the thing is or how generous the individual they tried to put down is. Canceling they negative words with your positive response will nullify their negative influence on you and address their negativity openly and proactively.

Stop Negative Talk/ Thought About Yourself

Negative self-talk is as damaging as negative habits. You can engage in negative talk but only focusing on the bad things happening in your life rather than the good ones. Negative talk can also apply to the way you think about yourself. For example, a night of hangout may be canceled by your pals. Rather than letting it go, you begin to tell yourself that it was canceled because of you. You use words like 'no one likes me that is why they don't want to hang out with me'. Another example can be something like this. After having a very productive day at work, you come home rather than being happy about your day; you begin to tell yourself how much work you couldn't get done.

Furthermore, negative talk means that you have a narrow-minded view of the world around you. When things are not working out for you and every turn, so there is no possible positive outcome in sight, which means that you have a feeling of imminent disaster coming your way.

If you engage in this type of talk about yourself, it is time you put an end to it, or you won't remove negative influence from your family and life.

Turn Negative Talk to Positive Ones

If you want to remove negative influence, you need to turn negative talk about yourself to positive ones. The power of the mind is crucial to the way you see yourself. Negative thoughts lead to negative speech, and negative talk leads to negative influence. You can change all that but having positive thoughts about yourself and, in turn, have a positive talk about yourself.

Start by evaluating any negative thought that comes into your mind. After evaluation, give a positive response to that particular negative thought. Make use of positive responses like ' I can do better than I did yesterday.' Make use of the ' can and will' phrase to dispel any negative thought that comes to your mind. Remember, you are what you think of yourself. Change must come from within before it can manifest outwards. Start your day every day with a positive affirmation of yourself. With consistency in your part, you will remove negative influence in no time from every area of your life.

Be Yourself

It's easy to impress someone or look good for someone, but it's not always wise. The simple fact is you can't always satisfy everyone. Instead of making yourself look good for others, why not focus on making yourself happy? Don't to impress anyone, let alone a negative person. Be yourself and spend quality time trying to figure out the things that make you happy. Spend time with people that will accept who you are and what you stand for. Don't pursue the wrong thing.

Determine Your Attitude

A person associating with a negative person does so at his/her own peril. They are toxic and introduce toxicity into your life. You don't have the will power to make your own decisions because you are surrounded by pessimists.

Don't allow negative people to dictate how you should respond or how your mood should be. You are yourself and in control of whatever that's happening to you. Choose how you want to behave. Choose how you want to be. Decide how you run your life because it's yours and no one else's.

Negative people can bring out the worst in you. It's quite normal. What's more important is how you let this negativity control you. Do not let your emotions get the better part of you. Determine your state of reaction. If you find yourself in negative situations, learn to control your emotions.

Reduce Negative Habits

You can't get rid of or remove negative influence if you don't remove negative habits first. These negative habits, like smoking, heavy drinking, and regular partying, could make you feel good momentarily, but they have a lasting negative impact on your dreams and aspirations. They generally leave you with a wicked hangover and a negative feeling in the morning.

This negative feeling in the morning will cause time mismanagement.

Time mismanagement means that you won't have enough time during the day to pursue your dreams and engage in those activities that will facilitate your career development.

Stopping all your negative habits will be a good way to handle negative influences in your life. Still, from experience, I know it will be difficult to stop all bad habits suddenly, so I suggest cutting back on your negative habits. This will go a long way to removing negative influence in your life. For example, rather than go out every night after work to the bar for a couple of drinks that usually lead to one too many, cut it back to once or twice a week.

Some people give the excuse of being stressed as the reason they drink every night. You can handle your stress by engaging in healthy activities like evening runs around your neighborhood. If you're not fond of running, you can get a bicycle and cycle around your neighborhood as well. You will feel less stressed after engaging in any of these activities. You might as well have friends over once or twice a week and cook for them. Social interaction is one good way to get rid of stress.

Have a Positive Lifestyle

You can get rid of negative influence by leaving a positive lifestyle. You can start by having healthy meals. Healthy meals should include a large portion of self-made meals and less junk. A balanced diet of protein, vegetables, and fruits, as well as milk, should be part of your meals. Remember to drink adequate water as well to stay hydrated. Cut down or soda or possibly avoid it completely as well as other sugary drinks.

The next part of your positive lifestyle should be to get sufficient sleep. This is one thing most people don't pay much attention to but, a sufficient amount of sleep every day plays a role in your mood and how you feel about yourself. When you get a sufficient amount of sleep, you won't get exhausted before the day even begin and you will be in a good mood. In the current economy, it is easy for you to neglect sleep, but it is essential you sleep at a fixed time to ensure you don't deviate from it. Set up your bedroom to ensure you get as much sleep as possible. If you maintain your sleep schedule, you will find yourself more relaxed and in a better positive frame of mind.

Furthermore, the recommended time for adequate sleep is nine hours, ensure you get up that number in a day.

Take Note of Your Unhealthy Habits

It is normal for an individual to have some unhealthy habits so you shouldn't feel that you are the only one with them. However, knowing what your bad habits are and looking for ways to eliminate them will assist you to remove negative influence.

To effectively take note of these bad or negative habits, think about habits that make you feel depressed and sad about yourself. Those habits that leave you with the feeling that your life sucks and drains your energy making it difficult for you to focus on doing things that will aid your development and influence your life positively.

The obvious examples of these habits are heavy doses of alcohol consumption, substance abuse, heavy partying and unhealthy eating habits. The less obvious ones are unhealthy relationships that leave you with senses of depression and sadness. Another example of this type of habit is self-esteem hate and loathing, low self-esteem. It's highly recommended that you document these bad or negative habits so you can know how to handle them.

CHAPTER 12:

Quiz to Assess Your Degree of Empathy

Read the statements below to yourself and keep a careful note of how many of them you agree with. Use a piece of paper and pen to tally the number of times you identify with the statements--this number will be your empathic score. If you agree strongly and frequently with a statement, mark down 2 points. If you agree somewhat, occasionally, or under specific circumstances, mark down 1 point for yourself. If you do not identify or agree with a statement at all, mark down 0 points.

Try to be as honest with yourself as possible. Answer with your gut, and don't overthink your responses. Also, remember that this self-assessment is designed to evaluate your current empathic abilities, which are fluid and in constant fluctuation. If you find you are torn on any statements, perhaps because you once identified strongly with them but now you no longer do, or vice versa, choose whatever answer resonates most powerfully with your present-day self.

It might be best to take this quiz when you are alone, calm, and able to focus, attending to no one else's needs but your own. If you are indeed an empath, your answers may be impacted by the feelings, judgments, or values of others around you, which can ultimately skew your scoring results.

1. I feel emotions more deeply than most.

2. I have been called "very sensitive," or perhaps even "too sensitive," by others.

3. I can become overwhelmed or uncomfortable in large crowds.

4. I sometimes feel the need for complete, uninterrupted solitude (maybe with quiet and or darkness, but not sleep) to gather my thoughts or "recharge" my energy.

5. I can tell when people are lying or trying to mask their feelings, even if no one else around seems to see it.

6. I am very conscious of how my actions will affect those around me.

7. I find the emotional reactions of other people--laughing, crying, scowling in anger-- be genuinely contagious, regardless of the emotional state I bring to the interaction; even if I am over-the-moon with personal joy, I can be quickly moved to tears by someone else's sorrow.

8. I am deeply bothered by situations of injustice, and often can't help but try to find a solution or remedy, even if it's none of my business or beyond my reach to do so.

9. I am drawn to animals, and I am more comfortable with them than in the company of some humans.

10. I am often told that I am a great listener.

11. I tend to take care of others before I address my own needs.

12. My emotional reactions seem to last longer than they do for other people--it might take me days or weeks to get over something that other people move on from in a matter of hours.

13. In a phone call (or another form of communication where I can't see someone's face) I can read someone's emotional state just from the sound of their voice, and usually gather this from only one or two words of greeting.

14. There are certain forms of graphic media that I just can't stomach--violence, for instance, or humiliation-based comedy is almost painful for me to watch, and I find it hard to shake the feeling off even after it's over.

15. People often open up to me, even those I don't know very well, sharing secrets, confessions, or other pieces of intimate knowledge.

16. I often find myself getting emotionally involved in other people's problems or successes; I might be deeply distraught over a friend's break-up or thrilled when a colleague receives a well-deserved promotion.

17. I frequently catch myself mirroring the body language of others, or mimicking accents and patterns of speech, during conversations.

18. I am more sensitive than most to temperature, and usually, feel chilly in places where others are perfectly comfortable.

19. I can't help reading between the lines or hearing the subtext of a conversation just as loudly as what is articulated verbally.

20. My emotions tend to resonate throughout my entire body; I have a hard time compartmentalizing or ignoring them.

21. I sometimes experience synesthesia, where two or more of my sensory perceptions are intertwined (a sensation of feeling color, perhaps, or seeing sounds, associating numerical values with musical notes, or feeling that certain days or months are linked to locations or emotional states, etcetera.)

22. I can be easily distracted by an external stimulus.

23. Anything that feels inauthentic--a book or movie, a business, or even someone's personality--is a huge turnoff for me, and I cannot stand to be around such things for more than a few minutes without experiencing pain or discomfort.

24. I do not mind being alone if I can determine how I send the time; I might prefer to stay home on Saturday night to read or paint or cook, rather than attend a party.

25. I am susceptible to bright lights, odors, and sounds, sometimes profoundly bothered by them while others can easily ignore them.

26. When conflict arises between people, I know but does not involve me, I still feel hurt, angry, confused or sad, and I am preoccupied until I've taken action to encourage peacemaking.

27. Miscommunication is profoundly frustrating for me to experience or witness, even between strangers.

28. I can sometimes experience two or more contrasting emotions simultaneously; I might be full of joy and fear and sadness, feeling each emotion equally and all at once.

29. I feel deeply connected to underdogs, both in entertainment media and in real life. I can be protective of friends and total strangers alike--anyone who seems especially vulnerable to victimization.

30. I have trouble accepting absolutes, believing that anyone is purely good or evil, that anything is decisively the best or the worst of its kind; I think the truth is always complex, multifaceted, and fluid, because it is largely a matter of perspective.

31. It is sometimes challenging for me to stay present at the moment; my mind is often stuck in the past or fixed in the future.

32. I react to most stimuli quickly and viscerally; I am not the type to sit back and wait to see how things play out before I decide how to feel about the situation.

33. Watching group interactions can be fascinating to me; I sometimes feel as if I can see or sense a complex web of emotions tying every member of the group together, like a game of cat's cradle, influencing their movements, behaviors, and attitudes.

34. The planned trajectories of my days can be thrown off course by fairly small triggers. Something as small as a sharp exchange, a missed green light, a good sign or bad omen, even a momentary sense of deja vu, might cast a ripple effect on my itinerary for the rest of the day or even week.

35. Music, movies, books, dance, and other art forms often give me a sense of being entirely transported to a different time, place, and reality; or, they might trigger an out-of-body experience for me. They can deliver a feeling of transcendence, even if I have no reason to identify with them.

36. I have an eye for small details that others frequently overlook.

37. When I connect with someone I like, we often form an extraordinarily deep bond, and we do so very quickly.

38. Conversely, I often meet people and immediately get bad feelings about them without being able to explain why. That may even be the case if the person in question displays kindness towards me at a surface level, which makes me even more uncomfortable.

39. I don't usually dominate conversations or feel comfortable talking about myself for long periods. I tend to listen or ask questions to encourage input from everyone involved.

40. I have a talent for bringing shy children, adults, or animals, out of their shells.

Your score

Tally up all your zeroes, ones and twos to find your current position on the empathy quotient scale. Remember not to let these numbers discourage you or give you too big of a head--empathy is fluid, and there is always room for growth!

0-20 - Little to no empathic connection

If fewer than twenty of these questions resonated with you, don't interpret that to mean you are incapable of empathy. This score might indicate an empathy deficient condition or disorder, but it also could come from an individual with average, or even heightened, empathic abilities who have learned to close themselves off temporarily. People sometimes reject or turn away from empathic sensitivity as a response to being hurt, having their ego severely bruised, experiencing trauma or grief, as a reaction to long periods of solitude, or a lack of privacy and personal space. Whatever the reason for your score, try to view this number as a jumping off point to start building your empathic energy. Try this test again in a few months, and you may be pleasantly surprised by your growth.

20-40 - Average empathic sensitivity

You are sensitive to the world around you, but selectively. You have a healthy sense of self, you know what you like, and you understand your value system. You recognize the boundary between your own emotions and other people's feelings but can still empathize fully in appropriate situations.

At this position on the empathy quotient scale, your boundaries need to be strong. If you surround yourself with people who display low empathetic sensitivity levels, you may find your score gradually decreases under their influence.

40-80 - Heightened empathic ability

Your empathic capability is above average, but perhaps not so strong that you have been forced to reckon with it entirely. You've found it helpful in some ways, but profoundly confusing and frustrating at times, too. That can be a turbulent awakening experience, as empathetic sensations come to you seemingly from out of nowhere, unpredictably and often at extremely inconvenient times. If your sensitivity is awakened but not trained, you are vulnerable to the whims of the world, like a rowboat in the sea without a paddle. You'll first want to enhance your empathic sensitivity and understanding, and then determine the specifics of your empathic type, before ultimately learning how to balance and ground your energy.

80-120 - Advanced empathic power

This score could alternatively be called "severe empathic sensitivity," depending on how well you've managed your abilities thus far. You feel a great deal more empathy than most, which leaves you quite vulnerable to toxic energy, emotional contagion, and depletion. With education, training and spiritual guidance, you'll be able to manage your power and maintain your energy levels, but it will take plenty of focus, determination, and patience to reach a point of emotional stability. With this degree of power, your reach may very well exceed your grasp, so it's important to seek out experienced mentors, metaphysical healers, and spiritual teachers to help guide you to a place of deeper understanding.

CHAPTER 13:

Practical Exercises for Empaths

Shutting yourself from others is incredibly harmful psychologically for anyone, not just for empaths. This increases the sensitivity we feel when around others. We want to be able to function at our best in all situations and not become overly sensitive to 'regular' people.

A method many sensitives use unconsciously to stop the constant bombardment of other emotions and energy, is to distract themselves. Distracting works to lessen the impact of external stimulus. But there are various negative forms of distraction such as alcohol, drugs, sex, porn and junk food which can lead to a reliance or an unhealthy addiction. Most of these addictions shift our perception into a state where we are not as aware, this allows us to escape feeling the pain in the world. Try to avoid these at all costs!

In this part, we will look at positive exercises and forms of distraction which will help support you no matter what you're faced with without relying on unhealthy vices.

Using Affirmations

Many people use affirmations nowadays, they have become incredibly popular in all walks of life. They're positive statements repeated over and over to help us escape negative thought patterns while promoting positive ones. They can help keep an empath strong particularly in an overwhelming situation. You can create your own affirmations if something in particular resonates with you. Here are a few of the ones which I have found helpful -

'I refuse to absorb other people's energy. I can acknowledge how others are feeling, but I now shield myself from absorbing anything from them'.

'I can allow others close to me, without taking on their energy or emotions'.

'I feel and connect with my own feelings before anyone else's'.

Assertiveness tip –

Do you struggle saying no to people? This is a common occurrence among sensitives, here is an idea which I found helpful when presented with something I wasn't sure about. If for example, a friend of colleague asks you out for drinks in the evening, instead of agreeing immediately, respond with 'Ok, I will just have to check my schedule and let you know' - This isn't saying no! But it is in fact giving you some breathing space to decide whether or not this is something you want to do. With this kind of response, you don't feel like you have been put on the spot and that you must respond immediately. This gives you time to process the request and hopefully muster up the courage within to say no (if you don't feel like doing what was requested). Beginning to honor your feelings is incredibly important.

Here are three unfinished sentences which you can work with to help build your sense of boundaries. Try to come up with as many different responses as you can. By doing this you are gradually beginning to reinforce and develop stronger boundaries.

1) I have the right to ask for.........

Some answer here could include - space, respect etc.

2) To have enough time and energy to function at my best, it is ok to..........

Examples - refuse invitations, do my own work first etc.

3) If I refuse others, they may......

Examples - not like me, talk badly about me, respect me more etc

Without talking care of your own boundaries, you are effectively hindering yourself from living a happy and successful life. That's what it comes down to. Over time, this becomes easier. Helping others at your own expenses is detrimental to the whole.

Exercise

Exercise is an absolute must. I have personally found it to be one of the main tools I use that helps me enjoy life as an empath. The right training will not only exercise the physical body but the nervous system also (the root of your sensitivity). By exercising to engage the nervous system, we can almost reset our minds and bodies. This is exactly how I feel after a workout, as though someone has pushed a button and I have been energetically reset. It works incredibly well to clear away negative or any stagnant energy. It also increases the flow of freshly oxygenated blood all around the body. These are just some of the many benefits associated to exercise.

Another important tip is to stay away from public mirrors. The ones you find in gyms and clothes shops. Empaths can pick up negative energies being reflected to them from mirrors especially if the people who have been looking at their reflections are egotistical or self-absorbed. The empath can often take on this negative energy as their own.

Clearing your energy to create healthier boundaries

Reduce negativity - Due to our sensitive nature, we pick up negativity very easily. To help overcome this, empaths should start distancing themselves from negativity as much as possible. This can include people you know, certain places, even the news and social platforms. The TV and social media can really impact the empath on a subconscious level, they may not realize it at the time but they are picking up a lot of negativity from these sources particularly from the news, world affairs, soap operas and even reality TV shows.

Balance - Living a balanced life, is important for anyone, none more so than for an empath. This includes all areas of life such as diet, work, health, sleep, exercise etc. Keeping all aspects in some kind of balance help avoid becoming over stimulated. Try not to overdo it, as you'll likely need longer to recover. I have personally found I can only exercise 2-3 times a week, any more than this and I tend to feel burnt out. Taking adequate rest is also important and will improve your overall health and well-being.

Determine what is not yours –

Sometimes we walk into a room or a situation and feel like we have energetically picked up a mood or a vibe which wasn't ours. Try to bring your conscious awareness to any feelings you suspect don't belong to you. If you don't feel it is yours then make a choice to discard it, send the unwanted energy away and down into the earth. This can be done easily, simply holding your focus and stating the intention in your mind while visualizing the emotion leaving you.

Declutter –

Since empaths fundamentally must claim ownership over their own energetic space and stop others intruding in it, they should also take the same care with their physical areas. If you are messy, untidy or have a lot of clutter, take the time to clear your physical space, doing this will clear your mind and energy also. Negativity tends to breed in clutter and mess.

Crystals for protection –

Crystals are a gift and a spiritual superpower for promoting self-care. Anything can be used as a symbol of protection whether that is a piece of jewelry or a crystal. The most important thing is that you believe in whatever you are trusting for your protection. This belief alone will help protect you. People find it easy to trust in crystals due to their natural Earthly healing properties and they're fairly inexpensive to buy. If you are interested in learning in depth knowledge on how to use crystals and how to get the most out of these powerful stones then please check out my other book - Crystal Healing: Heal Yourself & Transform Your Life.

Now we will take a look at some crystals which work incredibly well as protection for empaths and sensitives.

Rose Quartz

This is a great crystal for empaths to possess simply for its grounding properties. It is often referred to as the 'Love Stone', since is resonates and works to repair the heart chakra. These qualities give the user a boost while helping to keep others negative emotions out of their space. It promotes all types of love, such as self-love, romantic, unconditional and platonic. Since it is a quartz, this means it has a high energy that can help bring a positive loving vibration into almost all circumstances. By bringing more love into an empath's daily life, it helps to lower stress while carrying warmth to everyone who is present. It is also used to improve self-esteem and attract genuine love into our lives. All these positive qualities bring balance to the emotions while helping to reduce stress and anxieties.

Black Tourmaline

This has been referred to as the 'must have' crystal for empaths. Known for its protective qualities this crystal enables the carrier to shield and deflect away any negative or low vibrational energies. It does this by processing any bad energy which comes into the auric field whether it's from other people or the environment. It also acts as a filter to protect us, which only allows good energies in, such as love, joy and kindness.

When carried regularly it neutralizes and purifies our own negative thought patterns by filtering them into positive energy. It is renowned as an extremely effective grounding stone; it achieves this by creating a connection between the body and Earth. This contact helps to align and balance the energy centers (chakras) while channeling positive healing energy through the whole physical body.

Sugilite

This crystal comes in a striking violet color and resonates with the 7th chakra - the crown. It creates a firm impermeable bubble around the carrier which helps protect them from negative energies of the environment and unwanted thought forms from others. It's incredibly effective at preventing energetic attacks from energy vampires by dissolving the bad energy patterns headed our way. Its power enables the user to go through their daily activities with a sense of inner strength and grace. Due to its activation of the crown chakra, it helps bring healing light in from the head down to the 1st chakra - the root. This influx of positive energy promotes balance and well-being that keeps us strong when faced with negativity.

Lapis Lazuli

A very popular and attractive stone that has been used for many thousands of years, particularly prevalent with the ancient Egyptians. It is best known for its protective qualities and its ability to repair, seal and strengthen the auric field. This helps in dissolving any negative emotions or energies which have been picked up. Lapis is a crystal of truth which helps increase self-awareness within the empath, with this we become more conscious of what belongs to us and what doesn't. In the same way, it allows what doesn't belong to us to be released and 'brought to the surface'. Lapis works with the third eye chakra, which is the seat of perception, with this we are able to gain clarity and 'see' exactly what is occurring around us energetically. Although, empaths sense this, they do not always clearly understand what is happening. It also helps promote grounding and restores balance.

Practical Test:

1. What is rose quartz?

2.What is a gift and a spiritual superpower for promoting self-care?

3. How to reduce negativity?

CHAPTER 14:

Positive Affirmations to Be Made Daily

An affirmation is a positive sentence that will affect your conscious and subconscious mind. Repeating an affirmation has the power of helping it manifest. If you visualize and repeat your affirmation continuously, it will help in the manifestation of your desires much faster. Using affirmations will make the result more profound.

Positivity plays a very important role in your life. People probably tell you to stay positive all the time while assuring you that everything will be fine. There is more to this than just words. Positive thoughts and energy can be very powerful. If you focus on the bad things and negative thoughts in your life, this will result in the manifestation of those.

Thinking and acting positively will therefore help in the manifestation of positive results in your life. I'm not saying that a miracle will happen and you will get an expensive car just by saying you will get it the next day; however, if that car is what you want, use it in your affirmation sentence. When you practice and repeat this affirmation over time, it will help you get that car. You may be wondering how this is possible. Well, when you focus on that car or just anything else, you know what you want.

meditation will help to change your mindset and life to a much more positive one. This will make it possible to be determined and work singularly until you achieve your goal of buying that car. This is how the manifestation will work in your favor. When you keep lamenting your bad luck or anything negative, your energy and thoughts are focused on those. This drains you of the positive energy required to live your life more productively. Can you understand a little now?

Negative thoughts can arise at any moment, and they may be very overwhelming at times; however, with the help of Empathy, you can exercise control over these thoughts and turn them into more positive ones. Your negative thoughts should never overpower the positivity in you. For this, you need to maintain balance in your chakras, lead a healthy lifestyle, and practice regularly.

Healing with Affirmations

Affirmations are an easy and simple tool for healing. There is no complicated formula, symbol, or technique involved. This is why it is one of the easiest tools to use in your daily life, but it has a profound impact.

One of the ways to heal with affirmations is to chant. Chanting is a practice that is used all over the world and in various religions. Just repeating certain words with complete faith has a way of harnessing power into them. This is why you should try repeating your affirmation like a chant whenever you get a chance.

Use the affirmation chant to charge a bottle of water or some crystal that you can carry with you all day. You can also write the affirmation on some paper and place a glass of water over it. This water can be consumed or sprayed around your space when it is charged with the affirmation.

Another method involves using Empath more proactively. Write your affirmation on a paper and then practice over it with your palms. You can either hold the affirmation paper or hover over it with your hands. You can also do this by keeping a bottle of water on the table. Now use your palms to hover over this bottle. the associated symbols as you chant the affirmation. Try visualizing the outcome of your affirmation while you move your hands over the water. This also helps to charge that bottle of water with positive energy, and you can continue consuming it throughout the day.

Meditating on an affirmation is a healthy and effective practice. Take time out every day to meditate over your desired goal. Sit in a peaceful place and take some calming breaths. Close your eyes and begin chanting the affirmation. Meditate on the outcome that you desire. Visualize it happening. This can be a powerful tool and will strengthen your belief in the possibility of the affirmation manifesting.

Using crystals is another great alternative to try. Find the appropriate crystal for your purpose and cleanse it before you use it. Crystals absorb energy from each person they come in contact with, and you need to make sure the crystal you use is cleansed for your purpose. Now hold the crystal in your palms and use to charge it. Focus and use your complete concentration to repeat your affirmation as you hold the crystal. Direct the affirmation into the crystal and manifest the energy from your third-eye chakra. Visualize a white light coming from your chakra and beaming into the crystal. Then imagine the outcome of your affirmation happening. Use this charged crystal and keep it in a sacred space. You can also choose to carry it with you at all times.

All of the ways given above are just some of the options available to you. You can heal with affirmations in many ways. The affirmation that you create in the first place should be a powerful and meaningful sentence. This does not mean it has to be something complex and long; in fact, it should be a short and clear sentence. Think well about what you want to manifest and then use it as an affirmation.

Practical Test:

1. Is affirmation important?
2. Is affirmation to chant?
3. How to make and use an affirmation?

CHAPTER 15:

Avoiding the Negativity That Sometimes Plagues Empaths

Strategies to Avoid Absorbing Negative Energy

How to embolden yourself from the emotional effects of others

The transference of energy from other people is a real challenge in today's world. Highly sensitive people are often plagued with this phenomenon and wonder what to do about it. Signals carrying the energy from those around us is often involuntary. It just happens. Sometimes we can gain from these encounters but most often, they are a weight that can drag us down and ruin a perfectly good day.

When we absorb other people's feelings and emotions, they become mixed up within our own similar inclinations and thoughts. When this happens, things can get a bit more involved and interrupt the natural flow of our own lives so that things don't get done or become halted altogether. For this reason, we must guard against the potential for misinterpretations of these bundles of feelings in order to have an actively progressive flow of our own information and forward motion.

When you find yourself in a room with a very negative individual, their "bad" energy can actually very quickly be activated in you. In order to prevent this from happening, the first step to take is to take a moment and look inwards, try to identify the true source of the negative energy. Is it you and was it always there inside you, or is it the other persons energy invading your otherwise happy system? In most cases, you will be able to learn that it is indeed not yours and was not present in your immediate feelings and emotions until that other person walked into the room. You must then take steps to let it go. Close your eyes and visualize who you are. Embolden yourself with the strength that you know you have always had within you and hold on tightly to that which you believe. Since you are a positive life form, this will manifest in those negative energies leaving your body and your mind. Remove yourself from surroundings containing negative thought patterns and feelings. Just walk away from it and do everything you can to avoid repeating this type of situation and condition in the future.

Another trait empath all exhibit is that they are all hyper-sensitive to the effect of their surroundings. When an empath is in a space where harmony abounds, they are most at home, as they will always mimic the happy and harmonious qualities of the room. Consequently, when they are in an environment where there is negative and dark energy, the opposite happens, and they must remove themselves as quickly as possible which is exactly what they usually do. Actually, this is something all normally energized people should also do. Nobody should have to put up with those who simply drag us down with their whiny grievances.

Here are some things that you can do in order to protect and embolden yourself from the negative and nonproductive energy of those around you:

- Set your limits and boundaries. Negative people will recognize this in you and will generally move away from you.

- Be selective in where you go, who you are willing to speak with and always be sure to be in control of you.

- Don't get sidelined. Keep your antenna's up and use your special awareness to stay clear of others bad behavior and negative energies.

- Stay positive. Don't let anyone or anything drag you down. It is much easier to stay positive within yourself than to have to battle your way back up after being dragged down unnecessarily.

- Remember who you are and how much you love being you. You are above the fray when it comes to bad energy. Use your own "intact" systems to stay strong.

So if you've thought it over and wondered to yourself just how to stay positive when your find yourself in a negative environment; stick to the rules set out here and things will gradually begin to smooth out and become much easier for you. If these are people you just cannot avoid, and would really rather avoid, you must have a protection program in place, or you will suffer, and they will drag you down.

There is really no sense in letting this happen if your already know that it is a "given," with a certain person or set of people, that it has already previously been proven to be so. You can do this. Know the parameters, set up your own system in your mind when you know you must face them again, and keep it up!

You may want to think of in the abstract; be creative. Think of your next meeting with these low energy people as a heading. Think of the upcoming meeting, class, group, or whatever the case may be, as the heading on a part of a book. The heading tells the reader what is coming, and then the data pours out and is indeed, "as advertised." The heading predicted it because it knew for a fact what was coming next, and the data had to work closely with the heading because they work in tandem with each other. They are a team!

Now, breaking this theory down, you are the heading and the "people" in the group are the data. If your heading says, "Do not try to mess with me because I am protected, and it won't work!" They will take one look at you and immediately back off. Problem solved.

As stated, toxic people, whether they are consciously aware of it or not, do not do well with boundaries or "rules of engagement." These would be "your" rules, so you are in charge. When going into battle, be armed and dangerous. Be ready for the enemy.

I know that sounds a bit terse but it gets the point across and the alternative is having to set through hours of soul destroying and painful negativity that you know within yourself that you don't like and you don't need. Just do your homework and take control. It will be easy once you understand how to do it.

And there is more; again, why you know that you must see them, be with them, and interact with them, keep it short and concise so that there is no room for "small talk" or any unnecessary banter. Keep the communications brief and keep the material light whenever possible. Remember, toxic people will search for key areas in your speaking on which to pounce. This will create a scenario where they look better. This is their MO. If the conversation is by telephone, set a timer so you have control.

Weigh out the consequences of new topics that may arise in conversation and know which are worth dealing with and which are worth tossing into the circular file as soon as possible. Observe others intention in their speaking. Where are they attempting to take the conversation?

You really do need to protect yourself from what could be called "secondhand stress." Just being around people who operate out of drama can be very draining and as everyone must know by now, stress is not just a bad thing, it is a killer. You must come up with ways to avoid it at all costs. Research has shown that stress can be a bit like a yawn, it can actually be contagious. In an earlier part we tackled "mirror neurons" that are signals produced in the brain that provide some degree of ability for us to absorb and comprehend other people's feelings and emotions.

In the same way that we might understand others, we can also be a huge "antenna," for receiving those around us who may send us all their bad stuff. Negative energy and stress can be incoming in this way. Science tells us that even as we observe another's anger, our stress hormones may rise up to twenty-six percent in our bodies. Stress conveyed to us through other people can show up in a variety of ways. When we spend time thinking about the problems that someone else may be experiencing or getting nervous or afraid because that is the emotion that another person close to us is feeling is a stress maker for all of us.

Also, sustained stress can give us all sorts of extended health issues which means we must find a way to protect ourselves from the "outside" sources of errant stress. The following are a few suggestions that may help to immunize you against secondhand stress:

1. Do not let stress spread into your body! As social individuals, we see, and we feel. Prevent unfavorable "other peoples" stress and negativity by focusing on your own current feelings. This will contain your emotions and show you that these new apparent "inputs" are not yours. Thereby keeping tabs on your good feelings.

2. Empathize without swallowing the entire pill yourself! We are in charge of us and they are in charge of them and this focus can be a great deal of help as a filter or boundary locator. Put up your fence and play on your side, let them play on their side. This is actually a good time to do a lesson within yourself and know your passions and your own empathy. It's okay to substantiate their situation and do listen to their words if they need to "get it out," but remember, don't jump right in and share the agony. This is just not necessary.

3. Monitor your own stress levels on a regular basis and don't let them rise up! Get the endorphins going and observe your breathing. Utilize your mindfulness and meditate daily and if you can, multiple times a day. Any kind of exercise is also a great way to keep tabs on yourself. Your body will thank you when you pump up the body machine now and then.

4. Monitor your sense of boundaries! In a way, checking in on your boundary patrol is a healthy thing to be doing. Simply be vigilant and always know when to step away from and individual or a situation.

5. Boosting your sense of self, staying vigilant on boundary patrol, and monitoring your own feelings are all tools that can help to keep secondhand stress under control.

For the past few years, there has been a relatively new psychological theory in the works called "Emotional Intelligence." The idea is that just as people have an array of intellectual abilities, they also have a range of emotional abilities and skills. These emotional "tools," can be of immense assistance in the area of our thinking and what we do from day today. The bottom line here is that utilizing this theory makes you a better person and can help you grow in ways that you want to grow and not wherever the wind may take you.

Practical Test:

1. Is it important that you do not let stress affect your body?

2. Is monitoring your sense of boundaries part of the strategy?

3. When we absorb other people's feelings and emotions, they become mixed up within our own similar inclinations and thoughts? True or False.

CHAPTER 16:

Reducing Fear and Anxiety

Anxiety disorders are very common today, and it is estimated, according to data from several investigations, that 20% of the population will experience an anxiety crisis throughout their lives. One of the most known anxieties disorders are fears, among which we can highlight social fear. But what is social fear? What can we do to overcome it?

Fear is an emotion that has played a fundamental role in the survival of human beings. And also, this is fundamental in animals and in humans for survival. It mainly serves to guide us about the dangers that can threaten us at any given time, whether they are perceived in the external world or in the internal world. Activate in our body the escape or fight responses, as it is more convenient.

What Types of Fears Exist?

Simple fears generally occur towards a single object. They have a source, where they come from, usually in childhood, whereas children we get scared of certain things or situations. Being already adults and in similar scenarios, something acts as a trigger and makes us relive those terrifying feelings of the past, as if we were still small and helpless, developing a fear of something.

There are complex fears, which are related fears and intermingled with personality characteristics and character. They generally appear in the course of development in childhood or associated with various traumatic experiences in adolescence that intensify aspects already vulnerable in the first years of life. Mainly, they hinder the relationship with others, intimacy, commitment and aspects of self-concept, such as self-assessment. The social fear is an example of complex fears.

What Differentiates Fear from Shyness?

Shyness is a characteristic of introverted people, who are rather reserved, with a lot of inner life and who sometimes find it difficult to show themselves more socially, to appear, to have prominence and to develop socially with skills related to good conversation, to be entertaining or fun, Be the life of the party They are usually very thoughtful people with an intense emotional world that is little outwardly visible.

How Does Social Fear Affect the Lives of People Who Suffer from It?

It is very limiting. It can go so far as to make the person have to live in seclusion at home, avoiding contact with other people outside his family. Or also, it is observed when the person finds difficulties to attend usual social activities (study, work, shows) or exceptional (weddings, graduations).

The fear of being evaluated or being exposed is the predominant effect that these people experience, in addition to having many difficulties to show themselves publicly, to be the centre of attention of others or to stand out for some particular reason.

It is very great suffering that they suffer, reaching the extreme of not feeling worthy of being loved by others or having the feeling that there is a fault or a defect in them that they do not want others to see.

Social fear affects more in contexts with little appreciation of feelings, which are experienced as a sign of weakness, in environments of effective lack, where children are not offered safety experiences within the family so that later they become in children who succeed. Also in very overprotective and normative environments, where children do not develop self-affirmative feelings of their own value, where everything is resolved, and they do not have to work and put their own resources into play to get what they want.

A fear develops then to go out into the world, to connect with others as we are, with our defects and our virtues, to deal with our limitations to overcome those obstacles that arise. It may also happen that one of our caregivers in childhood has this same problem, and we learn somehow those fears or similar ones.

Anyway, even if we have grown up in an adverse environment, we can acquire from adults the security that we did not obtain in later rearing, develop new resources and strengthen ourselves to make our way into the external world. This sometimes occurs because there are new, more favorable contexts (partners, educational or sports contexts, a family of friends, gangs of university colleagues, work team) later in development or because people ask for specialized medical, psychiatric, help or psychological to overcome those difficulties.

In the case of complex fears, the treatments are longer since aspects related to the way of being and personality are worked, focusing on how to establish emotional ties and manage the emotional world.

One of the most commonly used techniques for the treatment of fears is systematic desensitization. Systematic desensitization consists of planning the very gradual and progressive exposure to those stimuli that produce the fear.

The person is developing the possibility of approaching what terrifies him with support at the beginning of the therapist, who sometimes acts as a counter phobic companion and through systematic repetitions, which increase the difficulty and time of exposure, it is justly desensitized, that is to say no longer feel fear and that the object of this fear becomes something non-frightening for the person.

Is It Possible to Overcome Fear Without Applying Exposure Techniques?

Of course. The exposure technique has been developed by the Cognitive Behavioral approach, and certain patients do very well and thus solve their problem.

But experts are very used to receiving people who have undergone this type of punctual treatment on a fear, based on exposure techniques, over time they develop another similar or the same intensifies, so it is necessary to apply here other types of targeted treatments at greater depth than allow the problem to work at its root, so that it does not reproduce again.

A person with social fear, or any other type of fear, can recover. You can return to experience much of its functionality, and you can develop roles and resources that allow you to go out into the world feeling safe and secure, safely and without fear, recovering a normal relationship with what generated so much fear.

Many times, patients are surprised to discover that something they have suffered for so long can remit resulting in new experiences and expanding the possibilities of experiences, which were previously not available.

In another perspective, social fear or social anxiety is a disorder in which people experience intense anxiety symptoms when they find themselves in social situations in which they irrationally fear feeling judged, humiliated or ridiculed.

A person with social fear cannot relate to or perform normal activities that involve being in a group, whether at work, at parties, or at sporting activities. Even acting in front of others also suffers, even if just to talk on the phone, ask for the bill or eat. It can be said that a person with social fear has an intense fear of relating

Zombies Representing the Social Fear

Although many people believe this is a kind of shyness, the truth is that social fear is not the same thing. A shy person experiences shame and, in some cases, fear, but in a very attenuated way; In fact, a certain degree of shyness is normal in most people. However, when suffering from social fear, the symptoms of anxiety and fear are disproportionately intense and disabling.

Physical symptoms experienced by a person with social fear can range from flushing, excessive sweating, dizziness and tremors, to nausea, gastrointestinal discomfort, tachycardia and even bouts of Anxiety. In addition, these symptoms are not limited to the time of social interaction, as one of the hallmarks of this disorder is exaggerated anticipation that causes people to live in states of anxiety weeks before each event they have to face.

The problem, as with other fears, is that in many cases, Anxiety leads people to avoid fearful situations, creating a vicious circle in which the main goal is to avoid relating.

Social fear impoverishes the life of the person who suffers it, making it difficult to find work, friends or partners and all kinds of experiences. In addition, whenever a situation that can trigger Anxiety is avoided, fear becomes stronger and more powerful.

Is It Possible to Get Out of the Vicious Circle of Social Fear?

Overcoming social fear is possible, but as with other anxiety problems, the road is long and requires commitment and effort. Recognizing and accepting the problem is the first step, but in most cases, it will be essential to seek professional help to overcome this disorder.

Some keys that can facilitate coping and managing social fear are as follows:

Be Aware of the Problem

Knowing what happens to us is the first step and then working with it. Now, it's important to be very clear that we are not the problem, but that we have a problem. Everyone has moments of weakness and overcoming. We all have the right to be nervous and make mistakes, and the important thing is to be on the road to overcome.

Working on self-esteem and self-acceptance is critical to overcoming social fear because it connects us with our essence and allows us to know ourselves. This will make it easier to accept what happens to us.

Face Fears Progressively

Moving to action is another key step. The important thing to overcome a fear is to face what is frightening but progressively. We can start practicing in environments that are not too hostile, such as in family gatherings, with a friend, or in small groups.

Another way to keep moving forward is to pursue our own challenges. If we are afraid of eating in public, we will try to take the snack until one day we are able to sit in the park to eat it. If we are afraid to participate in class, we will enroll in some activity where we know that there are few people to interact little by little. If what we fear is facing opinions, we can start by discussing a topic with a kind family member.

The key is to start little by little and move on to situations that generate the most Anxiety. Having a record of our achievements is very motivating.

How to Overcome Social Fear?

Learn to Manage Anxiety

Searching for our own ways to manage Anxiety will help us. For example, playing sports, meditating, or learning relaxation techniques… The less anxiety we experience, the less we will have to deal with at the most difficult times.

Seek Professional Help

If you feel that you cannot go it alone or that you need external support, do not hesitate to seek professional help. Research has shown that

cognitive-behavioral therapy, along with the development of social skills and techniques to control Anxiety, work to overcome social fear.

As we see, social fear is a limiting problem that impoverishes our relationships, but one that we can progressively overcome if we strive. Above all, we need to try.

Practical Test:

1. What are the types of fears?

2. Why is it important to be aware of the problem?

3. Is Seeking for professional Help relevant?

CHAPTER 17:

Channeling Your Unique Energy into Your Life

We all have natural gifts and talents. Some individuals are artistic, some are sporty or adventurous, and some are empaths. No gift should ever be hidden; following your passions is a way of finding purpose in life, which is something we all need to thrive. Consider some abilities that your gift has given you that you maybe weren't even aware of.

Empathetic Listening

Empathetic listening is truly understanding and being able to perceive what someone is saying to you. There is absolutely no judgment involved, but only raw compassion and understanding. Empathetic listening is not always easy as it means putting all your own personal needs and opinions aside to focus on who really needs your support. It's not necessarily about giving advice but about lending an ear to someone in need. Empaths are able to do this far easier than others, and, in fact, many empaths become psychologists and counselors because of it.

How comforting is the thought of having a space to release your emotions in a safe environment? This is exactly what someone with the gift of empathetic listening provides. It requires a certain level of thoughtfulness between the two individuals involved and can definitely create a bond. Through using their gift, empaths improve their ability to understand and console, which strengthens them in many aspects of their lives.

Attentiveness is given to what is being said, and this will make the individual feel important and cared for. It releases tension and can improve the mood, which is one of the things an empath lives for. The other person won't have to worry about being interrupted while releasing your emotions as an empathetic listener will constantly reassure them during the process. When someone's needs are put first and acknowledged, it increases their confidence and will forge a positive light on speaking up about how they feel in the future. It can never be a bad thing to be able to openly and honestly voice your thoughts.

Through empathetic listening, an empath can truly help someone in need. This is definitely a gift to be proud of. Use it often and you will never be without loved ones.

Empathetic Leading

Empathetic leading is sometimes viewed as a weak trait, but this is most definitely not the case. To be a good leader, sometimes it is required that you be able to put yourself in the other person's shoes for a moment. Empathetic leaders are also generally empathetic listeners as it is beneficial to them to be able to intently listen and understand the needs of those around them. Empaths that are in charge of others mostly don't have the "do as I say" attitude and are emotional thinkers which might seem like a poor skill to some, but in fact, is a unique kind of strength. If there is one thing that people being led by someone else want to feel, it is equality. Empathetic leaders make those around them feel like equals by considering them in every aspect of decision-making.

Empathetic leaders can use their gift to their advantage in more ways than one. They are able to use out the bad apples and pick up on some things that may be sketchy. They might even use the knowledge of someone else's feelings and emotions in a way that is beneficial to them if they deem it necessary.

The gift of being an empathetic leader is that those under you are likely to truly respect you and your opinions. It creates loyalty and clear communication, which helps to improve overall work ethic. The ability to put yourself in someone else's shoes is a fantastic one.

Empathetic Relationships

No relationship is ever perfect. For one to succeed, it requires effort from each partner, many sacrifices, and a lot of forgiveness. Above all else, you need to be able to compromise. If your partner is an empath, you may be much luckier than you think. They can be very difficult people to understand and deal with at times, but they have the traits that make up some of the best life partners.

Empaths are unbelievably loyal to their loved ones. They only wish to see the best in their partners, and they will give their partners their whole heart and soul. You see, when empaths dedicate themselves to something, they go all in. This includes relationships. You will be the main focus point in their lives, and they will do anything to make sure you know that you are loved and cared for. They are the type of people that will move mountains even if all they get back in return is a smile. Once they have devoted themselves to you, they will love unconditionally. This love is one of the purest forms you will ever find.

Since an empath's emotions and feelings are so intense, they are able to love just as deeply. They feel very passionately and will never deliberately hurt you as it would cause them great upset. They can often use their gift to read the situation and get a gauge on how you are feeling. When angry, they are very careful when selecting their words as they will not say anything to worsen a situation because their gift allows them to understand the situation on a deeper level. Openness and honesty are high up on the list of what empaths find important, and when they trust you, they will not do anything to hide their thoughts and fears from you. They are able to bring out the best in you through their joy and happiness and the optimism is only beneficial in a partner's life.

When an empath feels the pain of their partner, their natural healing instincts will come out, and they will do anything to subdue the pain and protect you. Some may not realize it, but with an empath by your side, you will possess the ability to make the world a better place. They are able to understand you on a different level due to their amazing ability to feel what you are feeling.

Change Your Mindset

I believe that success and happiness are all about our mindsets. It affects everything in our lives, even how we react and handle the world around us. To achieve your goals, you need your mindset to level up with your aspirations.

The Path to Self-Improvement

Your self-talk has a direct connection with whether or not you have a positive or negative mindset. Consider changing your negative self-talk into a full-on empowerment speech. Who better to encourage you than yourself? It'll have the biggest impact. One of the ways you can do this is by using the positive affirmations I mentioned earlier.

Your mindset is also a reflection of how you see yourself. If you constantly believe, for example, that you're a slob or a bad worker, you will eventually train your brain into believing and following these thoughts. Through reading, you might be surprised at how quickly you pick up on the author's way of thinking. Look into some literature that will lead you in the right direction and try to avoid dark and heavy reading until you're in a better headspace. Reading is an excellent activity for an empath to take up due to their ability to see how others feel and think. You may find that books help you feel more positive, depending on their genres and titles. Go for self-motivating and happy books and take note of how much your mindset changes by journaling.

Using your environment to exercise your way of thinking is maybe one of the best options for an empath. We tend to forget that there is a lot more out there than little old us when trapped in a certain mindset. You might think you're stuck in the worst situation possible until you see someone else in an even worse predicament than yourself. Nature can be your getaway and "mind cleanser" when you really need it. There is nothing like beautiful scenery to readjust your way of thinking and make you appreciate the beauty of this world and life. As a bonus, sunshine is fantastic for a natural mood-booster. Once your head is clear again, you can carry on with your self-improvement journey. Sometimes all we need is a bit of a break from our own minds in order to get back on track. There's no better break than a walk-in nature. You could even take that book along.

Surround yourself with people that have your desired mindset and try to celebrate your daily small achievements in life; it will lead you to accomplishing many more.

You Are Good Enough

Trust me, everyone on the planet has had a moment where they felt like they weren't good enough. Worse than that, I believe all of us have let the words and thoughts of others dictate how we feel about ourselves. No one can make you feel that way if you do not let them. Ultimately, you are in charge of your feelings and thoughts. Do not let anyone take that away from you.

A perfect example of what can make us feel like we're not good enough is the opinions of others and that little voice in our own head.

Shut down your inner critic. He's not doing you any good. You can talk back. The moment that little voice starts nagging at you about something that makes you feel inferior, shut it down. By shifting your focus onto something else or just simply saying "no," you are training yourself to recognize your self-worth. Make a list of what boosts your confidence on those days that you just aren't able to get rid of that voice. Perhaps you should consider saving or writing down messages that someone said that put a smile on your face. If they're truly worth it, stick them up somewhere you'll see them often, like the bathroom mirror.

It is so easy to compare ourselves to others on a daily basis as we always want to be the best that we can possibly be. The hard truth is that there is always going to be someone better than you. There will always be someone smarter, faster, or more attractive. You need to make peace with it, or it will eat you up inside. You don't need to be better than everyone else. You only need to be you. Trust me, being you is a pretty great thing. Being the best, you are what is important, not being better than someone else.

Social media is one of the things that is a major cause of people not feeling good enough about themselves. Many of us have at least one social media account and it is incredibly difficult to avoid, particularly since they are designed to be addictive

Practical Test:

1. What is Empathetic Relationships?

2.Why is it important to change your mindset?

3. What is the Path to Self-Improvement?

CHAPTER 18:

Being Yourself and Allow Your Creative Side to Flourish

Be Your Own First Priority

If you are completely drained, you will not be able to deal with the struggles of daily life or handle normal interactions with people. Even a person who's not an empath will struggle to control their emotions when they are exhausted and depleted. This is much worse for empaths, as they are dealing with their own emotions, as well as the emotions of the people and energy around them. Putting yourself first is not a selfish act. This is difficult for empaths to accept, but when they put this into practice, they will realize its importance.

Build Fences, Not Walls

Empaths tend to isolate themselves to prevent being overwhelmed by the emotions and energies of others. Don't do this! By all means, take time alone to decompress when you need to, but there is no reason that you can't have a healthy, active social life and be successful at work.

You can and should support the people in your life. However, it is important that you do not give them all your energy. You will be a better friend and a family member and lead a more meaningful life if you are not depleted. To accomplish this, you need to develop boundaries.

If you have a coworker who is draining for you to be around, you can still work with them. But you do not need to socialize outside of the workplace. If they invite you to lunch, politely decline. Use the excuse that you have to work for lunch. Next time tell them that you brought lunch, or you are on a special diet. They will eventually get the hint.

Keep your interactions with co-workers you find draining limited to what is necessary for your job. On days that you know you'll need to spend a lot of time with them for professional reasons, take some extra time for yourself in the morning to practice self-care. Make sure you take the time that evening to decompress.

If you feel your life would be better without a certain person in your life, you should cut them out of your life. For example, you may have a friend from your childhood that always needs something from you and always has problems they want you to solve but is who never there for you in return. Someone like this can be extremely draining for anyone to maintain a friendship with but is even more difficult for an empath. Empaths have a harder time saying no. It is harder to cut a conversation short. But if someone is bringing toxicity into your life, don't feel that you have to keep them in it just because you have a shared history. If this feels too selfish, try to reframe how you think about it: you will have a lot of time and energy to help other people if this toxic person is no longer in your life. Your friend will be better off if they have a friend without empathic abilities who is not so drained being around them. They can find another toxic person, and they can be toxic together.

For people, such as family members that you cannot cut out of your life, you should set clearly defined boundaries. For example, you may have a sister who you love dearly, but who is so needy that you always feel very drained after interacting with her. In this example, you could set boundaries such as limiting the time you spend with the person or on the phone. Your boundaries may be that you end your daily phone call after ten minutes and schedule a two-hour brunch every other week. Your boundaries should be based on your relationship with the person and how much interacting with them drains you.

At a certain time, each evening, turn off your phone or at least silence the ringer. Let your friends and family know that after this time of night, you are unavailable, except in emergencies. Don't be afraid to tell them that you consider an emergency a health crisis or similar. Your younger sister's fifteenth breakup with the same man she keeps going back to is not an emergency under this paradigm. You can talk to her about this the next day during your ten-minute phone call. You can support the people in your life and be there for them without being at the beck and call.

Many empaths find that touch intensifies the emotions they are experiencing through others and increases energy absorption. When you are in a crowd, you can try to navigate the edges, so you aren't bumping into as many people. You can give shorter hugs when you greet friends. You don't want to close yourself off completely to touch, but some people are just not as physically affectionate as others. Being one of them is fine. If you are meeting a lot of new people and want to avoid shaking hands, mention you feel like you have a cold coming on. People will appreciate the warning and keep their hands to themselves. Once you learn to shield yourself, you will not have to worry about making these excuses.

If you are in a social situation and are feeling intense vibes from someone that are making you uncomfortable or upset, you can move away. Do this kindly and unobtrusively. No one will think your behavior is odd or antisocial if you politely excuse yourself to refill a beverage, get some food, or use the restroom. If you are in a waiting room, you can always move seats. Grab your things, make a phone call outside, or ask the receptionist a question. When you return, simply sit elsewhere. Most people self-absorbed enough to not even notice.

Practice Separation

Empaths feel the emotions of others as strongly as they do their own. But it is important to remember that these emotions you are feeling through others aren't yours. They don't reflect what you are experiencing in your life. If your best friend is going through a divorce, the anger and sadness you are feeling through them is not your anger and sadness. Be there for your friend. Do your best to help and support them, but do not let their situation subsume you.

To practice separation, you first need to acknowledge the emotions you are feeling. Then, you mentally compartmentalize them as belonging to your friend and release them. Allow yourself to decompress and clear your mind after interacting with this friend.

Understand Your Own Emotions

Once you have separated the emotions you are experiencing through other people, it's time to concentrate on your own emotions. We'll continue with the example of an empath who has a friend going through a divorce. When you have released the anger and sadness you are feeling through them, think about your relationship. Do you have a significant other? How do you feel about the relationship? Does your partner make you happy and enhance your life? If you are single, are you content with this or do you want a relationship? What do you need and want in a partner? What do you expect to get out of being in a relationship?

Discover how you are feeling in your own life. Acknowledge and understand your emotions. Determine the source of these emotions. If you are sad, figure out why. Sometimes, the source will be obvious; other times, you will have to delve deeper. When you are more aware of your life and emotions, it will make it easier for you to separate your emotions from the emotions you feel through other people. Journaling can be a great way to examine your emotions, as well as practicing separation.

Are you happy? What can make you happier? Are you depressed? Why? What can you do to make it better? You give so much support to the people in your life; don't be afraid to ask them for support if you need it! You may decide you would benefit from therapy to further explore your emotions.

Release Responsibility

Empaths often feel they carry the weight of the world. They burden themselves with the suffering and problems of others. Empaths feel extreme guilt for not being able to fix other people's problems. You are not responsible for other people's problems. It's not your fault your best friend is struggling through a divorce. You cannot fix it. You would be overstepping your bounds to attempt to do so. You must let those around you live their own life and make their own decisions. This includes letting them make their own mistakes. You can actually do people a disservice by not allowing them to fend for themselves. They need to learn to rely on themselves and their own strength, not just yours. Concentrate on your own life and your own path.

If it is hard for you to change your mindset from fixing people to supporting them, consider that by controlling your empath abilities, you are allowing the people in your life to have privacy. You wouldn't want someone to read your every emotion. You can consider shielding a form of respect.

If you receive information through intuition that you feel it's imperative to share, be respectful of how the other person receives your information. You may get a bad feeling around your friend's significant other. If you choose to share this with your friend, be prepared that they won't want to hear it and they may be angry with you for telling them. You can tell them why you feel this way, but don't tell them what to do.

Celebrate!

There is a lot of pain and sadness in the world. This can weigh particularly heavily on empaths, who experience so much emotional pain that is not their own. Don't wait for holidays to celebrate the good things, whether large or small. Take the time to celebrate and bring joy into your life and the lives of those around you. If you got a promotion at work, treat yourself to a nice dinner. If you accomplished a workout goal, buy yourself a new training outfit. Is your 40th birthday coming up? Throw yourself a birthday bash! No "over the hill" paraphernalia allowed—good vibes only! Host a dinner party just because you have a new recipe you want to try.

Practical Test:

1.Is it important to celebrate?

2.What does Understanding your emotions contribute?

3.How to build fences not walls?

CHAPTER 19:

Using Your Gift to Your Advantage

To develop the gifts and talents of empaths, experts recommend a two-step approach: read properly the emotions of others and show how much you understand them. Take note that each step is dependent on one another. By doing these steps as a cyclic process, you would be able to significantly improve your empathic abilities.

Reading the Emotions of Other People

The first aspect of empathy that you can develop is your ability to read and understand the emotions of those around you. There are numerous ways on how you could go about this, but the main goal for every one of them is to gain an awareness of how another person might be feeling. Though reading the emotions of others is not an exact science—given the complexities of human nature—you would still be able to get valuable information that would help you learn how to act and think like a highly empathic individual.

To truly understand other people, you need to have the ability to recognize where they are coming from and figure out how they think and feel. Showing others that you are capable of this is usually a disarming experience for them. When you manage to disarm them, they would be more likely to take off their masks and share with you their real thoughts and feelings. Only then would you be able to offer the help that they actually need from others.

In a way, highly empathic individuals are selfless beings. They step out of their comfort zones to totally immerse themselves in the lives of other people. They are willing to open up themselves in order to figure out how to make things better for those around them.

So, how would you be able to walk in the shoes of another person? One of the most recommended methods by experts is a three-prong approach. The main objective, however, is to read between the lines. Listen to what others have to say but focus on how they are saying it. By doing this, you would be able to get a more accurate image of the person before you.

- Analyzing the Words of Other People

Highly empathic individuals are effective listeners. They are able to pay attention to what the other person is saying, and from there, pick out the points that really matter. They are not just listening to what others have to say. They are also processing as well as the information that they are receiving at the same moment.

There are times when words do not align with what the other person truly means. As such, empath needs to figure out what the other person is hinting at. Taking your listening skills to the next level needs time and practice. To make this process easier for you, do this exercise with someone you already know, and who is willing to tell you if your observations are accurate or not.

- First, let your partner speak about whatever topic that he or she wants to talk about at that given moment. Do not converse with your partner. Instead, just focus and listen to what they have to say.

For example, your partner, Anna, chooses to talk about her personal issues with her husband, Ben. Apparently, Anna wants to have kids, but Ben does not. Anna says that at first, it bothered her, but now she thinks it does not matter anymore.

- As you listen to her, take note of any emotion seeping through the tone of her voice. Check if there is any contradiction between her tone and the words, she is saying.

Following the same scenario given above, when Anna said that the issue is not bothering her anymore, you picked up the disappointment in the tone of her voice. Your ears heard her words correctly, but your intuition as an empath tells you that there is something else going on.

- Reflect on the meaning of the words of your partner and analyze them against the tone of her voice. Given the melody and rhythm of her voice, you believe that Anna still wants to have to kids and that she feels frustrated over her husband's refusal to have them in the future.

You can empathize with her by acknowledging her true feelings. Do not question the accuracy of her words. Instead, focus on what she truly feels to show that you understand the underlying meaning of her words.

When you have managed to say something back that correctly reflects the true meaning of your partner's words, the relationship between the two of you becomes closer. A deeper bond would begin to form since your partner would believe that you get where she is coming from. Continue practicing your skills as an intuitive listener so that you would be able to form more accurate conclusions about what people truly mean with their words.

- Understanding the Facial Expressions of Other People

Speaking to another person involves not only your ears but also your eyes. You have to observe the facial cues in order to get a fuller understanding of what others are saying. Even when someone is silent, their faces usually give away what they are really thinking or feeling at a given moment.

To help you practice this skill, here is a list of facial features that you need to observe, and the corresponding meanings of the common expressions that you might notice as you do so.

- Eyes

The eyes are a good source of information for empaths since most of its movements are automatic responses rather than controlled or deliberate. By observing them, you would be able to get a better idea of where the other person is coming from.

If a person's gaze is steady and does not back away when you stare back at him or her, then the person is likely not hiding anything away from you. If you two are conversing, then he or she believes in what you are saying.

On the other hand, a person who averts his or her gaze from you is most likely feeling worried about something. That person may also be hiding something, and he or she feels anxious that you would be able to uncover it. If someone's gaze shifts away whenever you make eye contact with him or her, it could either be an act of anxiety or avoidance.

- Eyebrows

The position of the eyebrows is indicative of a person's feelings. According to experts, human eyebrows move not only when the person is feeling happy or sad, but also whenever someone feels an extreme emotion in reaction to stimuli or information.

For instance, when the eyebrows are raised, the person could either be feeling surprised or curious. However, depending on the context of the situation, this position could also be taken as a sign of relief.

If the eyebrows are lowered, it could mean either that the person is experiencing displeasure, or that the person is trying to hide away something from others. The position is seen as an unintentional act of hiding one's gaze, similar to when the eyes dart away from the gaze of other people.

- Forehead

Check if the forehead of the person you are observing is wrinkled or smooth. If someone is deep in thought or confused, the forehead tends to become wrinkled. Smooth foreheads indicate that the person is feeling at ease or unbothered.

Signs of sweating on the forehead are also something that you should look out for. If the weather is not particularly warm, sweating on the forehead or any other part of the face could mean that the person is feeling anxious.

- Mouth

Observe if the person is exhibiting signs of a smile or frown. This is pretty telling of a person's true emotions, not just, because smiles and frowns are usually associated with happiness and sadness, respectively. If the emotion expressed in the eyes and mouth do not match, then the person is likely trying to hide his or her true feelings about someone or a certain situation.

To increase your level of empathy, try to practice reading the facial expressions of someone who can tell how accurate you are. However, please note that any variances between the expression and the words of a person do not mean that the person is deliberately doing it. Sometimes, a person is unaware of their facial expressions or what they are truly feeling.

Explaining how you have come about your conclusions is a more effective approach. Rather stating it like a fact, it would also be helpful if you would adopt a questioning tone when you try to assess someone's facial expressions. Here are some following guide questions that you could use for this:

- Are you feeling anxious right now?
- Do you feel happy about that?
- Is that bothering you?
- Do my words upset you?
- Decoding the Body Language of Other People

Beyond one's facial expression, a person's body language is also a veritable source of information for empaths. People with high levels of empathy are able to turn this information into a deeper understanding of the people around them.

Here is a list of tips on how you can effectively decode the meanings of one's bodily gestures:

- If a person is feeling comfortable or dominant, he or she would usually adopt an open posture—head is held up; the body is facing forward; arms extended outwards, or arms kept at the person's sides).

- A person who feels inferior exhibits a closed body posture, wherein he or she has her arms folded while facing away.

- A person leaning forwards shows that he or she is interested. If coupled with a tense body, it could mean that the person is feeling angry instead.

- If the shoulders are drooping, the person is likely feeling sad or tired.

- A body that is facing away can be indicative of a person's anxiety, embarrassment, or shyness.

- One can adopt a welcoming posture by standing or sitting with arms opened up towards other people.

- On the other hand, arms crossed in front of the body signals that the person is feeling defensive over something or towards someone.

Showing Others That You Understand Their Feelings

The other empathic ability that you can develop is your ability to show others that you understand their feelings. The timing and the manner of expressing this separates a highly empathic person from other people with average or low empathy.

Again, it is best to practice this with a person that you are close with. Learn how to pace yourself as well. Starting too intensely would make the other person feel uncomfortable. You can try to practice first with minor inconveniences of day-to-day to life.

Practical Test:

1. How to read the emotions of other people?

2. what is a source of information for empaths since most of its movements are automatic responses rather than controlled or deliberate. By observing them, you would be able to get a better idea of where the other person is coming from?

3. Is Decoding the Body Language of Other People part of using your gift as an advantage?

CHAPTER 20:

Controlling Your Awareness of Feelings and Emotions

Acknowledging Your Emotions

The first step when it comes to the emotions you are feeling, no matter where they came from, is acknowledging how you feel. Think of it this way, before you can start to heal from any situation in your life, you need to acknowledge it. You need to stand up and say, "This is how I am feeling" before you can start to understand why you are feeling this way. For example, you are hanging out with friends when you see a commercial about dogs in shelters. A local shelter is asking people from the community to adopt these dogs because their shelter is becoming too full. While some of the dogs look happily at the camera, one dog is curled up in a corner shaking. As you see this dog you say, "Oh, that poor puppy! He looks so scared and sad. It just makes me want to run up and hug him. No one should ever have to feel that way." In response, one of your friends laughs and says, "It's just part of the commercial. It's all so they grab the attention of people like you." You look at your friend and then start to feel self-conscious about what you said out loud. No one else seems to be reacting in the same way. You start to feel a little embarrassed as you look down at your phone thinking to yourself, "You need to be more careful of what you say out loud. Not everyone thinks like you do."

Throughout the rest of the evening, you are not as sociable with your friends. When they are laughing and having fun, you tend to give them a smile. You don't laugh as much because you don't feel like it. You start to get lost in your thoughts as you wonder what is causing you to withdraw from your friends. Why do you still feel bothered by what your friend said to you in response to your reaction to the commercial? You feel that other people would be move on from the situation and continue to have a good time, but you feel more out of place. How could you feel out of place amongst your friends?

The truth is you don't necessarily feel out of place with your friends. You know that they never mean to harm you emotionally or psychologically. What you are struggling with is acknowledging how your friend made you feel. You haven't acknowledged the embarrassment you felt. You haven't looked at the words they said that caused you to feel ashamed about the way you reacted to the commercial. When you don't acknowledge the way you feel, especially as an empath and highly sensitive person, you will hang on to the situation for a period of time.

Four Steps of Acknowledging Your Emotions

1. Note how you are truly feeling. People quickly try to push feelings aside. This is more common if you were not allowed to talk about your feelings or you didn't have parents teaching you how to open up as a child. This type of behavior will follow you into adulthood. It is also easy to tell yourself, "I feel kind of sad" and then not look deeper into the feeling.

2. Reflect on your feelings. You want to think about why you feel this way. Ask yourself when it started to find the possible source of your emotions. Take time to write down how you feel and why as this can help you process your emotions.

3. Stay open to your emotions. There is nothing wrong with vulnerability as it will help you be honest and open about how you are feeling. This isn't information that you need to share with anyone else, unless you want to. The important part is you stay open with yourself and begin to work through your emotions.

4. Go with the flow. You need to let your emotion run its course. Sometimes it will be painful, and this is something that is tough to get through. However, you cannot move on without fully acknowledging your emotion. It can take time to go through your emotion and you will find yourself wishing that you could forget about it and feel better. You won't feel better until you fully acknowledge the way you are feeling.

Understanding Your Emotions

Once you acknowledge your emotions, you need to start to understand your emotions. You will start this process when you begin to reflect on your feelings. To begin understanding your emotions, you need to know the five core emotions:

1. Hurt
2. Anger
3. Fear
4. Sadness
5. Joy

Any other emotions, such as guilt or jealousy, are known as secondary emotions. Secondary emotions are combinations of the core emotions. For example, you can feel hurt and anger when you are feeling jealous or fear and sadness when you are feeling guilty.

One of the first factors to know about understanding your emotions is that they don't always need to be positive. Like most people, you have no problem understanding your positive emotions. Positive emotions make you feel content and calm. They give you an uplifting feeling which helps you get through your day. When you feel negatively, you start to feel down. This has psychological effects, especially if you don't understand your negative emotions. For example, you meet your friend at the restaurant and see your ex-partner with someone else. While you have your own significant other, you still feel jealous seeing them. You see your ex is happy with their partner and you begin to wonder why you couldn't do the same for them. You are also confused with your emotions because it was your decision to end the relationship. If it was your choice, why do you feel jealous seeing your ex with someone else?

As a child, you let your emotions run wild. When you were unhappy, you let people know and you didn't see a problem with this. As you grew up, you started to scale your emotions back because you learned it isn't okay to be too emotional. This happens for different reasons. It might be because your parents told you to not act emotional or because society told you acting this way is bad. Now, to understand your emotions, you need to bring them back into the front. The only way you can understand where they come from and why you feel a certain way is by focusing on your emotions and the situation. To understand your emotions, you will ask yourself a variety of questions. For example, what happened before you started to feel this way? Is there something with your past that caused this emotion to come to the surface? For example, you are working in your office and you hear two of your co-workers talking about another co-worker negatively. You try to ignore the conversation but struggle to do so because it makes you angry. You don't understand how someone could be mean, especially when they work with someone five days out of the week. You don't feel the judgements from your co-workers is justified. You try to ignore your anger because it doesn't make sense to you. Your co-workers weren't talking to you, they weren't talking about you, and you don't know the co-worker they talked about well. Unfortunately, you are unable to ignore the anger as it continues to bubble up within you. On the way home from work, you start to think about the situation. You ask yourself, "Why did I get so angry?" and immediately think of the bullying you dealt with as a child in school. Therefore, you think this is one of the biggest reasons you feel so angry is because of the bullying.

Three Ways to Better Understand Your Emotions

There are many ways that you can start to understand your emotions better. For instance, you can use your own techniques that you develop over time. To help you start to understand your emotions better, here are three steps to follow (David, 2016).

1. Note the intensity of your emotion. You want to understand how strong your emotion is. For example, if you are feeling angry, do you have certain levels of anger? Do you feel like you could emotionally explode and yell at someone or are you more frustrated about the situation, like something is working right for you? To help you understand your intensity, rate them on a scale of one to ten.

2. Expand your emotional vocabulary. Like everyone, you know the words angry, frustrated, sad, happy, and fear. But there are many other words that can express the way you feel. For example, you can also describe angry as annoyed, disgusted, irritated, boiling, grumpy, and spiteful. You could describe happy as comfortable, thankful, content, elated, excited, and relieved. When you expand your emotional vocabulary, you can use different words when you make your emotional intensity scale.

3. Write about your emotions. Writing is an important part of not only acknowledging your emotions but also understanding them. There is a positive connection between writing and your emotions. No matter how you feel, writing about your emotions can help you overcome any negative emotions and understand them better. You don't always need to ask yourself questions. You can free write, which is when you write whatever comes to your mind.

Controlling Your Emotions

Once you acknowledge and understand your emotions, you can start to control them. There are many strategies that will help you stay in control of your emotions throughout any situation.

- Don't react immediately. Allow yourself to think about the situation before you react. For example, take a few deep and slow breaths to clear your mind. This will allow you to think rationally instead of jumping to conclusions.

- Understand your triggers. Generally, people feel happy and calm. However, this can quickly change at any moment because everyone has emotional triggers. You will start to find out what your triggers are when you are acknowledging and understanding your emotions. By knowing your triggers, you can further control your emotions as you will start to understand where they come from and prepare yourself when the situation arises.

- Change your thoughts. The biggest problem with negative emotions is they bring negative thoughts. This can create a cycle that you will struggle to get out of, so it is important that you replace your negative thoughts with positive thoughts. This doesn't mean that you want to ignore your negative emotions and thoughts. Always go through the points of acknowledging and understanding them as this will help you with control.

No matter what strategy you use, the point is to control your emotions, so they don't control you.

Absorbing Emotions

One of the biggest reasons empaths struggle with emotions is because they absorb emotions from other people. This means that the emotions people have when they are near you, you take on as your own. This is an important part of being an empath and a factor that you don't want to ignore because it helps you focus on healing other people. However, absorbing emotions can cause a lot of problems—especially when you don't take time to heal yourself.

Practical Test:

1. How to Acknowledge your emotions?

2. What are the ways to better understand your emotions?

3. How to avoid Absorbing Emotions?

CHAPTER 21:

The Pros and Cons of Being an Empath

Depending how long you've known that you are an empath, you may be quite familiar with the pros and cons of being one. We've already covered that one of the downfalls can be the way it is a heavy burden to bear due to the outside energies and emotions you are surrounded by. However, most things in life come with both negatives and positives. The experience of feeling those emotions around you can be wonderful and helpful in many different ways.

The pros and cons can't really be separated as they are often intertwined with one another.

Empaths are listeners. They can be all sorts of joy, being outgoing and enthusiastic and generally bubbly. Let's not forget the heyoka empath literally known for being humorous when you least expect it. Their journey can be one of emotional bliss, but it can also be one of emotional turmoil since empaths can be weighed down with mood swings galore. This is because their moods are not always their own. If empaths don't fully understand and differentiate their own thoughts and feelings from those of others, they can have fluctuating mood swings that literally change with the speed of flicking a switch on and off.

As with the good, being an empath can come with feelings of depression, anxiety, panic, fear, and sorrow. Without having any control over these feelings, you can be experiencing the suffering of others. It's a very difficult thing to have to handle and shouldn't be done so alone.

This is where compassion comes in. An empath should have at least one person they can turn to in the throes of these mood swings because being left alone can be detrimental to mental and physical health. Find someone, be it a friend or a partner or a family member, who you can turn to when things get too overwhelming for you. Whoever you find, make sure to tell them that all you really need from them is empathic love—the ability to show compassion without judging you. This may help you in recovery from these overwhelming moments.

Most empaths, unless they have gone on their own journeys of self-discovery and self-acceptance, don't actually know or understand what's going on within. They don't know that they're feeling another person's emotions like they are their own emotions. This can quite obviously lead to a myriad of feelings such as confusion, particularly if things were grand in one moment and terrible in the next. Understanding their empathic connection is a part of the journey.

It's easier for an empath to withhold their feelings and emotions than it is for others. They want to do their best not to be barraged by the feelings and emotions of others. In doing so, they often become reclusive and learn to block out these feelings. The downside of this is that they can end up bottling up their own emotions or building walls so high that they don't ever let anyone else in. This can definitely be bad for an empath—or anyone for that matter—because the longer you allow these feelings and emotions to build up inside yourself, the more power they build up. Eventually, they can explode and leave behind a lot of damage to both the empath and those around the empath. This can create an unstable environment, a mental/emotional breakdown, and/or an actual disease.

Expressing yourself honestly is a choice, but it is a great form of healing.

Cons of Being an Empath

Some of these can count as pros depending on how you look at them. You'll notice how short this list is compared to the list of pros. This is because being an empath is truly a positive blessing if you understand your gift properly.

- You are easily overwhelmed. Wherever there are lots of people, you can be overwhelmed with the feelings and emotions emanating off of those that surround you. Sometimes you can be in a room with one person and still feel this way. This is why it is so important not to bottle things up.

- Addictive personalities. Empaths are prone to looking for ways to escape or block out the emotions of others. This means that they sometimes turn toward addictive substances such as sex, drugs, and alcohol. Learning to protect yourself and your energy means that you won't be struck with the need to escape these things. Instead, you will know how to cope with them properly.

- Media can be devastating. Some empaths turn away from media altogether. They can feel the emotions of others so strongly that even reading a newspaper is too much for them. It is a harsh world out there.

- Empaths can pick up both mental and physical ailments that others may suffer from. This can happen even if you don't come into contact with the other person, depending on how strong your gift is. Needless to say, no one wants to suffer this way.

- Intuition can be hurtful when you know that someone you care about is lying to you or keeping secrets from you. The ability to know and feel these things can be difficult, particularly if you can't prove such things. Try to surround yourself with people who are like minded preventing feeling this way on a regular basis.

- We don't really have a home. Empaths are natural wanderers. After a certain amount of time, we can often feel foreign in places we once cherished. Our intuition implores with us to explore the great big world. Due to this, we're rarely ever satisfied with one place, but it does mean we make brilliant travelers.

Pros of Being an Empath

Well, we covered the cons, which I admit were pretty bad. Now we get to look at the reasons why being an empath truly is a gift. Bear with me here, because it's a pretty long list of reasons.

- Empaths are natural healers in many different forms: emotional, physical, environmental, animal, you name it. They can use their touch, their voice, and their creativity to do so. Most empaths end up on a path of healing because they simply have that pull toward their profession.

- As tough as crowds may be for an empath, the small circle they often end up building for themselves is a strong one. Once an empath makes a connection with someone, they are incredibly loyal and loving. We hold onto our loved ones tightly because we don't want to let the good ones go.

- Okay, we already know this one, but empaths love an insane amount. Their hearts are just bigger than most. Being so overloaded with all these feelings makes faking them difficult.

- That gut instinct is extremely strong and if you listen to it, I'm pretty sure you could conquer the world if you wanted to. Listen to that sixth sense of yours because it could save you from potential dangers if it hasn't already.

- Along with having an extremely strong sense of intuition, we also have amazing senses. It isn't only emotions and feelings that are heightened. If you find yourself enjoying a myriad of sensations with a lot more intensity than those around you, you can chalk that up to being an empath. We have heightened senses that allow us to better enjoy our food, beverages, flowers, essential oils, touch, and so forth. Admittedly, these can sometimes overwhelm us, but they could also help save lives. How, you might ask? Well, if you work on increasing a certain sense, such as smell, you could be able to track down death or disease in animals, people, and/or nature.

- I know we said that the weight of other people's emotions is a burden and we're really prone to lows, but we've also got the other end of the spectrum. We have great highs, too. Most empaths actually have a deep enthusiasm for life, and when we are enjoying it, we experience joy intensely.

- Empaths have an abundance of creativity! We think and see things differently. Our art is not the only creative aspect of our life, but so are our experiences, situations, and prospects. Now, you've probably had the misfortune of being told that the way you think about and/or do things is wrong, but it's a capacity all your own. Don't let anyone take that unusual creativity away from you, and let it shine brightly instead.

- This Is yet another con that also turns out to be a pro, but we can't be lied to. We are good at reading people's thoughts, feelings, and emotions. This means that we can tell when people are lying, we can tell when people aren't okay, and we can tell when people are bad news.

- Empaths can read emotional and nonverbal cues really well. It's a talent in numerous places. Due to our good senses, we can even sense the needs of those who do not speak, such as animals and plants, but also the body and babies.

- An empath generally has a craving to make the world a better place. This isn't a desire that you should ever feel ashamed of. We are capable of bringing plenty of positive changes to this world, and when we can, we should. There are already too many people turning blind eyes. Let's work on correcting the wrongs happening around us—together.

- It's especially important for us to change the world considering our pull to it. We are children of nature. It's one of the best ways to de-stress, and it can provide peace and comfort.

- To some, this might seem more like a con, but find that it's pretty cool to be able to recharge on our own. We require a certain level of alone time to recuperate. It is because of this that we are self-aware and think it's great to be self-aware.

Practical Test:

Which one is the Pro and Con?

1. We don't really have a home

2. Media can be devastating

3. Empaths are natural healers in many different forms

CHAPTER 22:

Traits of The Empath

Traits of the Empath

The empath is a highly emotional individual thanks to sensitivity to what is happening around them.

Have you ever been driving down the road, only to see a homeless individual begging on the side of the road?

If you are an empath, your first reaction is probably to feel that same sadness, discomfort, and cold that you perceive the other person to be feeling, especially if you have driven past in winter.

Overall, the empath typically has very predictable traits that go along with their massive capacity for emotional empathy.

These traits make it easy to identify who the empath is if you know what to look for.

Whether you yourself are an empath or you want to be able to identify an empath in your daily life, it can be essential to know what they look like.

This part will go over seven major traits that define the empath's personality type, touching upon each and how they can be beneficial or harmful.

Highly Sensitive to Emotions

The empath is perhaps primarily known as being empathetic.

This empathetic nature comes from the empath's natural high sensitivity to emotional states.

The empath only needs to look at someone or hear their voice in order to know what they are feeling, and those feelings will usually be deeply understood and felt by the empath as well.

The empath is incredibly in tune with those around them, and just walking into a room with high tension is enough to put the empath on edge.

The fact that the empath is so sensitive to emotions means that they are always willing to offer the necessary support to those around them.

They are willing to be there for those they care about, which is essentially anyone with a pulse thanks to their caring nature.

They will be there to help because they are so sensitive to emotions.

They are driven not by their emotional empathy, but rather their compassionate empathy—the empathy that drives them to act to help.

However, along with being sensitive to the emotions of others, the empath is also incredibly sensitive to their own emotions as well.

This can oftentimes lead to them feeling hurt over something that was not actually meant to be hurtful, which can also lead to being told that they are overly sensitive or overreacting.

It is common for the empath to hear that he or she needs to toughen up in some way, but really, that is counterproductive to who they are as individuals.

Highly Sensitive to Senses

The empath is not only emotionally sensitive, either—they are usually quite sensitive to physical stimulation as well.

The empath is largely highly sensitive in all senses of the word—physically and emotionally.

The empath is going to feel bothered by physical sensations that are problematic, which again gets them regularly told that they are far too sensitive and need to suck it up and deal with it like everyone else.

However, those who are telling the empath to suck it up and deal are likely not empaths themselves and do not understand the same level of distress and discomfort that can come from physical stimuli.

The empath, for example, may feel like wearing a tough sweater is unbearable because of the texture, or they may find certain sounds particularly grating, to the point that the sense is physically painful for them.

They may struggle to cope with these physical sensations and will go to great lengths to avoid them whenever possible.

The empath will deliberately design wardrobes to accommodate these physical preferences or make sure that they avoid living in an area with those senses being triggered.

This can mean, then, that you have an empath that will tell someone that they cannot deal with a specific sound or stimulus, and while others may think that the empath is being too stubborn and unaccommodating, really the empath is just trying to remain comfortable.

Certain scents, sounds, or textures can send them over the edge and further stress out the empath far more than it may stress out someone who is not as sensitive.

Mirror the Emotions of Others

That sense of empathy that helps the empath tune in to the emotional states of others also leads to the empath mirroring other people's emotions on a regular basis.

If you interact with an empath, the empath will likely appear to feel whatever it is that you are feeling.

If you are sad over a loss, the empath's heart is going to be hurting right along with yours.

If you are happy because you have just won something, the empath will be just as happy, cheering you on.

Because the empath excels in all three major types of empathy, cognitive, emotional, and compassionate, the empath is often readily swayed by the emotions of other people.

This, of course, has good and bad uses and implications.

While the empath may be able to aid someone if they are able to sense and understand the emotions of someone else, this also can lead to development and internalization of all sorts of negative emotions as well if the empath is interacting with a toxic individual.

This is problematic doing so leads to the empath developing toxic feelings as well, which are never productive for anyone involved.

This means that the empath has to be careful about who is allowed to be around him or her—when they are not careful, they are in a position where they may end up acting or behaving in unhealthy manners.

Introverted

Due to the sensitivity of the empath, they are frequently quickly drained by any interactions with other people.

Because they experience the world from an introverted perspective, they are usually easily exhausted, especially by anyone who would be deemed an energy vampire, such as a narcissist, who may demand far more than even the sensitive, caring empath can put out.

Because the empath is introverted as well, the empath also runs into situations in which they feel the need to separate away and regain their own energy levels for periods of time.

Effectively, though the empath is sensitive and loves to help other people because of the empathy they feel, the empath also needs plenty of alone time to recharge.

Unlike the extrovert, who feels energized in interactions with others, it takes a significant amount of energy for the empath to interact.

While this is not enough for the empath to entirely avoid people, they do take steps to accommodate themselves.

In particular, an empath is likely to limit their contact to small groups rather than going out for parties.

By interacting in one-on-one or small group settings, the empath is able to avoid some of the intensive emotional drain that being in a crowd can lead to.

Intuitive

Empaths are usually in a position where they primarily follow their feelings.

They are led by their intuition—those gut feelings they get when they see someone or are in a certain situation.

This is not because they are illogical or unwilling to reason, but rather because they are highly emotional people.

They live through their emotional states, and when you are so highly in tune with emotions, it can be easy for the empath to use those emotions as guides.

This can have its benefits, but it is also incredibly important for the empath to remember to pay attention to that intuition and learn to hone and trust it.

Sometimes, that intuition and empath can battle it out over one another to gain control of the empath's actions, and the empath needs to learn to find that balancing point between the two.

The empath needs to understand when to allow empathy to rule and when it is okay to step back and follow his or her intuition when they feel like the other person may be dangerous, even if the empath is likely to feel strongly for that individual and whatever situation that person is in.

Easily Overwhelmed in Relationships

Because empaths are all about the emotional connection to other people and need their space, relationships can become quite draining.

It is quite easy for the empath to become overwhelmed within a relationship, especially if they have a partner that is more likely to need more attention than others. Too much time together, even with someone they love, can be incredibly draining, and sometimes, they just need some time for themselves. This can lead to problems within a relationship, which can even just lead to the empath avoiding relationships altogether to avoid the problem.

At the heart of it all, however, the empath may be afraid of the loss of identity within the relationship.

If the empath is going to be reflecting back what they absorb like a mirror in their relationship, sometimes, they may feel that they will lose sight of themselves, and this can lead to them to hesitate in immersing themselves in that relationship in the first place.

Of course, they also tend to find relationships with energy vampires such as narcissists thanks to their caregiving nature, and that can make the relationship process seem that much more daunting.

All of the good of the empath lead to attracting many of the worst people out there, who may seek to treat the empath as a target to take advantage of.

Caregiver Personality

Thanks to empaths and their ability to feel compassionate empathy, they tend to develop a sort of caregiver personality.

They usually feel compelled to help other people, and if they are given the choice between taking the last of something else and giving it to someone else, they are going to give it to someone else.

They want to give and make sure that those around them, especially loved ones, are taken care of and happy, even if that can be an inconvenience or detriment to themselves sometimes.

This can lead to them giving too much, however—they may try to take on the problem that someone else is faced with, trying their best to help other people, but this can become yet another source of intense emotional drain that can cause all sorts of problems for the empath.

While it is absolutely natural to want to reach out to help someone else, it can also become unhealthy if instead of helping, the empath absorbs all of those feelings instead.

Nevertheless, this personality trait of being a big-hearted caregiver is an honorable one, and you can oftentimes find empaths in positions that are likely to help other people.

These positions, however, can also lead to burnout, as most of the time, when you are in a position of helping people, you are seeing people that are hurting in some way or another.

Practical Test:

1.What are the traits of the Empath?

2. Are Empaths sensitive?

3. Are Empaths easily overwhelmed by relationships?

CHAPTER 23:

Reasons for Not Healing

Reasons for Not Healing

Empaths often overlook the significance of their personal choices and actions in life. They even mistake some of their customs as effective to help them heal their core wounds yet the truth is, they are not. So, instead of having their inner wound healed, it just gets worse and worse each day. It would take a lifetime to discuss all the reasons that are possibly hindering the healing of an empath's core wound. So, I've come up with a list to present to you some of these reasons that are particularly important, as they are the ones that empaths normally do every day.

Living the People-pleaser Personality

You try so hard to be accepted when acceptance is not something you force in the first place. When people ask you to change, you'll more or less change yourself unhesitatingly. You project your false self in front of other people because you think it suits the society. You keep on trying to change what's on the outside without realizing that you are already hurting inside.

Letting Someone's Behavior Destroy You

With your desire to please people, you try to endure everyone's behavior. You let them hurt you, bully you, make fun of you because you think that is how you make friends with people. You think that getting used to their destructive behavior will eventually lessen your sensitivity and make you stronger but unfortunately, it won't.

Doing Others' Workload

You take "helpfulness" to the next level. You try to do others' tasks, works, or assignments because you think it will increase your chance of being accepted. You overwork, stress yourself out, and exhaust yourself just to find out that you are being treated as a pet and not as a friend.

Scapegoating Yourself

You keep on taking the blame on behalf of your friends, your family, or other people. Your guilt toward things makes you feel like you are responsible for everything and that it is just right to put the blame on you. You think catching the damage for others would help them cope with the situation and would help your relationship with them get stronger.

Tolerating Abuse

You keep on giving other people chances regardless of how much they wasted your time and your feelings. You often disregard the bad things that people did to you. You are afraid of losing them because you think your life will be empty once they leave. So, you keep on chasing after them at the cost of your own self-worth. Your core wound is getting worse and worse, but you can't feel it because your martyrdom is making you numb.

Depending on Drugs

You are so damaged that you think drugs are your safest escape. You take endorphins, antidepressants, anxiolytics or anti-anxiety drugs as they are the easiest way to drop down your sensitivity level. Yes, these drugs can temporarily provide relief and comfort, but they are not the only solution available. At the end of the day, none of them are making things better.

1.Empath Healing Techniques

Empath healing can be done in two ways: prevention of further infliction and taking measures to heal yourself. The first way is to let time alone heal it. The second way on the other hand, is done by healing the wound by yourself, using the following tools and practices:

Meditation

Meditation is the key to peace of mind and peace of mind is one of the keys to your healing. Meditation helps you clear all the chaotic and toxic thoughts that are poisoning your mental energy. It aligns the thoughts in your mind that are in complete disarray, as these are the reason you cannot come up with proper decisions in life.

Meditation comes in many types like the "mindfulness" meditation, originating from the Buddhist tradition, which is done by closing your eyes while sitting on crossed legs, with your back straight. The relaxation comes from breathing in and out and is meant to release depression. You can also try the visualization method of meditation that is a more modern technique. It is a guided meditation done by watching a sequence of scenes or images, along with a voice guiding you throughout the process. There are actually a lot of methods to perform meditation. You just need to choose which among them suits your needs.

Laughter

You release all the negative vibrations inside you when you laugh. Laughter serves as your personal vibe converter because it can transform negative energies inside you into positive ones. Laughing is the simplest method of healing yourself and the best thing about it is that, it does not cost anything. Brighten up your life by laughing every day as it accelerates your healing process.

Discovering Your Outlets

The good news is you can actually use yours to help yourself heal. Discover your hidden talents or in case you have already discovered them, nourish them. You may choose to paint, draw, write, sing, dance, compose, cook, or anything that could distract you, whenever you feel like you are starting to get covered by an unwelcoming atmosphere of varied energies. Use your talents to serve as your outlets for unreleased emotions like joy, gloom, hatred, or love. What's better than having an instant outlet to vent your feelings is the fact that you can also improve your talents through it.

Nature

An empath's spiritual energy is naturally linked to nature. This is the reason why some empaths possess the talent of geomancy in their subconscious. Provide yourself at least a weekly dose of nature interaction. Stay under a tree, swim in the fresh waters, or go into nature adventures. Your sensitivity allows you to absorb more of the positivity of nature so avail yourself of this healing method if you need a deeper contact to serenity.

Water

Dehydration does not only happen when you literally lack water in your body. It also happens to your soul. Fortunately, water doesn't just relieve physical dehydration but also the body's spiritual thirst. Water is your ultimate ally. It has a lot more function and importance to you than you think.

According to Dr. Masaru Emoto, a Japanese researcher, author and the photographer behind the volume "Messages from Water," emotional vibrations and emotional energies could change the water's physical structure. The conclusion was based on Doctor Emoto's water crystal experiment. Different water from different sources like river, lake, and water facilities, were frozen into crystals. The structures of crystals were observed to be different from each other. Frozen crystals from water that came from sources that are near industrialized areas didn't show beautiful crystals. On the other hand, crystals from fresh, virgin lakes and rivers developed beautiful crystal formations.

The experiment was further developed when Doctor Emoto started experimenting the effects of different actions to water as they are being frozen. Doctor Emoto tried playing music to water, showing letters and pictures to water, and praying to water. It was then found out that beautiful crystals are formed after offering prayer, giving good words, and playing good music to water while opposite actions resulted into disfigured crystals.

Based on Doctor Emoto's experiment, water can be considered as an element that absorbs energies that come from its environment. Let the water release the negative energy in you through cleansing and urination. And let clarity and positivity flow into your spirit through rehydration and refreshment.

Sea Salt

Seawater has a potent wound-healing factor. Sea salt, which is basically the solidified version of sea water and its minerals—can actually be an empath's healer. Since it is easily transferred into the bloodstream, it immediately helps clear out unwanted energy and dissolves negativity from your body.

Among the thousands of choices, the best one for an empath is the Himalayan sea salt. If the usual table salt has only four trace minerals and elements, the Himalayan sea salt contains 84 of them. You can pair your water intake with this salt to accelerate healing. Just dissolve a small amount on your tongue before drinking a glass of water.

Oils

Essential oils particularly target the skin, as well as the olfactory senses, to relax and balance emotional energy within your body. You can also inhale the vapors from essential oils. The limbic system is the part of the brain that is known to have a significant impact on one's emotions. Also, the oil's therapeutic benefits can be easily absorbed by the skin once the oil is applied on it. Oils are more into balancing the hormones and uplifting the spirit with its smooth texture and relaxing fragrance.

Lavender oil is the most versatile oil for an empath; it has tonic effects, and relaxing aroma. Plus, it has antibacterial and antiseptic agents. Basil and jasmine oils are perfect mood enhancers. Geranium and chamomile oils, on the other hand, are best for relaxing your mind state. Don't hesitate using oils as there will always be at least one that can address your current needs.

2. Repressed Sexuality

Among the aspects of an empath's life, his sexuality receives the least attention. Why? Come to think of it. The murder or bombing scenes in a tv show are seemingly normal to watch with friends or family but when the sex scene comes, everything just gets awkward. That exact moment, already exhibits how discouraged the subject sexuality is in our society.

Sex is a normal function of humans; or at least it was before society and religion decided that it's not. Since society and religion both hold enough power to influence the majority, expressing sexuality has been considered unethical and immoral. This caused sexual repression to take place.

Being an empath entails an extra challenge to control sexual urges and desires. Sexual energies can bother us just as much as emotional energies do. The hardest part of dealing with them is making the decision to whether release them or keep them, but my advice? Release them.

Repressed Sexuality Can Change Your Energy

One of the reasons why I gave that advice is that sexual energy can possibly affect the flow of energy in your body. Yep, we are also prone to unwarranted changes in our own energy, as if not being able to control the energies that enter us is not hard enough. Empaths need to maintain balance among different energies that flow in their body including sexual energy. So, any excess sexual energy can cause imbalance which can eventually lead to mood changes, distractions, or intensified desires for sexual intercourse.

Practical Test:

1. What is the key to peace of mind and peace of mind is one of the keys to your healing?

2. Can Repressed Sexuality change your energy?

3.It is when release all the negative vibrations inside you.

CHAPTER 24:

Understanding Energy

Understanding Energy

First, be aware that energy shields cannot be fueled by thought and intention alone. To keep your guard strong, you'll need a foundation of consistent self-care through proper rest, nutrition, physical activity, meditative practice, avoidance of toxic interactions, and the incorporation of an authentic lifestyle. Think of your energy shield as a set of turrets atop the temple that is your emotional self. The walls and foundation of the temple have to be solidly built and well-maintained to support the weight of their defense system.

You can use a physical talisman or crystal to activate your shield or to store energetic charge for it. Activating your shield is primarily a visualization technique. First, envision your aura, a halo of light surrounding your entire body and spiritual essence. It may have a color, or it may be pure divine light. Next, you'll need to determine what kind of shield you want to cast. Is your primary goal to avoid drama and stay focused on your goals? Or to preserve personal energy levels? Perhaps you want to absorb love but deflect negativity. Visualize each of these forces as a physical entity, and then imagine yourself forging a shield of light, buzzing with energetic charge, to suit your needs.

Many metaphysical healers and guides have their methods for casting energetic shields. Ask your yoga teachers, reiki masters, spiritual guides and fellow empaths if they have any advice for personalizing this practice or honing your technique.

Letting Go of Expectations

Empaths feel genuine, and it can be challenging for us to understand how their emotions don't drive other people. Sometimes, we expect other people to feel compelled, as we do, to do the right thing, express compassion to those in need, stifle the energy supplies of people with malicious intent, foster deep connections, and seek out higher truths. We are often in awe of people who can let things go smoothly; we may fear this behavior in other people, especially when they can quickly let go of things or people that we believe they ought to feel a sentimental connection.

It may sound cynical but learning to lower your expectations of other people can be incredibly freeing for empaths. In truth, many people you meet simply won't express any interest in the things that matter most to you. Deep levels of empathy are terrifying for some people and entirely inaccessible for others still. Throughout your life, you will encounter a significant number of people who never practice reciprocity or gratitude, and never pay any mind to their emotional bodies. If you expect them to do so, you will feel disappointment. If you expect nothing, what you will feel instead is either an impulse to ask explicitly for the attention you need, or an ability to accept things as they are, and be at peace with them.

If one is well balanced, he or she thinks positively, eats well, sleeps and gets enough rest and as such, the adrenal glands are not easily overwhelmed. During sleep, the levels of cortisol in the body rise naturally and peak just a few hours before we wake up. This increase happens so that a person can have a good start once he or she wakes up. It is also referred to as circadian rhythm, and it elevates and reduces energies accordingly so that the body can function effectively by staying awake when it is daytime and sleeping when it is dark.

When the adrenal glands are exhausted, an empath and any other person for that matter wake up feeling tired and disturbed even if he or she has had a long and otherwise restful sleep. This person will feel drowsy for the better part of the day, and then the cortisol levels will rise in the evening. The late peak will result in lack of sleep or difficulty resting at night.

It is very hard for anyone who has overrun the adrenal glands to get them back to a normal state. It can take a lot of time, but there are some changes that one can make and have an immediate positive effect on the glands.

For an empath, the most critical initial thing to do is to listen attentively to the body and take note of how it feels. If one pays attention to the feelings of the body, then he or she will stay aware of how the energy levels within are rising and falling throughout the day. This will help in noting the hours during the day which one feels exhausted than others; therefore, make the right moves to alter the patterns.

It is important that an empath understands why he or she is placing too much energy pressure on the glands. Once he or she identifies the root cause of the stress, emotions, and feelings, it will be easier to ensure that heightened state of alert is brought down, therefore removing the pressure from the adrenal glands.

In some cases, the empath may have to use medication to help focus on the body in order to identify any sensation that is taking place. Medication can also help one to sooth the mind and become calm so that he or she does not keep repeating the negative thoughts that will trigger adverse chemical reactions.

Another method that can help one to regulate the level of cortisol is spending time with friends, family and outside, doing social activities. Scientists have found that cortisol levels increase if one spends too much time alone. Loneliness, separation and isolation trigger feelings that we associate with negative experiences; therefore, empaths should learn how to balance alone time with social time. Consequently, cortisol will not be such an issue.

Other factors that affect the cortisol levels include diet and exercise. The regime that one uses for exercise and feeding determines the amount of stress placed on the adrenal glands. If one pushes the body too much, then he or she places too much demand on the adrenal glands, which then results in an overproduction of stress-related hormones. Bad practices such as skipping meals, intense workouts and eating junk foods force the glands to overwork. In the event that the person has food allergies, then the glands get additionally stressed. As such, it is vital to be attentive to the food that one tolerates.

An empath can keep the adrenal glands nourished and balanced by sticking to a healthy diet and getting enough exercise. An organic, nutritious, and well-balanced diet with healthy levels of proteins, and vitamins A, B, and C can go a long way in ensuring that the glands are functioning properly. It is also important to allow time for the body to absorb the nutrients before a person can engage in any physical activity. The empaths can also avoid large consumptions of alcohol and eliminate the intake of refined products and caffeinated foods.

If the unrest and sleeplessness occur due to disturbances in the mind at night, then we can create an environment that helps rebalance the glands. For instance, one can create stability, security, inner peace, joy, and optimism just before going to bed. The aim is to get a restful night's sleep and sometimes we can be startled by the thought of going to bed and failing to drift off as expected. Anxiety develops just before getting to bed when one realizes that he or she is going to stay awake for hours without getting to the highly desired delta state. The anxiety only makes matters worse.

When the adrenals are exhausted, empaths tend to wake during the night on high alert and to make matters worse, high stimuli dreams can add to the overanxious state of mind. Sleepless nights are particularly common for the empaths after they have endured an anxious and stress full period because even when they enter sleep, they can keep waking up at intervals during the night feeling the hormones circulating through the body even when they cannot understand the cause.

Disturbances in sleep are in most cases linked to biochemical reactions resulting from the flashes of high levels of stress hormones occurring throughout the body system between 2.00 am and 4.00 am. The high spike of these hormones affects the body so dramatically that it becomes impossible to remain calm thus the ability to stay asleep is interrupted. These disturbed sleep challenge can be rectified by making a therapeutic potion that consists of unrefined salts and organic honey. Mix one teaspoon of unrefined salt, for example, the pink Himalayan salt with five teaspoons of raw organic honey. The salt has healing properties, while the honey supplies the body cells with energy. One can take a teaspoon of the mixture about 20 minutes before sleeping; it will help to relax the mind and naturally regulate hormones. Consequently, one will be ready to drift into a restful place of rest.

Practical Test:

1. What is Energy?

2. Why is it important to let go of expectations?

3. can an empath keep the adrenal glands nourished and balanced by sticking to a healthy diet and getting enough exercise?

CHAPTER 25:

Putting Yourself First

Loving Yourself as An Empath

Empathy is one of the most interesting abilities one can have. An empath is often highly sensitive and emotional. This sensitivity often confuses and prompts empaths to believe others' emotions as their own. This is good when you are required to be sympathetic or empathetic toward someone. However, what will happen to your life if you stop experiencing your emotions and only live off the emotions of others? Obviously, it will become too much to bear. For your survival, you must ensure that you can distinguish between your feelings and those of others.

Since you are an empath, you tend to care a lot about everything and everyone around you. Whenever you are around others, you tend to give them a little of your energy. You tend to love with every cell of your being and are sensitive to feelings of others but what about yourself? Do you take care of yourself? Do you understand your feelings? At the end of the day, do you have any love left for yourself? How do you keep replacing all the love that you give out to others?

Empaths tend to give out a lot of their love and positive energy. Usually, they keep doing this even when the other person isn't deserving. Unknowingly, you are giving out your positive vibrations to those who are not in touch with their emotions. Essentially, they are energy vampires who suck out every ounce of your energy to make themselves feel better. Empaths tend to have an unexplainable magnetic pull that makes others gravitate toward them. It's as if they know that you will happily put them first and be quite willing to help them with their troubles. You constantly put a lot of your energy in the reaction or feelings you have toward others, instead of yourself. So, much of your energy is directed away from your personal truth and toward someone else.

If you are an empath, it is quite likely that you find it difficult to love yourself. It is rather tricky for empaths to put themselves first. They find it challenging to make themselves a priority. You must make yourself a priority. Treat yourself with the love and kindness that you show others. You deserve self-love, and it doesn't make you selfish. Empaths often feel the need to fix things for others. In this process, they overlook their own needs. In the long run, all this does is harm the empath.

You are entitled to happiness and love. You don't have to keep trying to make others feel better about themselves all the time. You have a certain responsibility toward yourself. Don't be under any misconceptions that self-love is selfish. So, start spending time doing things that you love. Do whatever you want, as long as it makes you happy and doesn't harm anyone else. When you are at peace with yourself and are full of positive energy, you are in a better place to help others. Self-love is the simplest way to heal yourself.

Importance of Self-Love

Growing up as an empath, you might have been told that you are melodramatic, extremely reactive or that you need to stop flying off the handle. You would have experienced a rollercoaster ride of emotions through your childhood and adulthood. Apart from this, you might have even grown accustomed to the anxiety you often feel. It's not just the lows, but the highs are quite potent too. Emotional music can make you feel sad; happy music can give you goosebumps or anything else along these lines. If you ever notice that you tend to get lost in the lives of the characters while you read a book, it is because of your empathic abilities. Needless to say, it is quite likely that you felt different all your life and out of place. It is time to realize that you are not alone, and all empathic people tend to face this.

You must never shame yourself for who you truly are. When you're growing up in a world that's riddled with chaos, where no one understands you, you might resort to shaming yourself. It is rather sad when someone tells you what you feel isn't valid or that you are reacting too much about something insignificant. When you think about it, this is a form of gaslighting, and you tend to feel like an outsider.

Since you have been called melodramatic so many times, you start believing them. You start doubting your thoughts and emotions. You start questioning yourself. Maybe you even start thinking that it is all in your head, so it clearly isn't that bad. Maybe you tell yourself that you must get a grip and learn to calm yourself down. This will wreak havoc on your self-confidence. The self-doubt you experience increases significantly. You start shielding yourself and hiding your true identity to fit in — even when your gut says otherwise. You start ignoring your intuition and kick yourself mentally when you realize that your intuition was right all along. As you try to keep up with the pace of others around you, you'd start feeling exhausted. All these things essentially mean that you start suppressing the hurt you feel. Well, you can certainly do this for a while, but there will come a time when it all comes crashing around you. Empaths are not meant to suppress their sensitivity, especially when every cell of their being is charged with empathic energy. Your sensitivity is the best trait you have, and if you suppress this, you tend to lose your identity. It is time to understand that your empathic abilities are a superpower, and not everyone is blessed with it. If you feel like you're falling behind in the world, it is merely because others are not able to keep up with you and it's not the other way around. Empaths are healers, dreamers, and artists. They tend to see the world differently from others. Empaths are capable of identifying the exquisite details of life that others often tend to miss out on. Your sensitivity is your gift, and you must embrace it. In this part, you will learn about the importance of self-love for an empath.

Self-love will help you set boundaries. As an empath, the pain of rejection is quite real and rather overwhelming. When you are capable of feeling everything deeply, you can easily avoid conflict and resort to pleasing others all the time. When you do this, it becomes hard to break free of this habit and stand up for yourself. It is time to understand that you're the only one who can dictate whether something is right for you or not. So, when you start planning and accepting yourself for who you truly are, you don't have to rely on validation or approval of others. When this happens, it becomes easier for you to set boundaries. When you start setting boundaries, it becomes easier to regulate the energy that you absorbed from others. This makes it easier to cope with your feelings and of those around you.

Self-love will help you understand the difference between a healthy and toxic relationship. Empaths tend to attract manipulators, narcissists, and other energy vampires, and hence end up in relationships that are abusive, codependent, and even downright toxic. A narcissist can be charismatic and fun to be around. Initially, they tend to make you feel like you're the best thing that's ever happened to them. They even pretend like they understand and accept you for who you are. This can make you feel like you've finally found someone who understands you and that you belong in this world. So, it is obvious that you will try to come to their rescue whenever they face any trouble. You might even start downplaying your needs to accommodate theirs. You keep giving so much of yourself that you forget that a relationship is a two-way street. One person cannot continue to give in a relationship while the other keeps absorbing everything. For a relationship to be healthy and wholesome, there needs to be a mutual give and take; it cannot be one-sided. When you start loving yourself, you start understanding your self-worth. You gain self-confidence and realize that if you keep on giving without getting anything in return, you are harming your self-respect. When you love yourself, you understand what a healthy and nourishing relationship is supposed to be like. This means you can easily recognize when a relationship is toxic and walk away from it.

High levels of sensitivity and low levels of self-esteem are often directly related. When you start loving and accepting yourself, it becomes easier to gain confidence. You can finally stop worrying about what others think about you and do things that you love. You can try your hand at new things that seemed daunting to you in the past. You will no longer worry about others' opinions and instead concentrate on your personal development. When you start believing how wonderful you are, you stop caring about what others say. Here are three simple steps you can follow well some self-love into your life.

Start trusting yourself and be your own best friend. You don't have to depend on others for motivation or encouragement. Everything that you need is present within yourself. All that you need to do is start looking for it. Empaths are quite understanding, kind, and loving toward everyone in their life. Why don't you start directing this exact energy toward yourself? If you want to, you can be your own cheerleader. Start treating yourself the way you would treat your loved one.

An empath's sensitivity is often thought of as a curse. Well, if you think like this, it is time to make some changes. Understand that your sensitivity is a gift you are blessed with. Not everyone can enjoy all the minute details of life. As an empath, you can experience all the highs of life like no one else can. Think of how you're lucky for being as sensitive as you are. Even if others don't understand you, it doesn't matter.

Empaths tend to be hard on themselves. Learn to accept the fact that failure is a part of life. You cannot attain success without running into a few obstacles. Stop treating every obstacle as a failure. Stop being hard on yourself and learn to forgive yourself. Show yourself the compassion you often reserve for others. Start monitoring your internal dialogue and ensure that you are kind to yourself.

Practical Test:

1.What will help you understand the difference between a healthy and toxic relationship?

2.Do Empaths tend to be hard on themselves?

CHAPTER 26:

How to Build Connections with Others

When you start becoming aware of what you want and how you can do it as an empath, that is your first step towards a change. It can be mind-boggling sometimes but when you have complete knowledge about your situation, things will automatically start becoming easier. Have you noticed children when they fail to make you understand what they are feeling? They start fussing or crying but when they find the right way to express their feelings, they can easily calm down. The same thing happens with empaths as well. When you learn to build connections and convey your emotions, everything becomes easier and sorted in life.

If you want to bring about any changes in your life, you need to start by accepting your qualities as an empath. You also need to accept the entire situation that you are in. You need to see yourself as someone worthy of love and attention, and you definitely do not have to be so hard on yourself. Empaths often fear that they might end up being egoistical and that acts as a barrier not only in forming connections but also in self-love. You need to build a healthy regard for yourself and that is not something selfish.

For empaths, the world is hard to describe, and so are their feelings. They do not have faith in their perceptions or their validity. But when they start to get a grip on why they feel or do what they do, that is when all the chaos starts to smoothen out. They can understand situations now because they have identified the patterns or structures that are there. But for that, empaths first need to learn how they can build the connections with others without hurting themselves and for that, I am compiled some useful tips for you.

Understand Energy Exchange

There are several ways in which you can understand and measure energy. Now, you have to understand that one of the most vital things that keeps you alive is energy, and it can be felt in various ways. Your emotions or feelings are one way of measuring your energy. If you are an empath, you will know how exhausting it can feel after you have had conversations with a certain person. These people are toxic for you and automatically drain the energy out of you. Even when you do not talk much, you can get exhausted simply by staying in the presence of such people.

On the contrary, you will also have people in your life who make you feel comfortable, and you will feel happy around them. This person can be your friend or even a family member. But what you have to understand that empaths always undergo these energy exchanges whenever they communicate with someone. You absorb the energy of other people and you let them do the same to you subconsciously. What you need to do is understand that you have your own aura. It is somewhat like your own personal bubble which determines your energy limits. All your emotions and thoughts are present in your aura. All your traumas are present there too.

So, when you connect with someone, you are taking in the energy that is present in their aura, and you are sharing your aura with theirs. This energetic field exchange does not always happen through talking. Sometimes, you can experience the same with a total stranger who is sitting next to you on the train.

Learn to Create Barriers

This is so important when it comes to effective communication. Empaths are so affected by what other people feel that they often mix up all the emotions and then confused about their own feelings. They cannot separate others' feelings from their own. That is why it is so necessary to create barriers so that you learn to ground yourself. If an event or a person has bogged you down, it is in your hands to stop it, and you can do so by creating a barrier. The simplest method is to avoid people or locations that give you that feeling but as you know, it is not always possible to avoid. Sometimes, you have to interact with people you don't want to and so that is when you have to make yourself strong. You can try to meditate or practice mindfulness to create strong barriers in your mind.

Use visualization to distract your mind from the negativity and tell yourself that what you are feeling is not yours. It is someone else's emotion that you have absorbed. You need to let that toxicity go because only then will you be able to see your true self.

Another way of creating barriers is by saying the right things. But this will take some time, and you have to work on increasing your levels of self-confidence. For example, if you are in the middle of a conversation with someone and you do not like where it is headed, then you can always ask them politely to change the topic because you do not feel so good about it. Or, you can excuse yourself from the conversation and take a break. You need to prevent yourself from getting drained of all the energy you have, and you need to do everything you can to keep yourself stable – that should be your ultimate goal.

Challenge Yourself

If you want to communicate better, you need to go out of your comfort zone. Communication is the key in all aspects of today's world, and if you keep yourself shut down, it is not going to do you any good. So, you have to learn to open up. Most empaths are introverts and opening up can be a big challenge for them. That is why, introvert or not; I always advise empaths to do something that is new to them because it will give you the lesson of handling anything that comes your way. You need to understand that there is room for improvement in everyone but change or improvement will only come when you take the first step. Here are some things that you can do to challenge yourself –

- Learn a new language – One of the best ways of challenging yourself is by learning a new language. Also, it won't go waste is you choose the language to suit your resume, and then you can even earn some extra cash on the side. This is not even difficult as you got plenty of apps providing free resources and also amazing YouTube videos where you can get language tutorials.

- Pursue a hobby – Everyone has something that they always wanted to do but couldn't because they did not get enough time. So, figure out what your hobby is and then pursue it. You can monetize this too once you learn it well.

- Do something you are scared of – Think about what scared you. Are you afraid of public speaking or maybe heights? Then, take a small step towards your fear, and once you do that, you can take another step towards it next week. Yes, the first try can be scary but don't leave it at that. You should look at your fear in the eyes and face it.

- Travel – When you travel, you meet new people from various cultures, and this will eventually help you in sharpening your communications skills as an empath. You will meet people outside your usual circle, and you will come to realize that everyone is different.

Practice Active Listening

Empaths are good listeners and that is why people come to them during their sorrows. But if you want to form better connections with people, you still need to brush up on your skills. Being an empath means you are absorbing other people's energy right from the morning. If someone impacts you too deeply, you might be thinking about that particular situation the whole day, and so when you try to communicate with the next person, you are not really listening as your mind has been diverted towards the previous person.

Also, not all empaths are active listeners. Some empaths listen for a while, and they wait to respond. You should be really listening to the person until the very end. Your body language also plays a big role in making the person in front of you realize that you are actually listening to them and not pretending to do so. Always maintain eye contact. Keep responding to them in full sentences. Simply saying single words like 'absolutely' and 'yeah' doesn't really count. You should come up with full sentences that have your judgment in them.

Engage in Self-Love

If you want to enhance your communication skills, you also have to work on loving yourself. You show empathy to others, and you are kind to them. Now, you have to practice some self-empathy. One of the ways in which you can do this is by trying to talk to yourself just like you do with those you love. Empaths have this habit of beating themselves up for every little thing but talking to yourself like a friend might help you in solving this problem. Take a piece of paper and write down any negative thoughts that you are having about yourself and then tell yourself the positive things that you would have told a friend experiencing the same thing in their life.

You can also get rid of the endless cycle of self-judgment by practicing mindfulness. Think about your feelings and emotions, but you should not be judging them. Just let them come into your mind and then let them go as if they are free flowing. Don't ruminate on anything and at the same time, don't push any of the thoughts away.

You should be able to forgive yourself. You need to remind yourself that you did what you could with what you had at that moment. Everything that happened has also given you some good lessons in life. But I am not asking you to shield your wrongs or pretend that they did not happen. What I am asking you is to accept that you made a mistake and then forgive yourself for it. Once you do this, you are practicing self-compassion. This means that you have learned to identify your own humanity.

Also, you need to stop comparing yourself with others. This is the era of social media where people are constantly checking through others' profiles and then comparing their life with theirs. But whatever you see on social media is just a photo. You do not know what is going on behind that. So, if you think that social media is making you upset, you need to reduce your time scrolling through the various social media accounts.

Practical Test:

1. How to Challenge yourself?

2. Is Engaging in Self-Love important?

3. Are empaths a good listener?

CHAPTER 27:

The Unhealthy Empath

The internet is full of stories of people who realize that they're not just sensitive, but empathic. Most of these people often find themselves distressed by it, even in pain from it.

Some people are so accustomed to reading between the lines when it comes to others that they forget that is not the norm in society. They expect friends to understand and anticipate their needs in the same way the empath does for them. The empath may not even realize they haven't expressed their needs to their loved ones. They find themselves feeling neglected. If this goes on, and they fail to communicate in return to others, the empath may isolate themselves further and further, not wanting to experience that perceived betrayal again. When left unchecked, this self-protection can turn into a full depletion of empathy in the once-sensitive person.

Sometimes, a lack of empathy sounds like a relief. Don't be fooled: the lack of empathy is directly tied to dangerous personality disorders such as psychopathy, sociopathy, and narcissism.

Instead of wishing your gift away, learn to harness it. When you can direct your empathy away from toxic sources and toward positive, clean ones, you can find peace and fulfillment anywhere.

Emotional health can be directly related to physical health. Those of us who are highly sensitive often experience a myriad of physical symptoms. These can include:

- Elevated blood pressure when triggered
- Irritable Bowel Syndrome (IBS)

- Skin inflammation, such as a rash or hives
- Abdominal cramping
- Vertigo
- Flushing of the face
- Weakness in the limbs
- Difficulty breathing / feeling like you're hyperventilating
- Weight loss to the point of cachexia
- Weight gain to the point of obesity
- Insomnia
- Muscle pain
- Joint pain

It's as if highly sensitive people are allergic to negative energy, somewhat in the way those with celiac disease have painful, disruptive reactions to gluten or the way dander can trigger hives and respiratory distress for those allergic to cats.

The human body's sympathetic nervous system, its fight or flight or freeze system activates when we are threatened. It creates slower digestion, increased heart and breathing rates, and triggers adrenaline and other hormones and neurotransmitters, which, in turn, increases muscle tension.

If you have ever had a near-miss with an auto collision, you probably experienced the following: you held your breath, your muscles seized up, bracing for impact, and your brain started looking for an escape route, even if it didn't have time to act on it. Minutes after, when everything is fine, and you're continuing on your way, your heart may still be pounding in your chest. You may still hear the thump of your blood moving through the vessels near your ears. You may experience pain in your shoulders and back from where you tensed.

But it doesn't take a life-or-death situation to launch the sympathetic nervous system into responding this way. Many people involved in high-stress relationships have similar reactions when they have to interact with certain people. Highly sensitive people often have a difficult time separating themselves from others' demands and ignorance of boundaries, and their bodies react in much the same way.

The parasympathetic nervous system works to counteract those things. When activated, it decreases the heart and breathing rates, it assists in digestion and relaxes muscles. Highly sensitive empaths need to create a lifestyle that will nourish the parasympathetic nervous system. We also need to indulge in rituals that can help us expel our negative emotions.

Roots in Trauma

Post-traumatic stress disorder, or PTSD, first appeared in American Psychiatric Publishing, Incorporated's Diagnostic and Statistical Manual of Mental Disorders, Edition 3 in 1980. Since its inclusion in the manual, it has become part of the American vernacular. Many people claim they have PTSD from watching a poorly made comedic film or being inconvenienced at the Department of Motor Vehicles. But for millions of people worldwide, PTSD is not something to joke about. It is disruptive and agonizing. When it triggers a severe anxiety attack, the sufferer worries she might lose her job, or not be able to take care of her kids. It can severely limit every aspect of her life.

PTSD can present itself in a multitude of ways, from obsessive-compulsive disorder, hyper-vigilance, attention deficit disorder, or depression. Most of us can sympathize with a soldier returning home from war. We don't understand his need to scan rooftops or be wary of suspicious packages. We don't know what it's like to leave the present moment and have to relive a battle when we're enjoying fireworks. We don't know, but we can imagine. We can accept that their PTSD is real and agonizing.

In cases of extreme childhood abuse, we can stretch our imaginations and conceptualize why survivors are afraid and why they are easily triggered. We can sympathize with them, and often, we can hurt for them even if we're blessed enough not to have endured anything like what they have gone through. Unfortunately, many peoples' grace doesn't extend to adulthood for the victims. Once they pass adolescence, childhood PTSD survivors seem to be expected to "be over it by now" or otherwise pretend that the abuse didn't occur.

The same could be said for adult victims of violence or psychological torture. It's been three years, Laura. Why do you still freeze when you hear that sound?

But some people are different. Some are ready and willing to be patient, to listen, and to accept a survivor in whatever state they come. A large number of empaths were once victims of trauma themselves. Instead of becoming cold to the world and using their injuries as an excuse to hurt other people, they chose to use their understanding to better the world around them. Many stepped into a deeper role and became empaths, whether intentionally or not.

Why Do Empaths Get So Tired?

Empath fatigue is cited as the most frustrating thing about being sensitive to energy. No one jogs for twelve hours a day, every day, with only a few short interruptions for rest. That would destroy a human body. Not many people can do any singular voluntary movement consistently for 12 hours a day without major repercussions coming to the body. Empaths, however, are expected to (and expect themselves to) be emotionally available during every waking hour.

For an undeveloped empath or intuitive who doesn't know how to protect and regenerate their own energy, any interruption in their flow can punch a hole in their dam, causing energy to leak out at an alarming rate.

Professions such as teachers, doctors, first responders, veterinarians, and counselors are often filled by empaths. When an empath is in a role that requires them to deal regularly with people who are hurting, they may experience secondary trauma. Some people go a step further and call this phenomenon empath compassion fatigue. When emotionally sensitive people are past their limit of empathy, they tend to shut down. They not only need extra sleep, but they also need a space to be awake but alone as they process everything that has come in. Sometimes this looks like an escape to an off-grid cabin in the woods. Sometimes this looks like going on a solo vacation and being pampered. Sometimes it looks like holing up for an extended weekend and enjoying your favorite foods while binge-watching multiple seasons of a new show. In 2012, Scientific American reported on research regarding the positive effect that intense special-visual processing video games can have on post-traumatic stress disorder sufferers. The subjects were instructed on how to play the game Tetris, then played it for around 20 uninterrupted minutes per day for a week. A control group was given no game to play. After the week was over, the group playing Tetris logged 8.7 "intrusive memories" such as flashbacks or panic attacks. The group that didn't play suffered nearly four times as many during the week.

While Tetris won't cure PTSD, it has been shown to alleviate flashbacks and panic attacks. Doctors have made correlations of this form of alternative therapy to the highly successful eye movement desensitization and reprocessing (EMDR) therapy that is gaining traction in the traditional psychology world.

This tells us that the human mind—empathic or not—requires time to process difficult things in the background while occupying itself in the foreground.

Processing Activities

- ☐ Reading a book
- ☐ Watching engaging television or film
- ☐ Listening to an audiobook
- ☐ Listening to podcasts
- ☐ Playing a video game
- ☐ Knitting or crocheting
- ☐ Boxing
- ☐ Play music
- ☐ Practicing yoga
- ☐ Writing fiction
- ☐ Driving
- ☐ Listening to music
- ☐ Cooking
- ☐ Walking a dog
- ☐ Running
- ☐ Painting
- ☐ Learning a new hobby
- ☐ Play with a pet

When engaging in media as your processing tool, you may feel even more tired or frustrated. Binging Game of Thrones or reading a forum may be fine for some, but it may compound stress in ways you don't immediately notice. Check in with yourself during your processing period to make sure you're improving and not spinning your wheels.

If you have taken time for yourself and feel like it's not refreshing you, or if you're just as anxious as you were before, please talk to a professional who's able to walk you through your energy depletion and see you to the other side of it. Your wellness is more important to the world than you know.

Adrenal Fatigue

In the Empath's Survival Guide by psychiatrist Dr. Judith Orloff discusses why and how empaths are so frequently misdiagnosed by doctors. Adrenal fatigue is likely to blame for the empath's sometimes sudden lethargy, and not laziness or physical diseases such as anemia or hypothyroidism.

Adrenal fatigue is said to be caused by stress. Our adrenal glands are part of the endocrine system and located over each kidney. They are small sacs responsible for the production of vital hormones, most notably here for adrenaline and cortisol.

Cortisol affects many different systems in the body, as there are cortisol receptors in nearly every kind cell. Cortisol is responsible for the regulation of metabolism, the reduction of inflammation, blood sugar levels, sodium balance, blood pressure, and even the formulation of memories.

When under stress, the adrenal glands snap into overdrive, producing the proper substances to keep you running at the required pace. The theory is that when they are in overdrive too long, they, too, run out of steam and are no longer able to produce the helpful hormones until given time and resources (in the form of lifestyle changes and dietary supplementation) with which to heal.

Often, adrenal fatigue is overlooked by medical professionals. In fact, regardless of growing research on the topic, the Endocrinology Society does not recognize adrenal fatigue as a condition. Mayo Clinic addresses these problems as adrenal deficiency, which suggests a different causality than the idea of overused glands. Holistic and homeopathic doctors, however, rarely overlook the symptoms and are willing to help treat the disorder. Still, the best practice is to first have a physician rule out problems like anemia.

Practical Test:

1. What is PSTD?

2. Is empath fatigue true?

3. What is Adrenal Fatigue?

Conclusion

While this book is dedicated to helping those, who suffer from debilitating negative emotions, it is also highly beneficial for those who just want to gain a better awareness of themselves. By practicing self-reflection exercises, increasing your self-awareness, and constantly turning your negative experiences into more positive ones, you allow yourself to not only master your emotions, but become a master over your entire life.

Once you begin to live a life that allows you to have so much control of your actions and reactions, you will question what was so challenging about it before. In spite of the fact that it can require some investment to build up the aptitudes and actualize the procedures, this time is all around spent and you get back beyond what you would ever conceivable put in. An existence of enthusiastic opportunity is conceivable, and you get the opportunity to settle on the decision to live it once you settle on the decision to control what is keeping you down.

When you show compassion and kindness to others, you increase your own happiness. Acts of kindness can take the form of many things — whether it is being more generous with your money, time, affection, or other resources, giving creates more positive emotions, which results in more pleasant feelings. Consider ways you can give more in each area, such as:

- Volunteering
- Scheduling one-on-one, uninterrupted time with your kids
- Treating someone to lunch
- Educating others
- Being more involved in your community

It can be easy to overlook the many ways you can express more kindness. Even something as simple as holding the door open for someone, buying coffee for the person behind you in line, or just smiling at others not only have a significant impact on the other person's life, but will also help you feel better about yours. In most cases, doing random acts of kindness on a daily basis creates a ripple effect, where the person you were kind to, be then kind to the next person, and so on. Just this thought alone can help cultivate more positive feelings.

Learn to really listen

Consider how much better you feel when you are having a conversation with someone who is actively showing interest in and understanding what you are saying. You probably have a deeper conversation and connection with this person who leaves you feeling better about yourself. If you learn to apply this same consideration to others when they speak to you, you will generally leave with the same feelings of understanding and connectedness. Learn to really focus and interpret what others say to you. Listen to hear what they have to say, as opposed to listening to respond. Often, this is all most people are looking for and it is something you can do without much practice or effort.

Even when you feel you fully understand and comprehend the effect your emotions have in your life, there is still a component you may not be able to gain full control over. Negative thoughts can be terribly discouraging. These thoughts have often developed and have been strengthened through years of negative self-talk. When you have such a strong connection with the negative dialogue in your mind, even though you try desperately to eliminate it, you can feel as if you are just not meant to be happy. These thoughts are what can greatly hinder your ability to fully control your emotions.

Thank you so much for reading book I hope you have learned something.

MASTER YOUR EMOTIONS:

A GUIDE TO OVERCOME NEGATIVITY. MOVE FROM NEGATIVE THINKING BY BEING EMOTIONALLY INTELLIGENT.

JUDITH HEAL

Table Of Contents

Introduction

Changing your brain means you need to keep your stress levels under control. This is because not only does it impact our health in both senses of the word, but it also takes up space in your mind. There are a number of reasons it inhibits your brain from functioning at its highest level. For one, it steals your ability to concentrate. You will not be paying attention to what is going on around you because your attention will be directed at whatever the source of your stress is. When you are feeling the effects of stress over a long time, it becomes the most active presence in your mind. It will take the wheel away from you if it is allowed to. It can even debilitate you because you can feel so much pressure that it is literally like a weight pulling down on you. You will feel unable to handle your daily life because doing anything will seem like too much. All you will want to do is lie in bed, and even then, you will still feel the symptoms- heart-pounding, limbs shaky, feelings that your world is going to implode at any second. You will not be able to eat or sleep. It will take over your life if it is not stopped.

There's no denying it- our lives are stressful. So often, we're on our way to work, getting prepared to host a family event, or cleaning a house that never seems to stay that way for an entire day. We're always on the go, which can lead to complications. There are also a lot of times where things happen that disappoint us. You might find out someone you thought was your friend was secretly talking badly about you or that you didn't get your dream job. The never-ending load of pressure can make us fearful about if we do not live up to the expectations placed on us by others and ourselves. When we feel rejected or betrayed, it can make us lose hope.

I can imagine that you have heard about anxiety and depression quite a bit lately, but what are these things, exactly? You might feel afraid at first when I tell you these are emotional disorders. I am not implying that people with them are crazy, or that if you have either of them that you are at risk for doing something drastic. These are both extremely common conditions to have, so much that most people struggle with them at least some point in their life. There are times where life brings more stress than our threshold can deal with. You might be dealing with a family crisis or the end of a long-term relationship. Sometimes it isn't even one big tragedy, but a culmination of smaller stressful events that add up to overload.

Having a problem does not make you crazy. It makes you self-aware. Everyone has met a person who does not have this quality. Think about a person you have known who never held themselves responsible for anything. Any time something goes wrong for them, they blame it on the shortcomings of others, and therefore, they never get better. What you are doing does the opposite. You will begin to get a handle on this problem. It will start the moment you admit it is there.

Anxiety is often equated with feeling afraid. This is only a basic understanding of this condition. Even though they often fear outside circumstances, what they have the most dread about is being inside of their own mind because it comes up with all kinds of crazy and scary situations.

When people hear about depression, they usually think it means being sad all of the time. However, this is not really what it is about. Depression is about a lack of motivation. It is not about feeling sad as much as it is about the notion that things will stay exactly as they are, which the person with the disorder is not happy with. "Nothing will ever change or get better." That is the sentiment that is constantly taken on by people who are suffering from depression.

While these disorders might seem like very powerful beings, they do not have to keep you down. I will show you how to keep that from happening. You are capable of combating these issues so you can be the one in control, not them.

Herein lies the major source of power that anxiety and depression hold. The sufferer does not feel like they have any control over the way they think or feel. To an extent, this might be true, but only on a surface level. We all have thoughts and even impulses that come to us out of the blue. We do not know how they got here, and they do not line up with what we want to feel or do, and that is precisely why they have so much power over us. To get a better understanding of how this is possible, imagine a child who has always gotten very high grades in all of their classes. Then they get into a class that they do not excel in. They are having a hard time comprehending the information they need to learn, and the grades they are getting are not what they are used to. This causes them to become fearful. They worry that they will not be able to move on to the following grade because of this class. Then the thought comes into their mind- maybe I am just stupid and that is why I am failing this class. What if I was only doing well in the other ones because they were easy and now, I see how stupid I really am! All of their life, they have thought of themselves as a good student and now things are happening to them to make them question that.

When someone is not happy with their life, a common response is that they should look on the bright side because other people are struggling with worse problems. This is not a fair thing to say to a person with this disorder because they do understand that their situation could be a great deal worse than it is. You know that others have it worse than you, but that doesn't mean your problems aren't significant.

In the case of both anxiety and depression, you will feel the urge to stay in one place that feels relatively safe all day, and you will not feel like doing anything. For depression, it is a special case, because the entire mission of this disorder is to make you feel drained of all energy. One of the biggest misconceptions about depression is the idea that it is about feeling sad all of the time. In reality, depression renders a person feeling emotionally bankrupt- meaning they have a hard time tapping into any sort of feeling. This creates a sense of numbness, which is the crux of the sufferer's internal turmoil. As humans, we want to feel emotions.

A strange thing happens when we are overstimulated. Let's say there is a worldwide crisis going on that has created a lot of changes in the daily lives of people as well as a sense of fear for their safety. There can come the point where you start to feel nothing. You have no motivation to do anything because it seems like too much work. What is happening here is a defense mechanism. You have been feeling a high range of emotions for an extended period of time, which your body knows is not good for you in any aspect of your health. As a response to this realization, your emotions shut down. In a way, it is your brain's means of forcing relaxation onto you because it does not see stress relief happening in the foreseeable future.

In times where you do not know what is going to happen following in your life, you need to take special care to keep a level head and stay calm. I know that this is especially difficult during the most frightening eras of your life, but if you do not do this, you will suffer from an overload of stress, which is a slippery slope to fall into.

During times where our conventional ideas of social interactions cannot be done, try to broaden your definition of that. Contact your friends and loved ones through messaging and texts. It may not be the same as seeing them in person, but it will be interacting with another human being, which is what you will need during this time more than ever.

In the management of both anxiety and depression, you must keep one important thing in mind- whatever is going on, no matter how troubling it is, it is not going to last forever. It might come back, but this episode is going to pass, and you will find relief.

One of the most crucial steps to overcoming anxiety is to accept it. You might think that sounds strange, but here is what I mean by that. A great deal of that distressed feeling comes from the feeling that you need to make it go away now and that something terrible will happen if you do not. It will cause you to feel abnormal. You will become afraid of losing control of your own mind. Let me tell you now- that is not going to happen. People feel anxious every day and do not lose their minds. Think of how many times you personally have felt that way and still managed to bring yourself back.

When you learn to ride out the feelings that come with anxiety, they will no longer be able to prevent you from living your life. Even if you are suffering from an episode, you will still be able to do whatever you want or need to do. This means there will be no more canceling dates or going home early from events because you are feeling overwhelmed. You will have the ability to tolerate the disorder, and that moment will be the end of you feeling debilitated by it.

Things are not hopeless. You are still here, and nothing bad terrible is really happening to you. The sensations inside of you might be very frightening, but they cannot do anything to you that they have not already done. You aren't helplessly at the mercy of other forces.

When you are feeling depressed, there will come points where you have to literally drag yourself out of bed. This will be the most difficult thing you have ever done or ever will do because whenever the will is not present, it is hard to find a reason to do this. To do this, refrain from giving yourself a long to-do list that will only make your desire to remain in bed all day long even stronger.

CHAPTER 28:

Programming the Mind

Many self-help gurus refer to us as having an inner child, which is supposed to be this pure and innocent side to ourselves. It is supposed to be creative, spiritual, and encouraging. Perhaps it is true. However, for most of us, the only child we have inside us is a screaming ADHD toddler who is hyperactive, never sleeps, feels that the world is against them, and that none of their friends want to play. That child is your subconscious mind. That child needs to be taught right from wrong, and they need to be raised to become well-functioning individuals within society (your mind). True, this child that we have inside us is creative, and they can come up with the most amazing solutions to problems if we let them. But every child needs a parent. You need to parent your subconscious mind (your inner child) and ensure that this child shares a belief system that you approve of. If this is not done, then your subconscious mind will begin to dictate what you do, how you do it, and how you feel about life. It decides these things based upon baser needs, such as your perceived safety, nutrition, and the reproduction of the species. Though this may have been fine and well during our early primitive times, it is no longer how we want to live our lives.

In the past, we used to silence the subconscious mind's patterns and behaviors to achieve a state of relative calm by using drugs and invasive "therapies." This theory of "shut it up" has in recent years become largely debunked. People no longer want their subconscious mind to be silenced; instead, they want to give it a voice and establish negotiations with it, making the subconscious mind your friend, not an enemy. The power of the subconscious mind is an amazing force that, if used correctly, can unleash our full potential and help us to achieve our goals through ingenuity and information processing at a level that our conscious minds can, as yet, not reach.

So, where does the concept of programming your subconscious mind fit in then? If we want to "negotiate" with our subconscious mind, how can we force it to do things a certain way? And that is where the confusion occurs. Words like "mind control," "programming techniques," and "methods" have been given a bad rep due to their abuse in the past. Modern-day approaches are much more moderate and inclusive than before. Your subconscious mind is included in the process, and it becomes your partner. In fact, the programming process is something that the subconscious mind already does every day by accepting and filing new information – you will now simply be selecting what you let your mind digest. It's sort of like a diabetic, who goes on a diet that supports their health (sugary sweets are not a good idea, but they can choose to eat healthily, although, they do sneak a treat now and again).

Now that you feel less guilty (or terrified) about reprogramming your subconscious mind, let's look at some techniques that are beneficial and fun, which will make a friend of your mind.

Imagination Is More Important Than Knowledge

Imagination is something that happens when your subconscious mind sends out a "random" series of memories or extrapolations to feed our conscious or logical mind; conclusions are reached, giving us imagination (or problem-solving). According to Earthsky.org (n.d.), imagination is where (when) the conscious mind "consciously manipulates images, symbols, ideas, and theories," and then creates the mental focus necessary to find solutions to issues and invent new thoughts about things. The brain (or mind) solves these problems by reorganizing the mind (our information). Andreasen (2011) believes that the mind is a system that creates new file-codes on an ongoing basis, like the root system on a computer. It decides what information is important based on our values, emotions, experiences, and conscious decisions. In layman's terms, the subconscious mind looks for connections between different memories and ideas. It then creates a range of possible answers or solutions to our problems.

An example of this would be if you need to decide what to wear for a Halloween party at work. Your subconscious mind would reference all the previous Halloween parties you have ever been to or seen. It would consider themes within the general idea of dress up parties, such as pirates, *Arabian Nights*, *Jungle Book*, and hospital themes. It would then use the information about what you have in your closet, consider how you could begin combining outfits (and even what it knows your friends have available for you to borrow). In the end, it will give your conscious mind some options, such as combining your black evening dress with biker boots and a leather jacket to create a gothic vampire look, or your white mini skirt with a sexy top and folding a white hat to play nurse. It would then be up to your conscious mind to decide on which imaginative option would be best received in your work environment. If your boss is very religious, they might not enjoy the vampire look (and you can put the ketchup back in the fridge). During these negotiations between your subconscious mind and the conscious mind, information is being exchanged both ways. You might end up adapting the nurse's look to rather become a nerdy scientist instead – since you know that your boss likes science, and you believe that impressing them will open future promotional opportunities for you.

Earlier, we indicated that the subconscious mind is in charge of maintaining balance. A challenge or problem creates tension in the body (and mind), which is not beneficial to the continued existence of the body. Hence, the subconscious mind sees problems (and their tensions) as a threat, and it will take the necessary steps to remedy the situation and protect the body (and mind). This is something that we can begin to consciously manipulate. If we continue with the Halloween scenario above, and one of your colleagues has been harassing you repeatedly at work or making you feel threatened, then your subconscious mind's creativity will be directed at protecting your survival. You might end up coming up with excuses not to attend that Halloween party, instead of thinking about costume possibilities. Your subconscious mind will be trying to remove you from the proximity of the fear-inducing person (your lecherous colleague), and this then takes precedence over the need to impress the bosses and win promotion.

Your subconscious mind is a "picture" brain. It sees solutions before your conscious mind can articulate them. If you were to be stranded on an island in the middle of the ocean, and you have only a pen, a box of dental floss, and a pair of ladies' pantyhose... (did you start thinking of a solution?) Without even completing the scenario, your subconscious mind had already sent through a mass of associations to your conscious mind, which considered the practicalities and came up with a possible solution. It realized in mere milliseconds that you would be hungry on this island, and it also realized that it could use the pen's cap tied to the dental floss to make a hook and line, while the pantyhose could be used to make a fishing net, to catch the smaller fish. This scenario also indicates how your subconscious mind assigned priority to your survival. It didn't think that you could use the dental floss to bind the leaves of the palm trees into a book (or make paper pulp with the pantyhose) and then write your memoirs with the pen. That is not related to your survival, and, therefore, it is not ranked at the top of your subconscious mind's "Google Search." In terms of the mind, it is not about what you would want, but rather about how you use what you know to sustain your continued existence.

This is not mere hearsay either, and scientists continue to investigate how our subconscious mind makes associations and uses those associations to reach conclusions. Neuroimaging studies have found evidence that people who are very creative experience increased brain activity in the areas connected with the making of associations when they are busy with tasks that involve finding solutions through associations (Andreasen, 2011). If those association cortices were blank, our subconscious mind would not be able to find a possible conclusion.

It is the putting together of information (and forming neural pathways or thinking paradigms) that gives us creativity. We have to motivate our subconscious mind to search for alternative solutions and not simply jump to the first possible option (track 101 of the mind's playlist).

So, how did the first person to make a pair of scissors, for instance, decide that putting two pieces of metal that are only moderately sharpened would give us a tool that can cut fabric in a straight line? While creativity may not be the mother of invention, necessity certainly is. In our island scenario above, the urgency (of having to eat to survive) is instrumental in motivating the subconscious mind to find a solution.

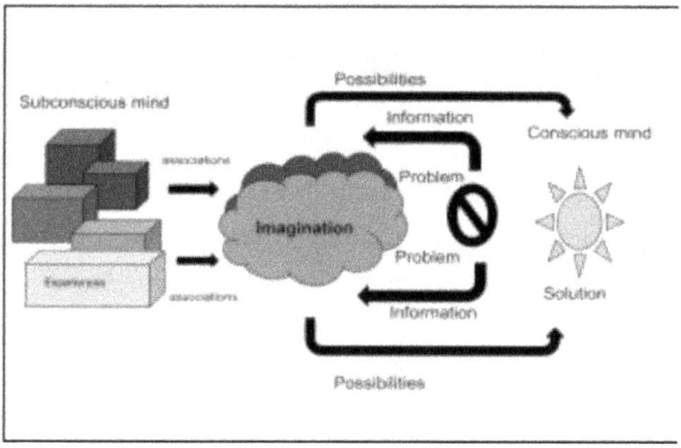

Your subconscious mind is the originator of imagination, due to the stored information it has and the associations it can make.

Man→ Strong

Rock → Build

Dog → Bark

Bicycle → Travel

Your subconscious mind does more than just suggest ideas to your conscious mind; it also takes action. Because your knowledge (which is kept in the subconscious mind) is based on past experiences, and the success or failure of our past actions, your subconscious mind is a bit of an expert at finding appropriate solutions, especially when it relates to your survival (just think of watching *MacGyver* on TV during the '80s or the new remake and all the incredible solutions that the character came up with –usually to save a life or to survive). A stimulated subconscious mind, which believes that it can find solutions, is an asset; however, a subconscious mind that has been subjected to mostly negative experiences (such as trauma) and has been conditioned to believe that it can't find solutions, will be in extreme survival mode. Cases where an abused woman stays with the abusive partner are prime examples of this. Their subconscious mind has been denied the positive past experiences to draw on to find a solution. Therefore, they cling to the dominant figure in their lives (the abuser) to keep them safe (even though the abuser is the cause of their danger). People who lack the knowledge to get themselves out of danger (especially emotional danger) will often be unable to see a solution, and therefore, lack the imaginative ability (and courage) to move forward. The good news is that imagination can be improved.

Practical Test

1.How do you program the mind?

2. Why do you think it is important?

3. What are the benefits of it?

CHAPTER 29:

Turning Negative Feeling Into Positive Attitude

If there's one group of emotions we should do away with, it's negativity.

Being plagued with negative emotions weighing on your mind only makes it that much harder to overcome your challenges.

It does beyond just "feeling sad" or "feeling unhappy". Negativity is an actual hindrance, stopping your brain from performing the clear-thinking process that it needs to deal with complex tasks.

When we can't think clearly enough to process the information on hand, it's easier for issues to seem bigger than what they are.

Add stress into the mix, and perhaps a dash of anger and it quite literally seems impossible to function normally when all your mind can focus on is how your emotions seem to be getting out of control with each passing minute.

Initiating change has to begin with you.

Tell yourself that you have no time for excuses anymore, the only action that is going to yield results.

Excuses only serve as barriers towards accomplishing your goals, and there is no room for that in your life.

Say yes when you feel like saying no and tell yourself you can do it even if it feels impossible.

You can overcome negativity. You can overcome anxiety. You can minimize your stress, anger, and anxiety. You can do anything you set your mind to, including mastering your emotions eventually.

Your mind is the very foundation of everything that you do. Your mindset affects your decisions, your thoughts, the actions and choices you make.

Changing your mindset is simply training your mind to see the world around you in a different light, and mindset matters because the way you view yourself and the world around you shapes the reality that you live in.

- **Think About It**

When a negative thought pops into our heads, we don't stop to think enough if this is a thought that should be taken seriously.

Is there really a cause for alarm? Or could be perhaps be exaggerating the thought in our minds, making it sound worse than what it really is.

Some negative thoughts and emotions are triggered by external factors.

You might be tired, hungry, exhausted, overworked or already feeling tense at the time of the negative thought, and it probably aggravated the situation.

When you're already not in the best frame of mind, a small issue can seem worse than what it is.

The following time you find yourself dwelling on a negative thought, stop and think about it for a minute and ask yourself if it's justified.

- **Have an Action Plan**

There are always going to be challenges which are unpleasant. We can't run away from it, even if we wanted to.

But viewing those challenges from a negative perspective is only going to make things much worse for you.

Having a plan of action on the other hand about what you can do to manage the unexpected un-pleasantries that life may occasionally throw your way will keep you moving forward and no longer be held back despite the negativity that you feel.

When Plan A fails, have a Plan B, a Plan C, and as many back-ups plans as you need.

Be as adaptable and fluid as water, ever ready to twist and turn to continue forging a path forward, because that's the only way to go forward.

Having a plan as opposed to having no plan at all, helps you manage the way you feel.

- **Think About What's Helpful**

Whenever you've experienced a setback, the last thing you might be thinking about is how this situation is helpful to you.

As bleak or negative as a situation may be, one trick mentally tough individuals use to help them maintain their optimism is to think about what helpful lesson they can take away from the setbacks they experienced.

It could be one lesson, it could be two, it could be as many lessons as you'd like.

No matter how bad things seem, there's always a silver lining, it's up to you to find it by asking yourself the right questions. Questions like what have I learned from this experience? What can I do to make it better moving forward? What's one positive takeaway from this situation?

- **Observe Your Surroundings**

Your environment has a big impact on the way that you feel. The place you spend most of your time is going to weigh on your mind subconsciously. You may not be actively thinking about your surroundings, but it's there in the back of your mind.

If you find it hard to remain positive throughout the day, do a quick scan of your surroundings and observe what the sources of negativity may be.

Your cluttered workstation? The toxic colleague who is constantly complaining and talking negatively about other colleagues behind their back?

Maybe that pile of paperwork you've been postponing for a while now and haven't gotten around to doing yet.

Once you've identified a potential source, ask yourself what you can do to rectify the problem.

Can the source be removed entirely? If it can't what else could you do to spend less time around this negative source in a week?

- **Stop Feeding into Your Thoughts**

Feeding into your negative thoughts is only going to fuel it to become even more out of control.

A thought may start off small, but the more you continue to obsess and dwell over the matter, the bigger that thought eventually seems to become.

The expression making a mountain out of a molehill is completely applicable to this situation.

We sometimes build up our fears so much in our minds that they seem disastrous until we eventually face them and come to realize it wasn't so bad after all.

- **Find Inspiration Daily**

The best way to cultivate a positive mindset and minimize negativity is to wake up each morning and make the first thing that you see something that is going to inspire you.

Pick a quote or a saying, stick pictures of inspirational quotes on your mirrors, in your cubicle at work, a note on your phone, make it your wallpaper on your computer, and just surround yourself with it so it's hard to miss.

Starting off on a positive note will help set the tone for the rest of the day, so wake up each morning and let positivity be the first and dominant feeling that helps to start your day right.

Every day is another chance, another opportunity to begin anew, and it is what you do today - not what has happened in the past - that matters most.

- **Cultivate Positive Dialogue**

We've established by now just how powerful your thoughts can be. If your thoughts have the power to influence negativity, they also have that same power to do the opposite.

You need to start tapping into that force and begin creating a more optimistic mindset.

You must push every negative thought you have about yourself out of your mind and start replacing it with something positive instead.

Imagine your negative thoughts as physical boulders in front of you, and you need to forcefully push those out of your mind and clear the path for newer, better things.

For every negative thought that you find yourself thinking, stop and immediately replace that thought with a positive one.

- **Reshape Your Failure Perspective**

Instead of thinking about them as failures, see them as lessons instead.

They're not failures, they're learning experiences that teach you what not to do, and what needs improvement.

We are constantly learning something new, always growing and developing into a better version of yourself.

Nobody can do everything perfectly, or always get it from the first go without taking a few stumbles along the way.

Every successful person out there today that has made their mark and becomes a household name didn't get to where they are without taking a few tumbles and stumbles along the way.

They too made plenty of mistakes before they got to the pinnacle of success.

Change your mind set by changing the way you see these failures, don't focus on how you failed but instead, start thinking about how you can improve following time or what you can do differently.

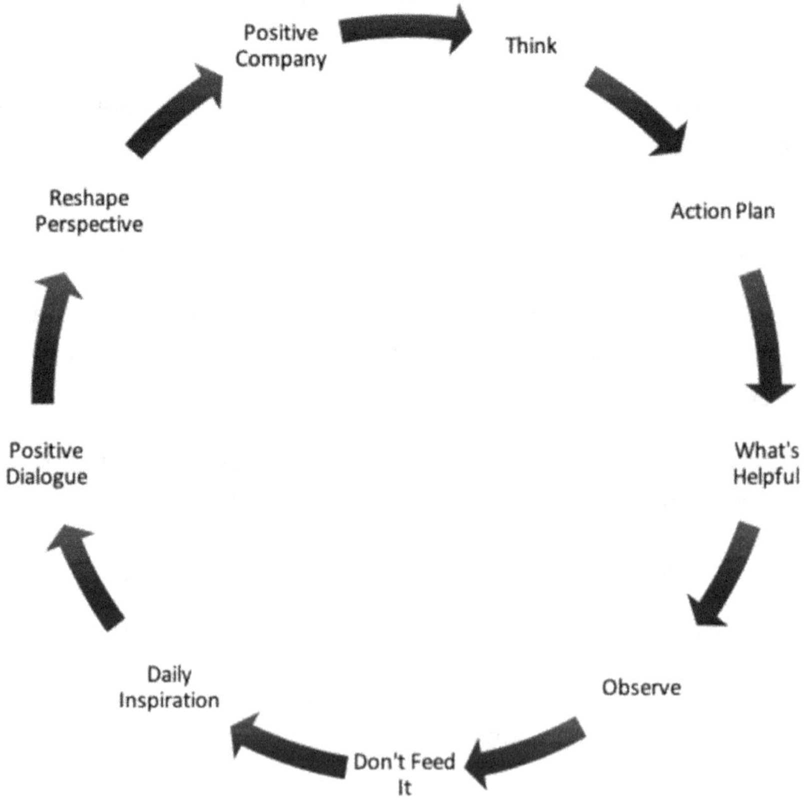

How to Overcome Negative Thoughts

You need to believe in yourself. Believe that you are stronger than you give yourself credit for, believe that you deserve to have a better, happier life.

You'll never truly achieve the level of positive mindset you hope for if you still have those nagging thoughts at the back of your mind that make you doubt yourself every step of the way.

Whenever you feel your emotions getting the better of you, stop and take a breath.

Focusing on your breathing will help you shift your focus and your mind from feeling anxious, nervous, scared or angry to calm, steadiness and peace.

By believing you can achieve it, you've already put yourself one step closer to making it happen for real.

- **How to Reduce Anxiety**

Anxiety is one of the things that could happen to you. You didn't ask for it.

Nobody would ever choose to feel tense and anxious over being happy and comfortable.

Those who tend to worry chronically are always surrounded by an impending sense of doom, or unrealistic fears that tend to magnify and increase their worries.

There's no one who would ever voluntarily want to put themselves in this position.

Anxiety just happen due to a number of factors and having them doesn't make you weak.

Anxiety is mainly caused by worry, and worry could stem from several factors.

For example, we worry that we might lose control of our emotions and react in a way we'll regret when it's done.

When we lose that sense of control, that's when we start to worry and obsess.

Not being able to fully control the situation goes against the very nature of some people who need to have that control to feel secure.

Because of that, they have a hard time coping and start worrying and thinking about the possible way's things could go wrong.

Eventually, this leads to anxiety.

Another possible cause for worry is our jobs. Job security is not a luxury that everyone can afford, and it is natural to worry on some level that we may be out of a job at any time.

Even if we lose our jobs, the bills still need to be paid because they never stop coming, and we worry about how we are going to do that with no income.

Anxiety over losing your job overwhelm you to a point where it starts to affect your productivity. Understandably, the stress of being made redundant is very real, and when combined with the external pressures such as the competitive job market, the worries seem endless and anxiety naturally follows suit.

Worry could be caused by several factors, each one as valid as the following.

Never dismiss your emotions and the way you feel; you have every right to experience the emotions that you do.

Practical Test

1. What are negative feelings?
2. Why is it good to turn your negativity into something good?
3. What are the ways to cope up with negativity?

CHAPTER 30:

Overcoming Fear

Fear is the feeling that you encounter when you think about a person or something that might harm you. When you experience fear, you get the urge to get away or avoid the threat.

As an emotion, fear is evoked in you when there is a concrete threat to your environment. For instance, the mere thought of a car that is fast approaching you or a spider that crawls on your arm can lead to the feeling of fear in you.

Fear is characterized by things that haven't happened yet – it is about what will happen in the future.

There are so many threats that can evoke fear in you; these include:

- The treat of getting harmed.
- Loss of financial or material possessions.
- Being afraid to say the wrong thing.
- Loss of friendship or closeness.
- Hurting other people.
- Fear of embarrassment.
- Fear of loneliness.
- Fear of disgust.

Usually, fear is evoked when you get into a situation that will evoke any of the emotions that have been described before.

When you experience fear, you will become occupied by the source that is the threat and look for a way to avoid or escape it. There are immediate threats that will make you react suddenly, or there will be threats that will make you plan to be more cautious.

When the system is working the right way, it will prevent you from getting into situations that are dangerous or that can harm you in one way or another.

Types of Fear

Some people have excessive amounts of fear, and these are called phobias. They will have a lot of fear for some stimuli that many people see as not being threatening.

Innate Fear

There are a lot of external factors that are known to make you get afraid, but studies have shown that we are born with some fears. These are termed innate fears. Other fears are called learned.

For instance, those kids that get bullied at school will start fearing to go to school; this is leaned fear.

Innate fear is the one that you are born with – fear of failure, fear of death, and so on. As you grow up, you get to learn about other things that make you become afraid.

Conditioned Fear

Apart from the fears that you get born with, there are other fears that are formed when you come into contact with a negative experience, and you become afraid that something bad will happen again. These fears are usually irrational, and they make us believe that similar circumstances will lead to the same outcome, which is wrong in most instances.

For instance, many people that were attacked by dogs when they were young will cringe at the thought of a dog coming near them. Well, the truth is that a majority of the dogs are very friendly, but just because you had a bad encounter with one, you avoid all of them.

We are also conditioned to fear the things that we are told to be negative. This is why you find so many people and families becoming prejudiced against other people.

How to Conquer Your Fear

When you keep on ignoring your fear, it grows to chronic proportions. When you decide to face it, it will shrink.

Every start of the year, people come up with resolutions which are goals that they desire to achieve during the year. Many of them fail while others make it. For those that fail, the main reason is that they fear that they won't make it. This prevents them from achieving what they are after, even if they have the capability to succeed.

Here are ways to overcome the fear that you have.

Understand Fear then Embrace It

Fear is there to keep us safe so that we avoid harm. Well, fear cannot be inherently good or bad, but it serves as a tool for us to be able to make decisions.

Fear has its good and bad sides as well, so make sure that you take advantage of the good side and you learn from the bad effects of fear. You can embrace fear so that it helps you to learn lessons but don't let out to control what you do.

Don't Be in a Hurry

When you are faced with a threat, you need to have a plan in mind on how to deal with it. Don't just stand there and wait for something to happen, rather you need to come up with a plan and explore your options.

One of the things that you need to do is to understand what you have at hand to use against the perceived threat. Many undertakings have been ruined because the person failed to make a decision based on what they had at hand. When fear strikes, you take time to consider whether the right action is to jump to the nearest decision or to analyze the various options and make the right decision.

Identify the Fear

At times when you are faced with a threat, try, and understand what kind of fear you are experiencing. Sometimes the mere act of stating what the fear is and then giving it a name will give you the strength you need to deal with it. Give the fear a name, then give it a size. The size is just the intensity, and it tells you how extensive the fear is so that you can decide whether you can handle it or not. The bigger the fear, the harder it will be for you to handle it. Remember when you try to ignore fear, it grows to unmanageable proportions, but when you decide to face the fear, it will become smaller.

Think Long Term

If you are a worker, you might think that you won't be available following month in the same position. This is too short a time to start worrying about issues; at times, you need to focus your brain on long term solutions so that you reduce the fear of the unknown. When you think about a long-term goal, you won't be able to fix the short-term issues, but it will allow you to think about stuff on a more objective scale and come up with the perfect solution.

Educate Yourself

No one is as afraid of anything more than what they don't know. If your fear comes by due to lack of information, then this is the right time to get the information you want so that you get the fear out of the picture.

Take time to understand what the fear is all about then go ahead to know how you can handle it the right way. There are various ways to get this information, including online blogs, research papers, books, and more.

Be Prepared

When you had a negative experience with something, and you failed to handle it the right way, you need to get prepared so that following time you won't have to react negatively again.

Many people have the innate fear of standing in front of people and saying something. So, if you have a fear that is related to your performance in a certain aspect, then you need to prepare for the task well in advance before you face the fear again.

Utilize the Push of Peer Pressure

If you have had a phobia for some time, it is usually good to have a few friends around to help you overcome it.

Have you ever done something that is scary like parachuting out of a moving plane just because you had your friends there to push you to do it?

Peer pressure can be good or bad; it only depends on how the pressure is used. Make sure you surround yourself with people that will help you to overcome fears that are making you fail to make it in life.

Visualize Success

Many people fall into the traps that fear lays because they have a negative mindset that tells them that they will fail. This is especially due to the fear of failure that comes up whenever someone wants to do something.

If you have seen athletes, you will realize that they do their thing with one goal in mind – success.

When they make it mental, they push forward, and then they end up succeeding at what they do.

You also need to adopt this mindset – success, at all times so that you will be prepared to succeed at whatever you try to achieve.

Gain a Sense of Proportion

You need to quantify your fear. For instance, you need to understand how big the threat is that it makes you run wild with fear. At times we get so caught up in the fear that comes with a certain threat that we fail to understand that it is manageable. So, when you are faced with a threat, try, and put a sense of proportion to it before you handle it.

Get Some Help

When you feel like the threat is becoming too chronic and you don't have something to do about it alone, it is time for you to get some help. You can approach a professional therapist to help you overcome your fear or go for friends and colleagues that will help you get over the fear.

If you can't find any of these, then look around for a support group of the issue to assist you. Don't worry if the friends that you work with don't have any experience with the issue at hand – all you need is someone that will guide you the right way.

When you are struggling with your fear, there is someone out there who has the solution that you are really looking for.

Are you doing something which has never been done before and you need to get some guidance on the same? Well, many people have a fear of failure when they go into unchartered waters.

If you are attempting something for the first time, then you need to know that there are some people that have done it before successfully. Is there a formula that they used to succeed? Is there someone that has written a book on the same, or can you use a formula from another area to meet their needs?

Have a Positive Attitude

You need to handle your fear of doing some things by having a positive attitude in all that you do. When you have a positive attitude, things get good and easy. It takes time to develop a positive attitude, but you will be able to get ahead in all that you do better when you have a positive attitude backing you up.

Practical Test

1. What is Fear?
2. What are the times when fear can be felt?
3. What is the best way to overcome fear?

CHAPTER 31:

Overcoming The Pureness Of Speaking

Now, let's get into the details, specifics, and how-to of actually doing it in the situations that matter most to you in your life. Overall, there are four kinds of speaking up for ourselves.

1. **Sharing Freely Socially:** This includes speaking your mind, sharing about yourself and your life, asking what you are really curious about, speaking up in groups, and generally feeling empowered to throw in your two cents in any social situation.

2. **Speaking Up at Work:** This includes speaking up in settings like meetings, among colleagues and peers, with potential clients and customers, or with supervisors, bosses, executive members, and other "higher ups." To be able to clearly and directly ask key questions and share your ideas so you can add value and make an impact.

3. **Objections, Disagreement, & Other "Difficult Conversations":** This can be in any relationship–business or personal. It involves noticing when you don't like something, or are upset, and being able to clearly and directly communicate this with the right person or people.

4. **Asking for What You Want:** This involves approaching others and asking for what you want, without shame or guilt. This can be in a work or business setting, with family and friends, or with your spouse or romantic partner.

As you read this list, which ones stand out to you? Is there one area where you already feel free to speak up? Perhaps you crush it at work and boldly share your ideas there, but are extremely uncomfortable and restricted sharing yourself when meeting new people, or out on a date.

Or maybe it's the other way around. You're great at asking for what you want in your relationship, but you're terrified to speak up in a room of "senior management" and other people who have more experience than you.

And, if you are thinking, man, I need to speak up in all of these areas! Well then, you're in the right place. Let's dive into each one with specific strategies and examples, to give you a clear sense of how you can begin speaking up for yourself in any situation, starting right now.

But before we do, I have to mention one extremely important thing. If you don't get this one distinction, your progress towards speaking up for yourself will be slow or nonexistent. How important is it? Super, duper important. Are you ready to know what it is, so you can finally break free and become the bold, expressive, unapologetic, fulfilled person you're meant to be?

You learn this by doing. **You learn the skill of speaking up for yourself, by practicing speaking up for yourself.** There is no other way.

Below you will find guidance, strategies, and examples. Things you can do and put into practice today. But only if you're willing to step outside the familiar comfort zone and actually do them. Reading about them, accumulating more knowledge on the exact right way to do it, and all the rest, will not set you free. Only action will.

Like all skills, if we're new at it, we might not be awesome at first. It might be a little clunky, or messy, or awkward a few times. Or a lot of times. And that's OK. That's the only way to really get good at this. Could you learn the guitar without ever missing a note, without ever messing up a chord? Absolutely not. That would be an insane expectation and would severely limit your progress. Yet that's how many people approach learning to speak up and be assertive.

Let that go now. Let yourself be a beginner. Let yourself learn, and be messy, and make mistakes, and keep going and growing. That is the path to mastery, and that is the path you are on.

Now that I've banged the Action-Drum yet again, let's turn our attention to the ins and outs of speaking up.

Sharing Freely Socially

This topic in itself could be an entire book. In fact, my book The Solution To Social Anxiety, my in-depth confidence training course, The Confidence Code, and my live event, Supremely Confident Conversation Master are all focused on breaking through social fear, maximizing self-esteem, and mastering all the ins and outs of being able to comfortably and confidently talk with anyone.

If you suffer from social anxiety, or if this area is a major challenge for speaking up, and you really want to master it, I encourage you to explore these other resources. You can find information about all of them on my website: www.SocialConfidenceCenter.com.

Since this book is all about shedding excessive niceness and people pleasing, that's what we'll focus on here. We'll explore the key shifts you need to make now to start boldly saying more, sharing more, and simply being yourself around others. You have set yourself up to implement these strategies quickly and easily. By asking yourself what you want, and owning your perspective more, speaking up will now come much more naturally.

You Get What You Think You Deserve

When it comes to social interaction, what do you deserve? This might be an unusual question that you've never really asked yourself. But unconsciously you have a set of beliefs that tell you exactly what you deserve. And socially, as with all areas of life, you get what you think you deserve.

What would serve you more is to have a healthy expectation of attention in a conversation. This means you think you deserve attention, for others to be present with you, and listen to what you are saying. What you say is significant and it matters, because it's about you. Even if it's you simply sharing something you read, or an experience you recently enjoyed in your life. That matters, because you matter.

One of my Mastermind clients recently shared about a first date she went on. She had been working on her dating confidence for the last several months and was starting to go on more dates, which the group celebrated with her. On this particular date, she said that she was very attracted to him physically, however whenever she shared about herself, he would listen briefly and then bring the conversation back to talking about himself.

"Did that feel good to you?" I asked.

"No, I didn't like it," she replied instantly.

I knew this would be the answer, because it doesn't feel good to anyone. We all want to receive attention when we're sharing, we all want to feel like we matter. Yet here's the fascinating part. She didn't enjoy the conversation that much, but she wanted to go out with him again, and she was anxious about whether he would follow up or not. Have you ever been in that situation? I know I have. And it baffles our conscious minds. Why do I care so much about whether this person calls me back? I'm not even that into them!

Yet we get what we think we deserve. On some level, my client still believes she doesn't deserve full attention, focus, and interest from a man she is attracted to. On some level she still believes she's not worthy of it.

This is something I really get. For years, whenever I was speaking with someone and they didn't seem interested, I would instantly conclude it was because whatever I was talking about wasn't interesting. The topic was stupid, or I was a boring and unengaging person. I wasn't good enough to keep their attention and I didn't deserve it.

Regardless of how long you've felt this way, now is the time to let it go. Raise your standard. You do deserve it. What you want to say and share matters. It is interesting. Own it. Expect more. Not in some crazy entitled prima donna way. In a healthy way that allows you to create the relationships that you really want, the ones that really nourish you.

So, the next time you're speaking with someone and they don't seem that interested in you and what you're sharing, pound the table with your fist and loudly shout, "Do you know who I am?!" No, I'm kidding. Actually, just notice it. Acknowledge that it's happening and notice that it doesn't feel good to you. Remind yourself you deserve better than this and act accordingly. Maybe you end the conversation and go talk with someone else. Maybe you decide not to pursue a second date even though he or she was really hot. There are tons of amazing, attractive, compelling people out there. Find one that excites you and gives you the attention that you deserve.

Side note: There is one caveat here. If virtually everyone you talk with seems disinterested, most likely you are doing something that is creating that response in others. It doesn't mean you're a boring person, it means there is some snag in your communication style that is blocking your connection with others. If that's the case, I strongly urge you to explore the resources I mentioned at the beginning so you can rapidly identify and change that pattern.

Practical Test

1.What do you think is the reason why you don't feel comfortable opening up?

2. Does having self-confidence make you feel more relieved?

3. What are the topics that you usually don't feel comfortable talking about?

CHAPTER 32:

What Are Emotions?

Emotions seem very real because we experience them physically and perceive them through our senses. Everywhere in the world, and even in the animal kingdom, the outward expressions of certain emotions are very similar. We can witness when a dog or an ape is angry, baring its teeth, or when a person tightens his jaw muscles in rage. When we ourselves are upset or afraid, our blood pressure and heart rate increase, and we feel the pounding in our veins.

When animals or humans are surprised, we see their eyes open wider, and their pupils dilate. Charles Darwin theorized that there must be some sort of physiological, genetic component to emotions that we share with other creatures who-although they may have a shorter range of emotions than we do-also experience fear, sadness, and anger.

The Physicality of Emotions

Like all people, you experience emotions physically. In fact, when you've felt a strong emotion before you could even identify it, you might have been aware of how your body felt-tense or relaxed, energized, or weary. Once you noticed your shallower breathing or your tightened neck muscles and thought about what you were experiencing, you were able to label your emotion.

Every day, you guess at what other people are experiencing emotionally by observing their facial expressions, body language, breathing, and vocal changes. You might have taken offense once at an e-mail or instant message that seemed curt, sarcastic, or unkind because you had no physical cues to help you figure out whether the sender was angry or irritated with you, and the writer didn't use an emoticon or an abbreviation such as LOL (laughing out loud) to indicate that he or she was kidding. Some children don't have the ability to read facial expressions, tone of voice, or body language; and unless they're trained in how to decode this physical evidence of emotion, they take words at face value, missing the nuances of communication that the rest of us take for granted.

Think of phony smiles that show muscle tension or eyes filled with tears that clue us into how someone feels even when a person's words give us a different message. People who are very good at perceiving emotions are picking up on many subtle physical cues. A top female poker player pays attention to her opponent's breathing and the size of his or her pupils to determine whether the person is lying. A lie detector can identify changes in heart rate so subtle that liars don't realize that they're showing physical evidence of discomfort with their false statements.

Our language reflects our awareness that emotions seem to be bodily experiences. If we're sad or disappointed, we say we're experiencing "heartache." If we're certain of something, we declare: "I feel it in my bones." But just as our emotions can chemically affect our cells, the chemicals in our body can impact our emotions.

Chemical Influences on Emotions

The theory that neuropeptides are emotions started with the discovery of receptors on the surface of cells that allow the neuropeptides to stick to them and transfer information. This was a crucial breakthrough for pharmacologists because it meant that we finally validated the theory of how drugs work in the body: They adhere to these receptor sites and download information that tells the cell what it needs to do.

When we laugh, our bodies create hormones called endorphins, which make their way to our cells' receptor sites-but those very same sites may respond to artificial endorphins that are created in a laboratory. This explains why mood-altering drugs such as morphine and Prozac can affect us. The chemicals in these drugs actually change our emotions.

Even if you aren't deliberately trying to influence your body and your mood with prescription drugs, you might be manufacturing your own biochemical that is impacting your emotional state. During some parts of their menstrual cycle, many women experience hormonal changes that make them more sensitive or irritable than they are at other times. Certain foods can affect mood, too. A number of women feel more relaxed after they've eaten chocolate, while some children become overly excited after ingesting certain food dyes or additives. And strange as it might seem, even sunlight can affect our mood: Absorbing it allows us to create serotonin, a feel-good hormone that we need to manufacture to avoid depression. Some people suffer from seasonal affective disorder, becoming very sad and pessimistic due to a lack of sunlight and serotonin. Full-spectrum lighting can improve their moods dramatically.

It's important to recognize just how strongly chemicals can influence our emotions. A woman I know who'd never experienced PMS was surprised that after giving birth, she felt a profound sense of sadness and loneliness. Holding her baby, she wept, and even as she did so, her mind clicked in and said, wait a minute—I bet this is that postpartum depression that the nurse warned me about. She remembered learning that after labor, the mix of hormones in a woman's body is changed drastically, and this can cause depression. Even as she thought about this and was intrigued, she still felt sad and lonely for several hours, despite her efforts to talk herself out of such feelings. However, she realized that these were emotions that would fade once her body's chemistry came back into balance.

The Energy of Emotions

Emotions have energy, and just as the sound waves created by a tuba and a piccolo are different, so too is the energetic vibration of each emotion. If you're experiencing joy, you're sending out a vibration of joy, and the universe will respond by bringing you more of it. If you're experiencing discouragement, you're emitting a vibration of discouragement, and you'll draw to yourself pessimistic people and disheartening events. This is why it's very important to experience positive emotions: Like a magnet, you can actually draw to your situations and individuals that will match the emotion you create. You have the ability to attract the life of your dreams by experiencing feelings that pull in circumstances, people, and opportunities that match up with your positive mood.

Creating a vibration of abundance-a feeling that you're wealthy and have all that you need-will actually create abundance. If you think, I'd like to have more money, you're admitting to the universe that you're short on wealth, and you're generating a feeling of lack instead of prosperity. If you state an affirmation about what you think is going to happen, such as "The right romantic partner is on the way to me," again, you're creating a sense of lack-in this case, that of romantic love and companionship in the present. To get what you want, you have to feel that you have it already. You might imagine yourself sharing a laugh with your partner, and experience what that feels like. Or you could create an affirmation such as "I have romance and companionship in abundance" and repeat it regularly to create the feeling and vibration of abundance. It's not enough to simply say the words. You really must experience the emotion of the affirmation in order for it to have powerful effects on your life.

As you engage in positive emotions more often, you may find that people who aren't vibrating emotions that match yours are still drawn to you. This is because they pick up on the fact that you're joyful, confident, inspired, and so on, and they want to feel those things, too. However, you won't be attracted to them because they don't match your energy. You can continue experiencing your strong, positive emotions and hope that they'll choose to match the vibration of your feelings and become joyful, confident, and inspired themselves. They may respond favorably, or they may block themselves from the positive emotions they're attracted to, turning away from you rather than changing their outlook. If clients say to me, "Peggy, I want to be confident like you, instead of worried and fearful about success," I'll work with them on creating confidence, but if they truly aren't ready to feel that emotion, they'll drift away. They choose not to match my vibration, and our partnership naturally ends.

The Reality and Unreality of Emotions

Now that I've explained the very real, very physical aspects of emotions, I have to tell you that ultimately, emotions aren't real at all, they're illusions. Of course, emotions feel real, just as the chair you're sitting on feels real, along with the sound of the traffic or the birds outside your window. The material world seems very real, and we believe what our senses tell us about it. However, the chair that you're sitting on isn't actually solid at all; rather, it's a buzzing mass of energy. It's made up of waves of light and tiny particles that seem to be pieces of matter but behave like energy or light, so you're actually sitting on a buzzing cloud. Everything solid around you is likewise a buzzing cloud—and indeed, even you are made up of light energy. The sounds coming into your ears and being interpreted by your brain as honking geese or car horns are actually vibrational waves of energy. So as real and tangible as the material world seems, the reality is that it's made up of energy and light.

Think for a moment about light. You know that it's clear and brilliant-without any color-but the moment that you break it up, it's split into different hues. You can see this effect when you place a crystal prism on a shelf by a sunny window. The shades of the rainbow will appear on your walls, as the sunlight is broken into rays of red, orange, yellow, green, and so on. The color green is still light, but it has its own vibrational energy, which is a little different from that of yellow or blue. The green flickering on the wall appears to be real because your eyes can perceive it, but when it's immersed in the light coming through the window, unbroken by a prism, you don't observe it. All you see is the light; the green has ceased to be. Emotions work in the same way:

When we're connected to Spirit, in a state of complete communion with divine caring, emotions don't exist. We don't enter into this world feeling worried, angry, or resentful. We don't even experience positive feelings when we come out of the womb. We only know one emotion, and that's love because Spirit is love. Just as white light contains every color, within Spirit, all the emotions are immersed in one gargantuan emotion-love. Engulfed by it, the unique qualities of each individual feeling dissolve. So, when we're connected to Spirit, deep in meditation and experiencing a much higher level of awareness, the emotions that feel so real and so very important to us when we're in everyday consciousness no longer exist, they're absorbed into light. And dark emotions, such as fear and sadness, disappear in the brilliant radiance of love.

Practical Test

1.What are emotions on your own understanding?

2. Do you think having emotions is a good or bad thing?

3. What kind of emotions do you usually feel and during what situations?

CHAPTER 33:

How Emotions Affect Your Life

Emotions have great impacts on our lives. It is the emotions that determine how well we spend our life. You will not realize the effects of your emotions in your life until something happens out of the emotions. Whether good or bad, the impacts will always be seen in the resulting situation. Emotions can either affect your life positively or negatively depending on how you handle them. You have all the power to decide how you want to live your life. If you let your emotions control you, then you are at a higher risk ending up with a bad life that you never desired.

Emotions can decide for you how you live your life if you let them do. Emotions ate very manipulatively. If given a chance, they control how a person thinks and if they have to, they destroy your life completely. Emotions can destroy your good relationship with friends, family and even colleagues. Remember positive relationships require time and effort to build. You have to be patient and wait for it to grow and win trust, but if you let emotions come in between, then this positive relationship will not take it time to brake. It will be gone even before you realize it is escaping.

Your emotions can make you care too much or get too attached to someone when you did not expect it to happen so. You can get attracted to someone through your emotions and be too much into them that you can't stay away from them even for the last time. They can tie your life around a single thing that you feel you are nothing without this thing and that you only need it to survive.

Emotions can also push you away from something and make you believe the worst about this thing. Emotions need to be managed by every person and if emotions are not well handled and dealt with the effects of someone's life are so severe and it always pops up when you left expect it. It makes things happen in conflict with what you expected and how you wanted it to be.

The effects of emotions in our lives can either be positive or negative, based on we handle our emotions. Carefully treated emotions normally result in positive results about everything. It makes ideas work as they were expected to and puts everything normal and easy to deal with. When emotions are not well attended to with a lot of intelligence, the end result will not be liked by anyone because of the negative effects that they leave in everyone's life.

There are positive emotions and negative emotions and they work in different ways and impact differently in everyone's life. It is therefore important to understand the effects of positive emotions as well as negative emotions in our life because if we ignore them, we will not be able to handle the effects appropriately and undo the danger that has occurred already.

Negative emotions are what normally awaken positive emotions. When negative emotions are experienced and you want to do away with it, the feeling that you have to deal with these emotions once and for all is what will bring about positive emotions in your mind.

There are some emotions that many people have regarded as part and parcel of life and these emotions are in most cases grouped to make up negative emotions according to some people. These emotions include pain, sadness, fear, and anxiety. They make us worry too much about life and make our lives stressful for no good reason. However, there are always positive emotions that come in between to resolve the conflict in the min to overcome these emotions.

We should always practice gratitude and try not to avoid the negative emotions to give them a chance to exploit and manipulate us to do exactly as they demand. When we think positively, we attempt to trigger positive emotions that will make us feel a little better. However, this should not necessarily mean that we avoid negative emotions. When we experience negative emotions, they come with their own benefit and give us the courage and ability to face them and deal with them appropriately.

For you to clearly understand the difference between positive emotions and negative emotions, you must first understand what emotions are. Emotions are our energy. In most cases, you must have spent time struggling to do something that we believe will result in good feelings. Emotions are connected to the experience that we realize when energy moves within our bodies.

Emotions arise from within us and most of them focus on specific parts inside the body. These are the feelings that we experience when sometimes we feel sad and try to sober up. The emotions are felt in our lungs in this case while when we receive an awesome message, we feel so high and the emotions are sent to our feet making them lighter.

Our emotions are our own enemies. When we try to ignore them, they become the worst fighters and insert in our bodies the pain that we never expected. Emotions should not be voided at all costs. They should be treated with maximum attention and well attended to in order to avoid too much pressure on our side.

Now here are how positive emotions being different from negative emotions.

Emotions are a matter of judgment. They determine how we think about ourselves and also how we feel towards other people and events. Positive judgment is associated with positive emotions. To see something good in other people and have a good feeling towards them, and judge them positively, you must have had positive emotions that are controlling how you think, feel and reason. Negative emotions, on the other hand, will make you judge other people and events negatively and only see the bad part of them instead of focusing on the entire thing and try to weigh between the positive side and the negative side of it.

When we relate to the normal functioning of the body, positive emotions are characterized by expansion. These emotions include happiness, joy, excitement, calmness, and peace. You will realize that whenever you feel some emotions that you label in these categories, you will have your lungs expand as the rest of your body relax to welcome the good feelings. It slows your breath; relaxes your muscles and you end up with a broad smile on your face that shows you are feeling amazed.

Negative emotions, on the other hand, are characterized by contraction. Think of emotions such as sadness, anger, pain, anxiety, and tiredness. When we fear something has happened or that we feel will happen and bring a bad result, we contract, become rigid and prepare to face the worst. It affects the normal functioning of the body and we may feel inactive on many occasions. Sadness also makes our body become heavy and we cannot be flexible enough to urgent changes that will require our full attention. It diverts our attention and makes us think of only the worst things that can happen to us.

Negative emotions result in excessive loss of energy in our body. This is because we concentrate more on the fears and worries about situations that are perceived and that we believe can bring the worst to us. The body is made to feel unrelaxed and our hearts beat so fast trying to fight back situations that are only perceived in our mind that in most cases might not happen as they were thought to be.

Negative emotions are what trigger positive emotions. When the body is allowed to contract freely, it will eventually relax and expand to welcome in good feelings and let go of the bad ones. Holding onto bad feelings only tie our bodies in one event and prevent us from moving on. When we all accept the positive emotions and allow our bodies to adjust to them and accept them ad normal part of life, we will eventually get over them since allowing the body to respond to the negative emotions automatically trigger the positive emotions that will help us to deal with the bad feelings.

Emotions are just some sensations of the body. They are what send signals to our brains enabling the braid to release hormones that either make us feel good or bad. The hormones that are released by the brain are what will determine how we feel all the time and it is also dependent upon the current state of the body and the emotions that cine along with it.

When we feel excited and high, the positive emotions will react to the body and sell signals to the brain to release positive hormones that will help us respond to the good feelings that we are experiencing. Negative emotions are triggered when the body sends bad signals to the brain that makes the brain to release the negative hormones. This normally results from sadness, fear, and worries that are perceived in our minds as a result of some events or people that make us feel uncomfortable.

How to Distinguish Useful and Functional Emotions from Dysfunctional and Harmful Emotions

It is not easy to not the difference between functional and dysfunctional emotions. Some dysfunctional emotions can sometimes be functional. In most events, we experience different emotions that are usually triggered by our current situations. The difference between useful and harmful emotions are dependent upon the adaptations of every individual to their environment.

Functional emotions can either be positive or negative. However, they promote an individual's adaptation to their environment and help them to attain what they want. The functional emotions are beneficial to a person's growth of mind and a positive attitude towards what they do or towards everything that happens around them.

Dysfunctional emotions on the other hand, whether positive or negative, hinders a person from moving on and prevent them from attaining what they want. They come with unnecessary thoughts that make a person feel like giving up on what they had started. The dysfunctional emotions slow down a person's adaptation to their environment and make everything seem difficult for them to handle.

Useful emotions guide our moves and lead us on the right track when we are making decisions all the time. Functional emotions help us to make decisions that protect us as individuals and also protects the entire community. They take care of everyone's feelings and in a situation where one is feeling low and demoralized, useful emotions help them get out of the situation and feel comfortable and cared for.

To finalize, emotions, whether positive or negative, functional, and useful or dysfunctional and harmful, both have great effects on human life. The effects are either positive or negative depending on the kind of emotions that are involved. People who chose functional and useful emotions will always end up with a positive impact on their lives. Those who chose the dysfunctional and harmful emotions also face the consequences of a bad influence on their lives. No one gains the fruits of another person's emotions. Choose your emotions right and make sure that while you are smiling at the effects of your emotions, someone is not crying because of your own emotions and not theirs.

Practical Test

1.Why do you think emotions affect our lives?

2. Is the effect good or bad?

3. What is the biggest impact of having emotions in your daily life?

CHAPTER 34:

Change Your Inner Thinking

With the amount of information, we take in every day, it is no surprise to know that our minds can get decluttered. Taking the time to focus on our mind helps us clear it up for future use.

Reframing Negative Thoughts

Research has shown that we have a bias towards negativity (Cherry, 2019). Well, who can blame us? Our ancestors needed to focus on the negativity. It's how they stayed alive after all. They didn't avoid predators by plastering a smile on their face and walking through the woods with the lyrics of "Oh Happy Day" running through their mind (well, their version of "Oh Happy Day.")

As we are used to focusing on negative thoughts a lot, it might not be simple to reframe our thoughts. But by being persistent and making sure that you are breaking the pattern of negative thoughts that arise in your mind, you will be able to prevent them from getting out of control.

Here are a few tactics that you can use to reframe negative thoughts.

Tactic #1: Watch Your Emotions

Your first step is to watch your thoughts. At this point, you are simply observing what is going on in your mind.

Don't judge any thought or try to analyze it. You are merely seeing what happens to that thought.

This tactic is most successful when you simply observe the way the thoughts occur in your mind.

You can perform this tactic anytime during the day, but I would personally recommend doing it while you are meditating since the meditation technique, I had mentioned focuses on observing your thoughts without trying to understand them.

Tactic #2: Distance Yourself from Your Thoughts

Whenever you are focusing on your thoughts, make a note of the fact that your thoughts and you are different entities. For example, if you are having the thought, "I am unable to do this," then think of another thought such as this, "I am thinking of the fact that I am unable to do this."

This way, you are not defining yourself by your thoughts. You are making it clear that your thoughts are independent.

Tactic #3: Learn to Say No

Whenever you find your thoughts start to stray away to other matters or worries, then you can say "No" out loud. Make sure you are firm and confident about saying "No." When you say no, visualize blocking your mind from wandering by imagining an unbreakable wall. Many people have different methods of visualizations. Some people choose to tie their thoughts down with a rope. Others imagine pushing the thoughts down into a room. Whatever visualization technique you use, make sure it focuses on anchoring your thoughts and preventing them from blitzing through your mind aimlessly.

Tactic #4: The Rubber Band of Defense

Put on a rubber band around your wrist. Whenever you feel that your thoughts are going astray and becoming negative, simply (and gently of course) pop the band on your wrist. This is a way for you to enforce Tactic #3.

Tactic #5: Understand What Triggers Your Negative Emotions

Every negative emotion is triggered by something. If you would like to gain mastery over your emotions, then make sure that you can understand your triggers. More specifically, start paying attention to things you frequently worry or stress about.

Ask yourself every time you notice a negative thought: what caused this thought to appear in my mind?

Make sure that you note down the triggers so that you have a list you can refer to anytime.

Teaching Your Mind New Habits

The idea that you can't teach an old dog new tricks does not apply here. Most people imagine the mind as a piece of concrete or a brick wall, sturdy and strong. But in reality, the mind is like a ball of clay. You can shape it how you want with enough focus and persistence.

Let us look at the ways you can accomplish that.

Lesson #1: Replace Your Thoughts

In many cases, your thoughts do not stick to the truth. They tend to be exaggerated. This is because your mind is trying hard to distract you or get your attention. If it notices that you are ignoring it, it simply amps up the intensity of the thought.

When the thought reveals itself to you, it is difficult to not feel defeated by it. It is easy to feel like you are a failure. However, upon closer examination, you will notice that the thought is not entirely true.

When these thoughts appear, do not let them get away with the effect that they put on your mind. Stop and focus on them. Question their authenticity. Try to examine them from every perspective.

Let's say that you were at a social gathering and you got to know that someone criticized your evening wear. Rather than feel dejected about it and listen to your mind (which is probably saying that you are incapable of wearing a good outfit), choose to reflect on the incident. You might find out that there were probably 20 people who really liked your outfit.

This way, your thoughts do not get the upper hand in the situation. They cannot make you feel bad without your consent.

Lesson #2: Accept the Scenario

What happens if the thoughts are the truth? What if you really did wear a rather awful outfit to the social event? What do you do then?

In such cases, know that your thoughts are exaggerating the situation as well. In a normal circumstance, you should shrug off the fact that the outfit was bad and decide that you are going to invest in a new outfit. Or wear something different following time.

What you are doing right now is accepting the truth. You are not rejecting what your mind is telling you, but you are rejecting how badly your mind is making the situation seem like.

One of the best ways to look at the truth is by asking yourself the following questions:

- What can you do to improve in the future or rectify the situation?
- Have you learned any positive lessons from it that you can use to motivate yourself?
- Can you find support from your friends or family to deal with the situation?

Lesson #3: Convert Your Thoughts

Overthinking gets you nowhere and neither does a runaway mind that is focused on taking you to the dark side of emotions. Rather than allow it to guide you, why not guide it instead towards positive emotions?

Think of ways you can come up with constructive solutions to your problem or situation.

The first thing that you have to do is break free from the negativity. Distract yourself with some form of action. Use the "I can" statements to find something to do that will help you feel better.

Following, start thinking of the ways that you can deal with the situation you are facing. For example, if your thoughts are reminding you about how badly you performed at your job that day and reminding you that you are probably going to get fired, think of how you can give a constructive spoon on your thoughts.

- What can I do to improve my work?
- Why did I perform badly today? Was I distracted at work?
- Was there a recent tragedy that affected me? In that case, I could try and ask my boss for a couple of days off work.

When you start finding solutions, you not only gain confidence in yourself, but you also overpower your negative emotions with positive responses.

Lesson #4: Designate a Time to Think About Your Stress

Sometimes, all you need to do is to vent out the stress that you are feeling inside. In which case, it would help if you set aside a small portion of the day to simply get rid of the stress you have been bottling up inside.

You do not have to spend a lot of time trying to figure out your stress. Simply take 15-20 minutes to exhaust your stress.

One of the best ways to perform this exercise is by keeping a timer on your watch or phone. When the alarm beeps, you know that you have reached your time limit. This way, you do not have to constantly worry about time while dealing with your stress (that would be even more stressful).

Practical Test

1. Why is it important to improve your inner thinking?

2. Do you always have to reframe negative thought?

3. What is the result on having a good inner thinking?

CHAPTER 35:

Program Your Emotions

Mastering your emotions is accomplished when you decide you do not want to be controlled by the negativity you confront in your life. This requires dedication and commitment but can be highly rewarding. When you learn to master your emotions, you are less likely to play the role of victim. Instead, you allow your emotions — the negative and the positive — to empower you. By developing your emotional intelligence skills, you have already laid the foundation to have complete control over your emotions. This can have a powerful impact on your success, relationships, health, and overall quality of life.

What makes mastering your emotions difficult is that we often automatically fall into negative thought patterns. Negative thoughts not only impact your emotional experience — they can completely dictate how you behave and react to emotional experiences, as well as determine which emotional experience you will have more of. By first understanding how these negative thought patterns affect your emotional health, you will be able to more clearly and intentionally shift your negativity to positive experiences and lessons.

How to change your emotional state from stressed and negative to positive and productive

As you can see, negative thoughts tend to be our default. They are often deeply rooted in our behaviors and outlook on life. One of the first things to do to adopt a more positive and productive state is to begin wiring your brain to search for the positives in each day. When you catch yourself having negative thoughts, opinions, or emotions, counter this with at least three positive emotional experiences. Up until now, you have wired your brain to seek out the negative — this is why it seems so easy to get caught up in the negativity. But by shifting the ratio of negative and positive experiences so that you have more enjoyable moments, it will become second nature and more natural to find these positive parts of your day.

Once you have gotten a better handle on actively searching for positive experiences, there are more steps you can take to shift your stressed out and negative emotional experience to ones that will serve you in a more productive and positive way.

Learn to Express Your Emotions

It is one thing to understand your emotions, but it is another thing to admit to the emotions you are experiencing. Often, we secretly deal with our emotions in private, because there tends to be a negative connotation associated with extreme negative emotions. For this reason, your emotions still have control over you. When you allow your emotions to force you to hide, deny, or cover up what you are feeling, you are not fully addressing them.

When you learn to properly express your emotions, you learn how to take control of them — and to control them in a way that moves you in a more positive direction. In order to express your emotions properly, you need to first be able to identify what you are feeling in the present moment. Practice properly expressing the emotion you are experiencing by stating these emotions out loud. When you announce these emotions, do so with confidence and empowerment. Stating your emotions to yourself out loud when you are alone will help you build confidence so you can properly state them out loud in front of others. When you feel comfortable enough, practice stating your emotions out loud to people you trust and feel safe with. You can begin this practice by focusing just on expressing your more positive emotions, and then begin to express your emotions when you are in more challenging situations. Remember that when you openly state your emotions, you are inviting others to do the same, and they may not feel the same way you do. Keep an open mind and remain confident about what you are feeling — don't let what others say sway you from your own experiences.

Tracking your emotions

One of the best ways to begin identifying how you handle stressful and negative situations is to keep track of them. Starting an emotional, or mood journal can help you better organize, understand, and change your negative thought patterns, behaviors, and emotional responses. Begin keeping a daily log of everything you experience throughout your day. How did you feel in each significant moment, and what were your thoughts as you were going through the motions?

When you do this daily over a long period of time, you will begin to take notice of some of your emotional patterns. You can clearly identify triggers that cause you to feel more negatively. This also allows you to pinpoint the thoughts that occur as you have emotional experiences. This simple exercise, which can be done in five or ten minutes, can help you strengthen your self-awareness.

Not only will journaling about your emotions allow you to change your negative experiences into positive ones, but the process can also be beneficial for your mental health. Getting these things out of your head can help reduce your risk of suffering from depression and anxiety. This is because you are not just keeping the experience stuck in your head and dwelling on one aspect of the event, which tends to be just the negative. When you write it down, you can clearly see what caused you to have such a negative reaction. This can then allow you to find a better way of dealing with situations like these in the future.

Take care of yourself

How you treat yourself can have a major impact on how you handle negative situations. As you learned earlier, the way you treat yourself impacts your confidence, and when you lack confidence, it will be more difficult to overcome your negative thought patterns. When you treat yourself with kindness and compassion, you're able to better confront negative situations and stress in a more calm and proactive way. In order to shift from constantly thinking things are stressful and negative, you want to be able to treat yourself in a way that allows you to make mistakes, take risks, and find solutions.

This is especially important when it comes to how you talk to yourself. If you find that your internal dialogue is one that constantly berates you, points out your failures, or keeps you feeling stuck and incapable, you need to first focus on shifting this negative mindset. A negative thought process will never allow you to see the positive in any situation, whether it is a joyful or unpleasant one.

Reframe your perspective

There are a number of ways to shift your perspective to better cope and to find the positive in most negative situations. You can begin by taking on a more positive outlook. Instead of being discouraged, hurt, or angry by a specific experience, learn to identify how the situation has healed you and allowed you to grow. You can also shift your perspective by looking at where you will be years from now. Many bad experiences are stressful and negative at the moment. Recall an event that you thought was the worst thing that could ever happen to you. Do you still have those same negative emotions? Chances are, you can probably look back and laugh at yourself for ever thinking that way. Before you begin to think about how bad a situation is, remember to look ahead and consider how you will view this situation in the future. Additionally, you can begin to understand your own worst-case perspective. This allows you to truly see the situation is not as bad as you are making it seem. To better utilize this shifting perspective, you want to identify the positive around each negative situation. You will begin to realize that there are plenty of things to be motivated and feel good about, despite things not turning out exactly how you had hoped.

You can also try taking an empathetic perspective to shift your attitude to a more positive and productive one. This type of perspective shifting provides you with the opportunity to see things from someone else's point of view. Many times, we can be so caught up in our own experience that we fail to recognize the other people around us and how they may be interpreting the same situation differently. When you take the time to look at things from another person's point of view, you can gain an understanding of how to let go of your own hurt feelings, resentment, and negative emotions to truly embrace the positives that are present.

Practice forgiveness

Forgiveness can provide you with a number of benefits, especially when it comes to accepting negative events. When you forgive yourself and others for any negativity, you will reduce your emotions of hurt, anger, and disappointment. Forgiveness is simply the act of acknowledging what occurred and letting it go so it does not have a greater negative effect on you.

Regaining positive emotions

It can seem impossible to experience positive emotions to the fullest extent when you have spent so much time allowing the negative ones to control your life. When this occurs, your brain is programmed to seek out more negative experiences, as this is what it is currently wired to do. When you want to attract more positive experiences your way, you need to first focus on retraining your brain to find them.

It can be easy to become overwhelmed by negative emotions, and these can quickly spiral into a state of mind that leaves you feeling lost and out of control. When you begin to notice you are feeling stuck, chronically stressed, and indecisive, there are simple steps that can help you have more positive experiences.

Ask yourself a lot of questions

Question what you are feeling, why you are feeling that way, what has occurred in your past that could be triggering your emotional response, and if the way you are behaving in reaction to these emotions causes you to look at these emotions in an adaptive or maladaptive way? Analyzing your emotions, the situation, and your behavior is one of the first ways you can begin to experience more positive emotions. Once you have answered these questions, you can use your answers to help you visualize better solutions. When you want to change your negative emotions to more positive ones, visualizing can allow you to clearly develop a specific solution for dealing with emotions.

Practical Test

1. How does programming your emotions work?

2. Do you think it is effective?

3. What are ways you can reprogram your emotions?

CHAPTER 36:

Factors That Influence Emotions

What impacts emotions? This is a valid question to ask if you want to understand and master your emotions. From the context of this, we will be looking at two important things that impact emotions; the brain and social norms/culture.

The brain is a grand master in manipulating emotions so even when you think you know the source of your feelings or emotions, it could be really tricky. We like to think we are in control of our feelings and the triggers behind these feelings, but the truth is our brain has a much more profound impact than people like to admit.

Every single moment, there are lots of activities going on in your head and the brain is at the center of all these activities and somewhat complex processes. A lot of process is involved in how we interpret situations and react to them. Remember that emotions are defined by three important things: cognition, responses, and reaction. The brain determines every of these activities which makes us wonder how our brain actually impacts our emotions. What happens in your brain right before you experience an emotion?

Again, your brain exerts influence on emotions because it is central to how emotions are formed. The brain consists of different parts that are all responsible for generating different emotions. The part of the brain responsible for processing emotions is the 'emotional brain' which is generally referred to as the limbic system., helps you measure the emotional quality or value of a stimulus before initiating an appropriate response; it is the part of the brain responsible for initiating the fight or flight response. The hypothalamus helps you regulate your responses or reactions to emotional triggers. There are also other parts of the brain like the hippocampus which all impact your emotions due to its memory retrieval functions. In fact, the hippocampus determines your emotional responses to triggers. Since different parts of the brain process different types of emotions using different methods, damage to any part of the brain can have a huge influence on your emotions and moods no matter how mild. Central to all of this is the limbic system which takes a generalized and simple approach to stimuli.

Sleep

When do you struggle with sleep the most? It is probably the times you had so much on your mind, and rest seemed to be a far-fetched idea. Anxiety and negative emotions can cause a person to become restless, and this has adverse effects on sleep patterns.

Quality sleep is one of the prerequisites for a healthy body, and when your body is deprived of sleep, it can create a ripple effect that affects you mentally and physically. Sleep loss affects your attention span. You will realize over time that you don't pay enough attention to your work or what others say to you.

Sleep deprivation also prevents the body from strengthening its immune system with the cytokines needed to fight infection. When you don't have enough cytokine in your body, it will take a longer time for you to recover from illnesses.

Anxiety, worry, fear, panic attacks, and sadness are some of the negative emotions that affect your ability to sleep peacefully daily. If you don't find a way to manage such feelings, you will be dealing with more problematic health and physical issues.

Sports

This has been proven to be true over a series of studies. So, if you want to put your feelings in check, stay away from junk food, eat balanced meals, and maintain a good routine of exercise.

Keeping your feelings in check overtime can be tough. This is why many persons do not make much effort and give up eventually. Sometimes, you will lose the plot, but this should not deter you from moving on.

A person who can manage effectively manage his emotions and put his feelings in check will be viewed as one with logical reasoning, an effective conflict handler, a person with high emotional intelligence, inner peace, and self-confidence.

Food and drinks

When a person is dealing with negative emotions, food is usually the last thing on their mind. Not eating may or may not be intentional in that state. But anxiety always paves the way for eating disorders, and this is true because most people who are diagnosed with eating disorders struggle or may have struggled with stress in the past.

Eating disorders are illnesses. The people who experience them observe a sudden change with eating, which is usually caused by their anxiety overweight gain and how they look.

Relationships

Once you've raised your social awareness skills and learn how to understand what other people are feeling, you are ready to work on maintaining your relationships. Let's clear it from the start – this is not an easy job. You will need to use all other areas of emotional intelligence to help you build and maintain them.

Four Things You Need to Know

The first thing you need to assess and manage is the effect different people have on you, as well as recognize what they are feeling and what is the cause that they are feeling that way. If you fulfill that, you will be able to make a decision on the best way to communicate with them to achieve the result that suits your or their needs.

Four different criteria determine the effectiveness of managing relationships:

- Deciding which course of action is the most appropriate for a given situation. To discover this, you will need to recognize the current feeling of the other party and the reason behind that feeling. You will probably have several choices to interact based on the research you conducted, and each of them will cause a different reaction. You will also recognize and appropriately manage the effect they have on you

- Interacting with the other party based on your research

- The result is what should guide you to choose what to say and how you will communicate your message. That means that your actions come with a particular goal in mind, making managing your relationship an intentional activity

- Your needs will be what will cause you to want a particular outcome. It might be your personal needs or the needs of your business

Seven Competencies

Certain competencies might be best related to workplace relationships, but they can also be applied to relations outside of work. The reason you might primarily connect them to your office is that they have a lot of similarities with leaders.

Goleman defined the competencies, and they include:

- **Influencing** – the ability to persuade other people into doing something that fits your, their, or joint needs

- **Inspiring** – the skill to motivate other people by inspiring them

- **Developing** – the ability to give useful feedback and help others build their knowledge and skills
- **Being a catalyst for change** – knowing when change is required and starting the process
- **Managing conflicts** – the ability to efficiently settle or misunderstanding, differences of opinion, or disputes
- **Creating bonds** – building networks and maintaining them
- **Collaborating with others** – creating effective teams and nurturing them

You can use each of these competencies to maintain your relationships. However, before you do that, take some time to think about them.

The question you should ask yourself is "Do you perform these competencies right now and are you good at them?"

It's always a good idea to write everything down. Think about various areas of each competency and note what you are doing well and what can be improved. For example, providing feedback for other people is something that you surely do right now. On the other hand, you can also write where you could use some improvement (yes, it might be the same competency, just a different area).

The following step is to think of two actions that you will take to develop yourself in that area and write them down. Taking an online course, conducting your own research, reading a book, or trying to mirror the behavior of someone you respect are all included. Finally, try to actually perform these actions and work on your competencies. You will notice that it will improve managing your relationships with others.

Let's take a look at the example of giving feedback. You are already giving it to other people, but you would like to work on it and make it more supportive. You conduct an online research and discover some tips and try to apply them the following time someone asks you for feedback. You will notice that they will more appreciate the feedback that's supportive and constructive and your relationship will benefit from that.

Work environment

For emphasis, it is not possible to eliminate all difficult situations because of the nature of human interactions and the need to take risks as well as adventure. There are also external factors that are beyond the scope of individual control. Avoiding circumstances that trigger adverse emotions is among the effective ways to condition the mind to handle setbacks. An example is where an individual feel irritated when a deadline is fast approaching. It might help if the person started planning and working earlier by splitting the work into modules. One can go further and inform colleagues that short deadlines may make the person react adversely. Change the environment where possible to get away from triggers, especially where the triggers are non-human entities. The bottom line is to ensure that the mind is prepared and has little pressure when handling a challenging issue.

It is important to learn to change thoughts. It might appear an easy strategy, but most people struggle to let go of their thoughts. As indicated earlier, thoughts impact emotions and subsequently, emotional reactions. The persistence to current thoughts occurs because the mind is trying to solve pending issues, and this is sometimes useful. Through the use of cognitive reappraisal, one can replace adverse thoughts with constructive thoughts. Sticking to negative thoughts could also be linked to low self-esteem.

Words that we use

You cannot take words back, so when you are about to use abusive words in a fit of anger, rest assured they will go a long way to harm the person you are saying them to. You can say you don't mean them later, but the words have already had their effect. Sometimes the use of hurtful words stems from a desire to make them feel the hurt you're feeling, but it's not necessary.

Practical Test:

1.What are 3 factors that usually affect your emotions and why?

2. How do you control the things that you say especially when you feel angry?

3. Do you think sleep can really make you feel better?

CHAPTER 37:

Breathing Techniques

Breathing is a fundamental principle of our lives. You must breathe in and out to live. Many times, people suffer from breathing-related problems, which later on affect them. Some have lost their dear lives because of having difficulties in breathing. Others are suffering because they are unable to breathe well. Therefore, it is essential to note the exact significance of breath.

The first important of breathing is that it reduces anxiety. Breathing also helps in the elimination of insomnia. It has the power to manage your day to day cravings, and also it can control and manage your anger response. Breathing brings your whole body into more excellent balance as it can initiate calmness within you. You will realize your entire being becomes normal again after a proper process of breathing and level of stress will be no more. For those having a high level of emotional frustrations can also apply breathing techniques all through the day so that they might get well too. Nothing is as sweet and pleasant as having an excellent relaxed body.

Before doing this breathing process, try as much as possible to adopt a good sitting position. The position should be comfortable and relaxing. You can also place your tongue behind your front upper teeth and do the following:

1. Start by making sure your lungs are empty. You can do this by allowing the air inside to escape through your nose and mouth. You can facilitate this process by doing some enlargement of your shoulder and chest and contracting your stomach so that you increase the exhale process.

2. Now you can breathe in through your nose. It should be tranquil and silent. Remember, it is supposed to take only 4 seconds.

3. The following step is to hold your breath, let's say for about 7 seconds. Don't rush here as your breath should just come naturally.

4. Then go ahead by breathing out. You have to force all air out through your mouth. You can purse your lips too and making some sounds of your preference. This should take at least 8 seconds.

5. Repeat this process four times.

Therefore, this breathing technique to delete stress in life is seen as a formidable way to control anxiety. Therefore, your level of anxiety will reduce. You will start having a perfect life without stress and anxiety. Remember, this process takes time. It is now recommended that you perform it in a sitting position that's not only affordable but also comfortable. This type of breathing is the famous 4-7-8 breathing.

We also have roll breathing that you can eventually use to delete some sorts of anxiety, stress, depression, and even unpleasant feeling within you. Roll breathing has several important in your body. Roll breathing enlarges your lungs and, as a result, makes you be able to pay a close watch on your breathing. The rhyming and rhythm of your breath become your full focus. You can undertake this breathing anytime and anywhere. However, as a learner, you should use your back on the ground with your legs bent. Then start by doing the following:

- Place your two hands on your belly and chest, respectively. Take a note on the movement of your hands as you concentrate on your breathing process. Continue breathing in and out.

- Focus on filling the lower lungs so that your belly moves up when you are inhaling while your chest does not move an inch. It is better to note that breathing in should be through your nose while breathing out must be through your mouth. You are allowed to repeat this process even ten times so that you can realize better results.

- After filling and emptying your lungs, you can now perform the other step of filling your upper chest. You can manage this by first inhaling in your lower lungs then increasing the tempo so that it reaches the chest. Here, you should breathe regularly but slowly for quite sometimes. During this process, note the position of your two hands. One placed at the belly will slightly fall as the stomach contract. The one put on your chest will rise as more air is breathed in your chest.

- It is now your time to exhale. Go ahead by exhaling slowly through your mouth. You should make that whooshing sound when your hands start falling, respectively. Always, your left hand will have to fall first, followed by your right hand. Still, on this, notice the way tension leaves your body as your mind becomes relaxed and calmed.

- Repeat the whole process of breathing in and out for at least 3 to 5 minutes. In this case, make sure you are observing the movement of your chest and belly. Take note of the rolling wave's motion.

- Your feeling matters a lot in the whole process. Take a more exceptional look at how you feel in the entire rolling breathing.

Your body regains its full free state, and you will feel more relaxed. You can, therefore, practice this rolling breathing process daily and make sure this goes for several weeks. By doing so, you will be able to perform this kind of breathing exercise everywhere. Also, you can eventually achieve this instantly on most occasions. It will help you regain your relaxation and calmness back. At the end of rolling breathing, your anxiety will be at bay. However, this process is not for everyone since some may feel dizzy during the exercise. You can reduce the breathing speed and accelerate slowly. You can then get up slowly after feeling relaxed, calmed, and lightheaded.

The following breathing exercise throughout the day can also involve **skull shining breath**. The skull shining breath is also known as kapalabhati in another language where the term initially originated. It is a dominant type of breathing that enables you to acquire a relaxed and calm mind and brain. It always boasts of the right way of killing the anxiety in you by eliminating the tension, especially in your skull. Remember, it is good to note that the pressure of the head can negatively influence your whole day, and the impact can remain with you for long.

Skull shining breath is not difficult to undertake, and this will give you that morale of even performing it throughout the day. You can start by having long breathing in then follow it with a quick and extremely powerful breathing out. Exhaling should originate from your belly, especially the lower part.

However, after getting familiarized with the whole contraction process, you can now start on inhaling and exhaling at a faster rate. Increase your pace here and make sure all the breathing process takes place through the nose. In this process, do not involve your mouth at the initial stages. You can go on with the process repeatedly until you start feeling very much relaxed.

You can now take note of your feelings at the end of the breathing exercise. Remember, this breathing process can eventually prevent muscle tension too. It also helps in releasing abdominal pain. Your worries, stress, anxiety, and even clogged breathing sites will be well.

Breathe Deep

Throughout any day, there are bound to be things that cause your stress levels to rise slightly. There are also going to be thoughts that pop into your head and cause you to feel anxious. Our mind can be our own worst enemy, but the good news is we can take control. There are many ways that we can help ease our fears, and deep breathing is one of them!

These techniques are extremely easy to do and can be done anywhere, even at your desk or on the bus to work! If you find it hard to concentrate, you can also purchase a guided relaxation tape, or download a stress-relieving app, as these will guide you through breathing exercises until you get the hang of doing them yourself.

Try this:

- Close your eyes and breathe in through your nose for a count of five, hold it for five, and then exhale through your mouth for five, in a slow and controlled manner. Repeat that for as long as you need to gain control.

- Once you're feeling a little calmer or in control, picture the thing that is causing you stress or anxiety as an item or a color. For instance, it might be a black ball, or it might be a gray cloud. It doesn't matter what it is; it simply needs to symbolize the thing that is negatively affecting your day.

- Now, visualize yourself forcefully pushing that item far away from you, and visualize it disappearing into the distance.

- Finish off with the same breathing technique you started with, before gently coming back into the room.

This is a method you can use for any type of stress or anxiety that is bothering you, and it's a great way to get rid of an issue that is upsetting you at any stage during the day.

Another essential breathing technique is ensuring that we are taking deep, full breaths. When we are even the slightest bit stressed, we start breathing shallowly. These shallow, short breaths do not give us enough oxygen and can even lead to full-blown panic attacks. To stop poor breathing, place your hand an inch or two above your stomach. Now, slowly breathe in through your nose until your stomach touches your hand. Go with our usual 5 counts inhales and hold for a few seconds before slowly exhaling out through your mouth.

When our breathing is shallow, we only fill up the top portion of our lungs with air. Placing your hand above your stomach ensures that you are breathing deeply enough where your entire lungs are filled!

Deep breathing is the foundation of many calming strategies. It can be done on its own or with other methods like meditation, tai chi yoga, etc. Deep breathing is easy because we need to breathe to remain alive, but strongly and efficiently for mental relaxation and stress reduction. Deep breathing focuses on breathing the stomach thoroughly and clean singly. It is easy to learn that you can do it anywhere, and it regulates your stress levels. Sit down with your back straight, inhale through the nose as the belly grows. Inhale as much clean air as possible into the lungs. It makes it possible to get more oxygen into the blood. Exhale the mouth as the belly drops to force as much air as possible out and close the abdominal tract. If you find it difficult to do this sitting, first try to lie down. You could put your hands on your chest and stomach to see if it's wrong.

Practical Test

1. Why is it important to learn some breathing techniques?

2. Which one is most effective for you and why?

3. Do you think that this can really help ease stress?

CHAPTER 38:

Meditation

Meditation is a technique for relaxation and self-awareness. It is an exercise that plays several crucial roles in the lives of those who engage in it. Several forms of meditation have been defined by several health experts, spiritual leaders, and educators for many purposes.

Meditation improves both the physical and emotional wellbeing of a person. By definition, it refers to the act of stilling the mind and reflecting on the true essence of self in a conscious manner. It involves focusing attention on a particular subject as a way of increasing awareness.

Meditation has been in existence for several decades and is practiced by thousands of cultures around the world. It is available in almost all religions, and nowadays people practice it for medical reasons as well.

Types of Meditation

Meditation is available in several different types. Today, we look at some of the most common ones.

Concentrative Meditation

This is a kind of meditation where you drive your attention to a single object or point. You switch your concentration off anything else that is going on so that you gain maximum experience of whatever your attention is focusing on. This can be your breath, a set of beads, staring at a flame, or repeating a given word. In most cases, concentrative meditation becomes difficult because it is not easy to focus at one point for a long time. Beginners are advised to start with a few minutes and keep building on their meditation time as they master the technique.

Metta Meditation

This is also referred to as loving-kindness meditation. It concentrates on generating a positive attitude and affection towards things, people, and sources of stress. You can achieve this kind of reflection by opening your mind to emotions of love and kindness towards others. In the process of meditation, you are required to send messages of loving-kindness to others as many times as is possible or until the stressful feeling is over. This kind of meditation seeks to build love and compassion towards oneself and also towards others. It is commonly used by people who are frustrated, angered, and those in conflict with others. Its primary purpose is to create positive emotions that suppress feelings of anxiety and depression.

Transcendental Meditation

This is one of the spiritual meditations that entails slow breathing while sitting down. It aims to bring you to the point that is above the normal state. When engaging in this form of meditation, you should concentrate on repeating a set of words depending on the complexity of your challenge. You are given a chance to select the kind of words you use.

Mindful Meditation

This meditation technique teaches you to concentrate on the present while shielding any memories about your past or future. It makes you more aware of your current surroundings without having to worry about what will happen following. One advantage of this kind of meditation is that you can do it anywhere, at any time. It is also one technique that is involved in most of the other forms of meditation. Most people engage in mindful meditation because it helps improve focus and memory. It also helps overcome negative feelings and lessens the impact of any reactions one has towards negative emotions. Physically, it has been found to lower pressure in individuals suffering from high BP.

Progressive Relaxation

This is also known as body scan meditation. It is a form of meditation that checks the body for tension so as to release it. During a body scan session, a relaxation expert works on your entire body, starting with the feet upwards. This happens as you tighten and relax your muscles while visualizing any changes in your body.

Body scan meditation's ultimate goal is to improve your overall feeling, thus causing you to stay calm. It also relieves the body from some types of pain through relaxing muscles. As the muscles relax, most people always end up asleep.

Breath-Related Meditation

This involves mindful breathing where you are required to breathe in deep, but slowly while concentrating on each breath that you make. The aim is to focus on breathing alone, and this shuts the mind entirely on other things.

Yoga

Kundalini yoga is a very popular type of meditation that combines mantras, breathing, and specific body movements. You need a teacher for this kind of meditation although once you master it, you can do it by yourself in the comfort of your home. Yoga is mostly used in reducing body aches and improving a person's mental capability.

Zazen Meditation

Fondly known as Zen meditation. This is a kind of meditation practiced by the Buddhist religion. It entails certain calculated moves and body postures. Mostly, Zen meditation is taught in class. This form of meditation aims to assume a particular position while breathing deeply and reflecting on a person's thoughts. It is correlated with mindful meditation, although it somewhat involves a lot of practice and patience.

The Meditation Process

Meditation is a straightforward activity that takes place using various procedures. However, the most fundamental process is as indicated below:

1. Lie down or sit comfortably. You may sit on a comfortable chair or lie on a bed. There are also unique kinds of meditation cushions and chairs that you can invest in
2. Close both eyes
3. Start breathing naturally – either faster or slower depending on the type of meditation
4. Concentrate on how the body responds as you breathe. Significant parts of the body to focus on are the chest, belly, and rib cage.
5. If your mind begins to wander, redirect it back to the breathing.

This is only a basic form of meditation. You can do this several times each day and maintain it for a specific period. Other more advanced techniques will involve activities like repeating words, maintaining specific body posture, and the like. Before you start meditating, you will first need to identify a particular time and place that is suitable for you. Studies show that meditation is more effective when you do it as a routine. This means that you should practice it at the same place and time each day. Once this is done, you can then set the amount of time you need for each session. If you are a beginner, you can start with small-time periods like three minutes for each session. The time you set must be one that is achievable so that you do not struggle with your sessions.

You must also ensure that you get a comfortable place to sit or lie on. When seated, you must always remember to keep your back straight. Do not cross your legs and arms.

Another thing you need to establish before starting your meditation is whether you need your sessions to be unguided or guided. Guided sessions are those led by an expert. This can be face to face kind of sessions, or you can use audio or video recording. These are commonly used by learners with little or no knowledge about meditation. Unguided meditation is for experienced meditators who do not need to be instructed. Some meditation techniques are best suited for beginners, while some are more complex and ideal for expert meditators. Ensure that you understand what each type entails before you get started.

As you start, let go of any form of expectation. Just sit or lie down and remain calm. Do not fight your thoughts but be sure to maintain focus on the main object of meditation. The more you meditate, the more relaxed your mind becomes. Breathe normally, unless the method of meditation demands that you do otherwise.

While most people close their eyes during meditation, you can choose to keep them open so long as you remain focused on the session. Besides the many things you need to know to get started, here are some tips you can employ in your sessions to ensure success:

- **Start with Short Sessions -** The recommended duration is two minutes a day, for a period of one week. Then keep increasing by two minutes each time.

- **Start in the Morning -** Doing your meditation sessions every morning helps a lot because you may get too engaged during the day. You may also forget about the session entirely and concentrate on other things. Set reminders for your ideal time

- **Check How Your Body Feels -** Always check how you feel before, during, and after the session. Start with your feet, check how this feels and slowly move upwards to your ankles, belly, chest, up to your head.

- **Monitor Your Breath -** Count your breath as you inhale and exhale. This will help you to concentrate more
- **Avoid Wandering -** Control your mind. If you do not, it will keep wandering, and you may lose focus. Any time this happens, relax and bring your thoughts back to the breathing. However, do not force your mind to clear since this will happen automatically as you continue with the session.
- **Focus on What is Right -** Do not worry about any mistake that arises since everyone faces them. Understand that there has never been a perfect way of meditating and ignore anything that you do wrong.
- **Allow Feelings to Grow -** As you meditate, some feelings will also arise, and you may want to connect with them. This is fine. Just seek to understand what made the feelings to occur but do not suppress them.
- **Focus on One Spot -** Keep your eyes glued in one place. Monitor the light, energy, and sound in the room. You can spend one day concentrating on the noise alone, then another day on the music and so forth.
- **Get Guidance -** If you get stuck during a meditating session, feel free to ask for assistance. You can even get some friends or family members and do the meditation as a team. Alternatively, you may also identify a community of meditators and become a member.

It is always advisable that you eliminate any distractions that may hinder you from focusing on the subject of the session. For instance, you may need to switch off your phone or put it on silent mode. Remember, meditation is meant to make you relax. Therefore, it is vital that you do not strain during the sessions since you do not need to work too hard for you to achieve the benefits listed above. All you need to do is to make it a daily practice and ensure each session is as comfortable as possible. You may start with the basic forms of meditation and keep advancing as time goes. Even if things do not go as planned, avoid being judgmental. Instead, learn from every mistake and seek to improve following time. Allow yourself to have fun, enjoy each session as you observe your body's response.

Practical Test:

1. What is meditation?

2. How does it help relieve stress and anxiety?

3. What is the best type of meditation for you?

CHAPTER 39:

Making Decisions

Before we begin, let us understand the simple fact that the methods and techniques for improving your concentration and focus are not tailor made for our core purpose of learning a new language. Instead, these methods are universal and apply to everything. The ability to focus and concentrate well is something that is reflected in whatever you do. The truth is that these methods are not a foolproof way of learning a language; they augment your ability to study and help you get through by allowing you to focus and concentrate on your work – which is something that is required in all fields, not just the area of language learning.

Given below are some of the simplest and most effective techniques for improving your concentration. You may have even heard of them before and you may even consider them cliché at times, but they have been tried and tested again and again – they are recommended repeatedly because they **work**! The problem is not practicing them diligently; most people lose steam halfway through and end up throwing in the towel – the best way to get these techniques to work for you is to **keep** practicing them daily! Do not miss even a day; you don't need to get stressed out if you do forget or don't have time on one day, but the greater number of these sessions you miss, the lesser you will feel their effects. Now, let us begin!

Before we get into the details of anything, let us first try to understand what the word focus means. When you are working on something, and you pay attention to nothing but the job you are doing – that is focusing. Simply put, it is the ability of a person to completely devote all his attention to a singular issue. This may involve detaching the mind from anything that is not ancillary to the attainment of that object or issue. In other words, it includes the ability to allow you not to get distracted.

What you must remember is that your focus cannot be absolutely perfect – that is an inhuman expectation. As human beings, we **will** get distracted. We cannot shy away from taking breaks either; in fact, pausing work for a little while before jumping back into it is actually an effective method of improving attention span! What we must remember that is focus can be defined as a continuum; you can never achieve the perfect focus, but you can work daily towards being **more** focused than you were yesterday!

What to Focus On

Following in order is deciding **what** to focus on. Now, this may sound very simple, but it is actually not so. One of the prime reasons why a person cannot focus on a task at hand is because of his inability to pin down his concentration on one issue at time. Multitasking is all well and good and sometimes, it is unavoidable. But what we tend to forget is that when we multitask, we tend to divide our attention among several different things, which means that the amount of attention we give to each is lessened. For menial jobs, this may work, but for something as difficult as learning a whole new language – it obviously does not! Listening to music or watching something on television, for instance, while studying vocabulary lists – that is definitely a bad idea! The trick is to prioritize and mentally rank the tasks in such as a manner that the one needing urgent and maximum attention is picked first. Choose a task and then devote your full attention to it – you will find that not only does it get done better; it gets done faster, too!

Deal with distractions

It is a commonly known fact that a person can focus better when the distractions are minimum. But you may not be accorded this luxury every time. Just when you sit down to learn those tough new words in Japanese or try to understand the logic behind the conjugation of

French verbs, the radio starts playing your favorite song or your phone will not stop pinging, since everyone will choose just now to start posting message on your friends' group!

Distractions tend to be highly individualistic though. There are some who are distracted by music; there are others who cannot work unless they have something playing in the background. These people have trained themselves such that the music is not a distracting stimulant, but an encouraging one instead – the moment they hear tunes, they start focusing on their work! You will need to figure out **what** your distractions are in the first place and then learn to work around them. It may take you some time – do not get discouraged and try to think creatively so that you can overcome these little hassles!

Here are a few, quick, generic tips that can set you on the right track!

- Develop a routine and stick to it. When you start working things according to your schedule, your brain automatically gets tuned to what you must do at what particular time. If for instance, you have trained yourself to sit and study your new word list in a foreign language at 4 pm every day; you will instinctively go ahead and do it at that time, no matter where you are and what you are doing! It takes time to make a routine, however – studies say that it takes at least twenty-one days for a practice to become a habit. So, make schedules and then keep working them until things become so routine that you don't have to think about them anymore!

- Capture your distraction and keep working. Keep a notepad or a sticky note pad close to you. For all those work-related distractions that interrupt you at exactly the wrong time, this is a very workable idea! Every time something distracts you, write it down on the notepad – you have captured it this way. This is something similar to the many visualization techniques psychiatrists recommend – essentially, you are convincing yourself that the distraction has been captured and is trapped within the paper, allowing you to continue your work. Now, once your work is over, open up your notepad and go through the list of distractions – anything important you can get back to right now. If for, instance, a friend had called while you are working, you can now call him/her back.

- Find yourself a '**study spot'**. Once again, you are attuning your brain to think in a certain way. Pick a quiet spot, where you will not have many distractions – in your room, for instance, there may be books or magazines or laptops that will distract you, no matter how comfortable the place itself is. Choose a place where you will not be disturbed and use that place to **only** work – now, make this part of your daily routine. Soon enough, you will find that every time you go to that place, you automatically feel the urge to study or work.

- As is the most obvious thing to be done – turn off all electronic devices! The phone is, indeed, a marvelous invention; it is also the most marvelous of interruptions! You will never get anything done so long as the device sitting so innocently on your table keeps lighting up every time someone feels the needs to share what they are doing on Facebook. Keep it switched off or at least put it on silent, so that it does not distract you. Of course, language learning may involve the use of the internet or watching videos online and the like, so for those, use your computer and strictly restrict yourself to only the websites you need to access. You will have to exercise self-control!

- Schedule your distractions. Yes, you heard me right – **schedule** your distractions! It may sound counterproductive to everything I have said so far, but it works. Like I mentioned earlier, our attention span as human beings is something that tends to be very limited. If you work for more than three-four hours straight, chances are you will get super tired you will undoubtedly get distracted. Your work will suffer, and the quality will no doubt go down. What you need to do is give time for those distractions that you have kept away from yourself. Take a break – spend time doing those things that you would typically consider your distractions and attend to them. This way, when you return, you will be relaxed, and your mind will be able to work better.

- Work in the 50-minute hour pattern. This is a very simple technique that will help you maintain your focus for long periods of time. In fact, it is actually an extension of the last point. What you must do is this – when you sit down to work, set a timer for exactly fifty minutes later. When it goes off, stop working. The brain generally starts getting tired after an hour and begins to lag in attention; you are, essentially, pre-empting this and working with it instead of against it. For the following ten minutes, do not do anything, and do not think of your work. Simply relax, perhaps meditate, and allow your brain some rest. Now, when you begin again, don't jump into your work right away – spend the first fifteen minutes reviewing whatever you have learnt/worked on so far, and then reset your timer to the following fifty minutes. This way, you enforce what you have absorbed and increase both your attention and retention spans.

These are but a few quick hacks to help you overcome your distractions! Practice them daily, or they will not work. And remember, they are not set in stone; like I said; distractions are very personal things, so you will need to figure out what works for you. What I have given you are general, simple things to get you started – keep them as a guideline and make your own way forward!

Practical Test

1. Why do you think you should have the right mindset when making decisions?

2. How do you deal with distractions?

3. How do you concentrate when making decisions?

CHAPTER 40:

Setting Goals and Curing Insomnia

Do you know where you will be in five years' time? Do you have a clear objective of what to work on now? Do you know what you wish to accomplish at the end of each day?

As you have already read, goals are the stepping-stones that lead you to a successful life. Without them, you are swimming in a pool lacking in direction and focus. Setting and planning goals give you the power to control your life and the direction it takes, giving you a benchmark in deciphering if you are prosperous or not.

To accomplish goals, you need to know the proper way to set them. You cannot just tell yourself that you want something and expect it to happen. It is a process that begins with a serious consideration of what your desires are and what you wish to achieve. It requires you to work hard.

Thankfully, some steps are easily defined to help transcend the specifics of all your goals. Getting to know each of these steps is essential to your overall success in forming goals that you can accomplish and feel proud of. They are known as the "Five Golden Rules of Goal Setting." Let's dive in, shall we?

Create Goals that Motivate

When you set goals for your life, you need to know the importance of motivation and accomplishment. They go hand-in-hand, which means you need to choose goals that are genuinely important to you. This means that they need to hold some sort of value in achieving them. If you don't have very much interest in the outcome of your goals, they become irrelevant and you will not put as much work into them. Motivation is the vital key to accomplishing your goals.

Set goals centered on your high priorities. This gives you the focus that keeps you from creating too many goals. Achieving goals requires commitment. When you feel a sense of urgency to complete them, this maximizes your success levels. When you feel you don't have to complete a goal, you will continue to put it off until the end of time. This will leave you feeling frustrated, which only feeds the unmotivated portions of you. It also fuels the "I am incapable of being successful" mindset.

Tip: To ensure your goals motivate you, jot down why they are valuable to you. Use this as a value statement to assist you when you begin to doubt yourself.

Write Goals Down

Physically writing your goals down makes them tangible and real, erasing the need to make the excuse to forget about it. As you jot down your goals, use words like "will" instead of "would like to."

Frame your goal around a positive statement. For instance:

"I will hold onto employees that exist for the first quarter" instead of "I will reduce the employee turnover rate." The first one is more motivating while the second is just a get-out clause allowing one to succeed.

Tip: Make a to-do list for yourself regarding your goals. When you use a template with your goals on top, then you can view them as the top priority.

Remember to place your written goals in a place that helps remind you every single day what you want to do. Place them on your fridge, mirrors, computer, desk, walls, etc.

Create a Plan of Action

This is an often-overlooked step in the process of planning goals. We become so focused on the outcome we desire that we forget to plan all the steps we need to fulfill those desires.

Write down each individual step and cross them off as you accomplish them. This is how you will realize that you are indeed making progress towards the goal. This is important, especially for long-term goals.

Stick with It

Setting and planning goals is an activity you will continue to do for the remainder of your life. Do not view it as a means to an end. They are built-in reminders that keep you on track to your ultimate goal and allow you to review them. While your destination may look similar for a long time, you will find hat you will always be changing exactly how you get there along the way. Ensure that the necessity, value, and relevance of the goal remain high for you.

Setting goals are so much more than saying you want something to occur. If you continue to live life without clear, defined goals and understand what you truly desire, you have few odds of reaching success. Following the golden rules of goal setting will help you gain the confidence you need to enjoy the satisfaction of achievement that comes with doing what you want to do. What will you accomplish today?

CBT Techniques for Eliminating Insomnia

For some reason, most people seem to attempt to treat their sleep deprivation by swallowing pills. It has long been established that pills don't help. But this is not mean that there are no other ways of treating sleep deprivation. One of the best ways of overcoming insomnia is through Cognitive Behavioral Therapy. The following are some of the CBT techniques that help in overcoming insomnia.

•Stimulus control therapy

This technique is aimed at eliminating factors that set your mind to resist sleep. The practitioner might ask you to set consistent sleep time and wake time and avoid taking naps during the day. This technique requires that you use your bed for only sleeping. If you climb onto your bed and for some reason, the sleep won't come, you should go to some other room, and only come back when you are feeling sleepy.

•Alcohol avoidance

If you have a tendency to drink alcohol late into the night, you will find yourself struggling with sleep issues. Alcohol tends to influence your nervous system, and it becomes hard for you to get sleep. This technique aims at keeping you away from alcohol so that you can be pretty sober when you go to sleep.

•Caffeine avoidance

Like alcohol, caffeine is just as bad. People that drink caffeine a few hours before they go to sleep will experience difficulties getting sleep. The practitioner might ask you to stay away from caffeine a few hours before you sleep. This means you will not be stimulated, and sleep will come to you much more naturally.

•Improving hygiene

In some instances, sleep deprivation might be tied to poor hygiene. Can you imagine having to sleep in a dusty, bug-infested bed? Anyone would have trouble closing their eyes. But when you clean up your bedroom and use clean sheets and mattress, it becomes a lot easier to fall asleep.

•Improving the environment

Another way to fight sleep deprivation is through making improvements in an individual's sleeping environment. This means you only have to keep the necessary things in the bedroom and get rid of the unnecessary stuff. It may not be easy because you may have developed an attachment to various things. For instance, the tv and radio have to go.

•Relaxation

This technique aims to make a person feel more relaxed. You're obviously not going to fall asleep if you're feeling tense most of the time. But then relaxing helps you fall asleep much faster. This technique involves things like meditation, imagery, and deep breathing exercises.

•Paradoxical intention

In this technique, a patient has to fight away the fear of not being able to sleep. Usually, what happens with people who have insomnia, they will throw themselves onto the bed, and start worrying that they're not falling asleep. But this technique is designed to make a person resist that kind of worrying.

•Biofeedback

This technique aims to keep watch over your heart rate and muscle tension and show you how to adjust them. Your professional mental health assistant will hand you a device for taking various measures. This will help you understand how your body is responding to the environment.

Practical Test

1. Why is setting goals important?

2. What is CBT and how does it work in curing insomnia?

3. What are the things that motivate you?

CHAPTER 41:

Sedona Method

The Sedona Method is a one of a kind, basic, amazing, simple to-learn and copy procedure that tells you the best way to reveal your regular capacity to relinquish any excruciating or undesirable inclination at the time. The Sedona Method comprises of a progression of inquiries you pose to yourself that lead your attention to what you are feeling at the time and delicately direct you into the experience of giving up.

A Sample Releasing Process

The accompanying clarification and procedure will give you a comprehension of what The Sedona Method is and a little taste of what The Sedona Method discharging strategy can accomplish for you.

Keep in mind, this is only an example. For you to get most extreme advantage and continued outcomes, we energetically suggest that you work with our sound program or potentially go to one of our courses.

There are three different ways to move toward the way toward discharging, and they all lead to a similar outcome: freeing your regular capacity to relinquish any undesirable feeling on the spot and permitting a portion of the smothered vitality in your inner mind to scatter. The main route is by deciding to relinquish the undesirable inclination. The subsequent path is to invite the inclination, to permit the feeling just to be. The third path is to plunge into the very center of the feeling.

A basic exercise

Let me clarify the strategy all the more altogether by requesting that you take part in a basic exercise. Get a pen, a pencil, or some little article that you would drop without even batting an eye. Presently, hold it before you and truly grasp it firmly. Imagine this is one of your restricting sentiments and that your hand speaks to your gut or your cognizance. On the off chance that you held the item long enough, this would begin to feel awkward yet recognizable.

Presently, open your hand and roll the article around in it. Notice that you are the one clutching it; it isn't joined to your hand. The equivalent is valid with your sentiments, as well. Your sentiments are as connected to you as this article is appended to your hand.

We clutch our sentiments and overlook that we are clutching them. It's even in our language. At the point when we feel irate or dismal, we don't normally say, "I feel furious," or, "I feel pitiful." We state, "I am furious," or, "I am miserable." Without acknowledging it, we are misidentifying that we are the inclination. Frequently, we accept an inclination is clutching us. This isn't correct… we are consistently in charge and simply don't have any acquaintance with it.

Presently, let the article go.

What was the deal? You let go of the item, and it dropped to the floor. Was that difficult? Obviously not. That is the thing that we mean when we state, "let go."

You can do something very similar with any feeling: decide to release it.

Staying with this equivalent similarity: If you strolled around with your hand open, wouldn't it be exceptionally hard to clutch the pen or other item you're holding? In like manner, when you permit or welcome an inclination, you are opening your awareness, and this empowers the inclination to drop away without anyone else—like the mists going in the sky or smoke leaving behind a stack with the vent open. It is like you are expelling the top from a weight cooker.

Presently, on the off chance that you took a similar item—a pencil, pen, or stone—and amplified it sufficiently enormous, it would show up increasingly more like void space. You would be investigating the holes between the particles and molecules. At the point when you plunge into the very center of an inclination, you will watch a practically identical wonder: nothing is truly there.

As you ace the method of discharging, you will find that even your most profound sentiments are simply on a superficial level. At the center you are vacant, quiet, and settled—not in the agony and haziness that the majority of us would expect. Truth be told, even our most extraordinary sentiments have just as much substance as a cleanser bubble. Also, you realize what happens when you stick your finger into a cleanser bubble: it pops. That is actually what happens when you plunge into the center of an inclination.

If you don't mind remembering these three analogies as we experience the discharging procedure together. Discharging will assist you with freeing yourself from the entirety of your undesirable examples of conduct, thought, and feeling. All that is required from you is being as open as you can be to the procedure. Discharging is a basic procedure will free you to get to more clear reasoning, yet it's anything but a reasoning procedure. In spite of the fact that it will assist you with accessing uplifted innovativeness, you don't should be especially inventive to be successful at doing it.

You will benefit from the way toward discharging the more you permit yourself to see, hear, and feel it working, as opposed to by pondering how and why it functions. Lead, admirably well, with your heart, not your head. In the event that you wind up stalling out in attempting to make sense of it, you can utilize the indistinguishable procedure to relinquish "needing to make sense of it." Guaranteed, as you work with this procedure, you will comprehend it all the more completely by having the immediate experience of doing it.

So here we go.

Deciding to Let Go

Make yourself agreeable and concentrate internally. Your eyes might be open or shut.

Stage 1: Focus on an issue that you might want to rest easy thinking about, and afterward permit yourself to feel whatever you are feeling at this time. This doesn't need to be a solid inclination. Actually, you can even keep an eye on how you feel about this activity and what you need to get from it. Simply welcome the inclination and permit it to be as completely or as well as can be expected.

This guidance may appear to be oversimplified; however, it should be. The majority of us live in our considerations, pictures, and anecdotes about the past and the future, as opposed to monitoring how we really feel at this time. The main time that we can really take care of the manner in which we feel (and, so far as that is concerned, about our organizations or our lives) is NOW. You don't have to trust that an inclination will be solid before you let it go. Truth be told, on the off chance that you are feeling numb, level, clear, cut off, or void inside, those are sentiments that can be relinquished simply as the more conspicuous ones. Basically, do as well as can be expected. The more you work with this procedure, the simpler it will be for you to distinguish what you are feeling.

Stage 2: Ask yourself one of the accompanying three inquiries:

- Could I let this inclination go?
- Could I permit this inclination to be here?
- Could I invite this inclination?

These inquiries are simply posing to you on the off chance that it is conceivable to make this move. "Truly" or "no" are both worthy answers. You will frequently give up regardless of whether you state "no." As best you can, answer the inquiry that you pick with at least idea, avoiding re-thinking yourself or getting into an inner discussion about the benefits of that activity or its results.

All the inquiries utilized in this procedure are intentionally straightforward. They are not significant all by themselves but rather are intended to guide you toward the experience of giving up, to the experience of halting hanging on. Proceed to Step 3 regardless of how you addressed the principal question.

Stage 3: No issue which question you began with, pose yourself this straightforward inquiry: Would I? As such: Am I ready to give up?

Once more, avoid banter as well as can be expected. Likewise recollect that you are continually doing this procedure for yourself—to pick up your own opportunity and clearness. It doesn't make a difference whether the inclination is legitimized, long-standing, or right.

On the off chance that the appropriate response is "no," or on the off chance that you don't know, ask yourself: "Would I rather have this inclination, or would I rather be free?"

Regardless of whether the appropriate response is still "no," proceed to Step 4.

Stage 4: Ask yourself this more straightforward inquiry: When?

This is a solicitation to simply release it NOW. You may end up effectively giving up. Recall that giving up is a choice you can make whenever you pick.

Stage 5: Repeat the former four stages as frequently varying until you feel liberated from that specific inclination.

You will presumably wind up giving up somewhat more on each progression of the procedure. The outcomes from the start might be very inconspicuous. Quickly, in the event that you are steady, the outcomes will get increasingly observable. You may find that you have layers of emotions about a specific theme. Be that as it may, what you let go of is away for acceptable

Practical Test:

1. What is Sedona Method?
2. Why do you think this method is helpful in mastering your emotions?
3. Summarize the steps of letting go.

CHAPTER 42:

Using Emotions Properly

Emotion is a psychological state generated subconsciously. It is stimulated by certain internal or external bodily responses. Sometimes, people interchangeably use the words' emotions and moods together, but there are differences in meaning. An emotion is intense, short-lived, and has a cause. On the other hand, a mood may not have a definite cause, is milder, and could last longer.

Basic Emotions and How to Use Them to Grow and Change Our Lives

Below, we identify some of these basic emotions and their effect on our daily life's and behavior.

Happiness

Most people strive to achieve this emotion called happiness. It is an emotional state of feeling pleasant brought about by feelings of well-being, satisfaction, gratification, joy, and contentment. It is expressed through:

- A smiling face
- Having a relaxed stance
- Pleasant tone on your voice

Happiness is considered as a basic human emotion. Things that influence happiness in people are normally culture. For example, attaining some high standards in life like owning property and having a good job could result in happiness. However, the truth is that happiness is dependent on personal belief, and what may bring happiness to one may not necessarily mean anything to another.

Happiness and health are related. Ill health can deprive one of the emotions of happiness. Both mental and physical health contributes to emotions of happiness. Also, to be noted, marital satisfaction is a great contributor to emotions of happiness.

Emotions of happiness are linked to poor health, anxiety, stress, loneliness, and depression. This has brought about lowered immunity, inflammations, and a decrease in life expectancy to such individuals.

Sadness

Sadness is a transient emotion characterized by bad feelings of disinterest, hopelessness, grief, disappointment, and dampened mood. Emotions of sadness happen to everyone from time to time. If prolonged, it can lead to depression.

Sadness is expressed in various ways including:

- Crying
- Withdrawal from people
- Lethargy

- Quietness
- Dampened mood

Depending on the root cause, people can be assisted to cope with its severity so as not to sink into deeper complications like depression. Also, this emotion can be prolonged resulting in negative thoughts, if not well-managed.

Fear

Fear is one of the most powerful emotions and an important role in survival. When something causes you to fear, you are likely to develop a fight-or-flight response. All of a sudden, you become tense, your respiration and heartbeat increase, your sensory organs become alert, prompting your whole self to either fight back or run from danger. This response can cause you to do the unplanned in a way you cannot explain.

This kind of emotion can be expressed as follows:

- Facial expression: widening the eyes, opening your mouth, pulled back chin
- Action: run, fight back, and hide
- Physiological reaction: accelerated heartbeat, breathing heavily, panting

Different people express themselves differently in incidents of fear. Some people can become numb and even collapse in incidents of fear depending on the cause. For example, the sight of a snake may cause one to run, another to fight back, and another to become numb and motionless.

Fear can also be a result of thought regarding a potential danger, resulting in anxiety not knowing what exactly to expect.

Some other individuals love attempting fearful ventures, like extreme sports ventured by people who enjoy the feeling of attempting fearful things.

If consistently exposed to a fearful situation, it could lead to familiarity hence reducing the feeling of anxiety and fear. An example would be one who fears hearing gunshots. If they move near a barrack where gunshots from training soldiers are the order of the day, then the fear of gunshots reduces with time.

Disgust

It can be displayed in the following ways:

- Turning your face away from the scene of disgust
- A physical reaction like vomiting
- A facial expression like closing eyes and wrinkling your nose

Disgust can be brought about by an unpleasant sight, smell, or taste. Food that has gone stale can cause a disgusting emotional reaction.

Other things that may trigger a disgusting emotion include decomposing body, rot, blood, untreated wound, and poor hygiene. The sight of immoral actions can also be disgusting.

Anger

Anger is also a major powerful emotion characterized by feelings of frustrations, agitation, hostility, and antagonism. Same as fear, anger can cause body fight-or-flight response to respond promptly. When feelings generate emotions of anger in you, you are likely to arise to fight back or defend yourself.

It is normally displayed through:

- Facial expression: glaring or frowning
- Body language: staring strongly at the source or turning away from the source
- Voice tone: yelling or speaking gruffly
- Physiological response: turning face color, sweating, shaking
- Aggressiveness: throwing objects, kicking, hitting

Most of the time, anger is presumed as a negative emotional reaction, but it can be constructive because it helps one to express themselves in full, expel all the stored pain from within, and clarify your dissatisfaction on the cause of anger. Expressed anger hits the 'enough' button, and the situation has to be addressed.

However, anger can become uncontrollable leading to an unhealthy, dangerous, and harmful way of expression. For example, the aggregated can hit the other with an object leading to injury or even death. This is where uncontrolled anger turns to violence, abuse, and aggression.

Some health conditions in individuals can lead to uncontrolled anger when provoked. Such cases should be handled soberly, bearing in mind that it could run out of hand leading to unprecedented events.

Some people, due to uncontrolled anger, have resulted in having diseases like coronary heart disease and diabetes, while others have found themselves in behaviors like smoking, alcoholism, and aggressive driving.

Surprise

This emotion is normally brief. It is a physiological startle response resulting from an unexpected response. This kind of emotion can be negative, positive, or neutral. Example of a negative surprise could be arriving home and finding your pet dead, whereas a pleasant surprise could be an award from your boss for a well-done job.

It is characterized by:

- Facial expressions: raising eyebrows and opening the mouth
- Physical response: jumping up and down
- Verbal reactions: gasping, screaming, and yelling

Surprise emotion can also trigger a fight-or-flight response. There is a burst of adrenaline that causes the body to either flee or fight.

Surprise moments tend to linger more in the mind standing out in memory. Surprise news can get hold of people attention, and that's why newsmakers are more inclined to breaking news.

Other Significant Types of Emotions

Other significant types of emotions that may not necessarily trigger expressions include:

- Amusement
- Shame
- Contentment
- Satisfaction
- Excitement
- Guilt
- Contempt
- Pride in achievement
- Embarrassment

- Relief

Advantages of Emotions

Emotions have three components, namely:

1. Subjective (experience)
2. Physiological (body reaction)
3. Expressive (behavior response)

1. **Motivate to take action.** Let's take for example when one is about to do a final exam that determines whether they step up or re-sit, there is a definite feeling of anxiety. The most emotional response will be to study. The motivation to study will outdo the anxiety to ensure you stand out with good grades.

Naturally, everyone will strive to engage in activities that bring positive emotions and avoiding those that are likely to trigger negative emotions.

2. **Boost our survival tactics and help us avoid danger.** Charles Darwin believed emotions drive both humans and animals to manage and reproduce. Anger drives to confrontation, fear may cause us to move to areas of safety, and love may cause us to look out for our mates for reproduction purposes.

Emotions are adaptive drivers taking us to a place of action that guarantees survival and success.

3. **Help in making decisions.** Our emotions are major influencers in our decision making, right from what we take for breakfast to the leaders we choose during political elections.

Even though logic, rationality, and statics are key factors in making decisions our emotions determine the final move. Emotional intelligence has been proven to play a major role in our decision making.

4. **You are understood through your emotions.** You should not be afraid to express yourself through your emotions. You can express your emotions through body language such as facial expressions of whatever emotions you are going through.

You can also express your emotions verbally, hence your listener will know your position on a particular issue and be advised how to react or help.

5. **Through emotions, you can understand others.** Just as expressing our own emotions can help convey valuable information to others likewise can we be able to understand others through the emotions of their display. It's important to be able to interpret and respond to others through the emotions they display. This enhances effective communication in dealing with different people as you consider their predicaments through their emotional expressions.

Charles Darwin, an early scientific researcher on emotions, indicates emotional display can save anyone from impending danger. For example, a spitting and hissing animal indicate that it's angry and possibly defensive, so the best thing is to back off and avoid it.

Understanding others through their emotional display will help us know how to respond in a way that is calm and amicable.

The Relevance of Both Positive and Negative Emotions to Daily Life

Some of the common positive emotions may include:

- Awe
- Serenity
- Happiness
- Amusement
- Interest
- Contentment
- Satisfaction
- Joy
- Love

Negative emotions include:

- Annoyance
- Melancholy
- Loneliness
- Rage
- Sadness
- Disgust
- Anger
- Fear

Both positive and negative emotions happen and for a good reason. For example:

- Disgust – we can reject unhealthy stuff.
- Trust – you can connect with genuine people.
- Sadness – you get to connect with our loved ones.
- Joy – it reminds us of what is important.
- Surprise – have a focus on new situations.
- Anticipation – you can look forward and plan.
- Fear – it protects us from anger.
- Anger – it enables us to fight against problems.

Unpleasant negative emotions are also important in our lives. Some seemingly positive emotions can be a major contributor to stress. For example:

- Planning for a wedding
- House moving (exiting at the same time stressing)
- Having a baby
- Starting on a new job

The above activities are positive and exciting but can bring negative emotions with them; hence both positive and negative emotions are inevitable in life.

10. Understanding Your Emotional Needs

Understanding your emotional needs must tackle any emotional pain or dissatisfaction. A baby could be crying because they are wet and they need a change of diaper, but someone may fail to understand that and instead, bring the baby food. The baby will continue to be frustrated because his need has not been addressed, so is when we fail to understand our emotional needs.

Emotional needs are developed early in life most probably related to upbringing. The area in which your emotions were starved will most probably be your greatest emotional pain. If you suffered rejection in your upbringing there is an inner need for acceptance wherever you go.

These negative emotional pains will cause you to fight for acceptance because it's a void inside you that needs to be filled. So, we should not fight our emotional needs. Instead, we should strive to achieve what seems as emptiness.

Emotions should not be suppressed whether positive or negative that one should strive to achieve what seemingly seems to be the need.

Practical Test

1. Why does using emotions important?
2. Do you think you have used emotions properly?
3. How do you balance your emotions daily?

CHAPTER 43:

Emotional Triggers

In developing your emotional intelligence, there are things that you should start and stop doing, things that are not obvious but have a big impact, like little drops of water compared to an ocean. As small as they are, each of them incrementally makes a big impact on your growth, both positively and negatively, and if it's the latter, it might be too late to fix the issue. It's not enough to know just how you can grow your emotional intelligence. It's important to note the things you do that tamper with the growth and begin stopping them, not tomorrow or following week—now!

How Do You Know These Things?

Some of the things that tamper with the growth of your emotional intelligence hide in between everyday habits that are considered normal, so finding them can be a tad bit difficult. When there are certain things about you that put people off constantly, it's important to note that these things are detrimental to the growth of your emotional intelligence.

In finding these things out, pay attention to how you are viewed by people. It's okay to say, "I don't care about what others think of me or my lifestyle," but if the things you do that seemingly do not make a difference to you negatively affect those around you, it's okay to start thinking about changing those things.

See how your actions reflect on others around you. In watching how these actions reflect on them, you are exposed to what you are doing that is detrimental to your own emotional intelligence. This is important because one of the characteristics of people with high emotional intelligence is the positive impact their actions have on those around them. So, if your actions are constantly affecting those around you in a negative manner, that's one way to know which things should be stopped.

You can also go simply ask. Meet friends, people who are close to you, converse with them, and ask them, "How do my actions affect you?" "The things I do, do they hurt you?" "Am I insensitive?" Another characteristic of a person with high emotional intelligence is empathy. So, when you are told that you do not know how to empathize because of a certain thing you are doing, then know that that action is detrimental to the growth of your emotional intelligence.

Subtle Bragging

Subtle bragging, or humble bragging, is the act of bragging in a way that is not exactly noticed as bragging. You don't realize you are bragging when you practice humble bragging, because by your standards you are just being modest. This is something we do among friends, sometimes innocently.

An example of subtle bragging is watching your friend talk about how bloated he feels and how his fitness regimen seems to not be working. At this point, the only thing you are supposed to offer is a word of advice on how he could start making his regimen work. Instead, you may start yapping on and on about your water therapy and how you eat right, your low carbs diet, how much time you spend at the gym, and then you go on to slap your abs and move your arms to expose your biceps and end with the statement: "Even after all I've done, I still don't look as good as I want to." Although you thought you looked and sounded modest, you weren't.

Being Overly Serious

This might look like a good trait because it yields productive results, but it can be a problem in disguise. There's a difference between being serious and taking yourself too seriously, and the latter is indicative of underlying insecurities that individuals may have. For instance, humor may uncloak weaknesses which may leave them emotionally naked. Although it takes times to accept your own weaknesses, being too serious will leave no place for creating relationships. If you examine the relationships, you have in your life and realize that you only have business inclined relationships then you might be exhibiting this trait.

Being too serious detaches you from your coworkers and friends. Nobody wants to say something funny they found online to you, because they would come off as not serious. You unknowingly miss out on the beautiful things in life and it might begin to reflect on your family and kids too. They cannot say, "Daddy, I saw and played with a clown today," because they know the only thing you want to see or talk about is their schoolwork.

You don't find yourself laughing at anything, because it seems mundane. So, a joke is usually met with a harsh remark from you rather than a smile or laughter. Being overly serious is a bad thing, wrapped up in good results because it makes you unapproachable. It is bad for relationship building and should be stopped as soon as possible.

Going through Your Phone in the Middle of a Conversation

This is a very disrespectful act that is unfortunately very common nowadays. Some people are so attached to their phone that they can't bear to take their eyes off of it for an hour; hence they tend to go through their phone even when an important meeting is going on. This can mess up your relationship because it makes the person think you're insensitive. Bringing out your phone and going through it in the middle of a conversation is not only insensitive but it's disrespectful too. You're telling the person that whatever they were saying to you, as important as it was to them, is unimportant to you, and that can make the person feel insignificant. You should definitely stop using your phone in the middle of a conversation.

Calling the Names of the Important People You Know

If you cannot go through a conversation without mentioning the names of the important people you know, this is you trying to make yourself look better than every other person sitting in that room at that moment, and you do not necessarily have to drag that kind of attention to yourself. You have met the president nice. Your father's brother is the one on TV—yeah, that's nice. Not everyone needs to know. Instead of making you look interesting, you come off as a braggart in want of attention and that sincerely puts people off. Name dropping might make you feel better about yourself, but how do you think it will make others feel about you?

Screaming at People

No one likes a screamer. No matter how much the person deserves your screaming, it's not necessary. You make people feel small and insignificant when you scream at them. Especially when it is a constant habit of yours to scream when you are mad at others. You can say that it's just your way of reacting when you're mad, and that screaming makes you feel a lot better, but have you ever stopped to consider how the other person feels about your screaming?

Using Abusive Words When Angry

You cannot take words back, so when you are about to use abusive words in a fit of anger, rest assured they will go a long way to harm the person you are saying them to. You can say you don't mean them later, but the words have already had their effect. Sometimes the use of hurtful words stems from a desire to make them feel the hurt you're feeling, but it's not really necessary.

Gossiping

"It was just a harmless conversation," you would say. But it did involve you talking to one person about another and spilling secrets that you were meant to keep. It did involve you saying things that were not exactly great about another person. Now, exactly how harmless was that conversation?

When you gossip about another person, it says more about you than it does about the person you were talking about. It doesn't make sense to base your discussion on the life of another; relationships that thrive on gossip have a very shaky foundation and are bound to crash sooner than later. Gossiping is a horrible habit, and it depicts a very low state of emotional intelligence.

There are a ton of other things you could talk about when chilling with friends. It doesn't necessarily have to be about other people. Unless you are talking about ways to help them, there is no need to talk about their situation. Gossips depict disloyalty so it should be avoided at all costs.

Talking a Lot More Than Listening

When you talk more than you listen, it limits your chances at learning and unlearning things. You are literally shoving your opinion down the throat of others without giving them the time or the chance to air theirs. This is an attitude that repels people. For communication to occur there has to be more than talking, there has to be listening too. And when you talk more than you listen, communication has not taken place, because you were the only one talking. Listening most times helps you to make a better decision. Not listening to people when they talk and being too concerned about airing your own opinion will make you look ignorant. At some point, you will begin to say things that do not make a lot of sense because you were not listening in the first place. You will suddenly begin to look ignorant, and no one wants to associate with an ignorant person who is also not willing to learn.

Posting Too Much of Yourself on Social Media

A lot of people are guilty of this action. It depicts a want for acceptance, and it's usually captured by the phrase "putting it all out there." Well, news flash, you do not have to do this. You do not necessarily have to tell the world all the dreams you have or all the things you do after you wake up and before you go to bed. You do not need to be validated by social media and those online. They don't really care that much about you. They should not know so much about you. It's needless throwing these things in their faces. Save some information for yourself. Remember, the internet has a good memory; it never forgets.

Being Closed-Minded

This is a very big problem. It is important that you view things with an open mind. Keeping a closed mind makes you unapproachable. It also means that you already have a formed opinion about a certain thing, and when you are approached, you are unwilling to listen and make changes to your initial thoughts, making you inaccessible. It's very sensible to keep an open mind and be open to changes. Learn to see the world from the eyes of other people. It makes you more sensitive.

These habits are associated with people with low emotional intelligence, and they should be stopped now. They are harmful to you, to the people around you, and to the growth of your emotional intelligence.

Practical Test

1. What is emotional trigger?

2. What do you think is your own emotional trigger?

3. How do you deal with emotional trigger?

CHAPTER 44:

Emotional Intelligence

Emotional intelligence is the capacity to monitor your emotions as well as to be able to handle the emotions of other people. For you to be emotionally intelligent, you need to distinguish between the different emotions then label them the correct way. Once you do this, the following step is to use the information that you have gathered to guide your behavior and to think as well as to influence the behavior of other people.

Emotional intelligence is what we use when we put ourselves in the shoes of other people, have deeper conversations with our spouses, or manage an unruly child. It lets us understand ourselves better, connect well with others, and live a happy life full of good decisions.

Components of Emotional Intelligence

Before we can look into anything else, we must understand the components of emotional intelligence. As a person, I have gained a lot of insight into emotional intelligence after I mastered the components of emotional intelligence.

Let us look at these components because they also form the skills that will allow you to interact better.

1. Self-Awareness

Self-awareness has smaller components that make it one of the best components of emotional intelligence. First, emotional awareness means you recognize another person's emotions and its impact on the environment. Additionally, you need to have accurate self-assessment so that you know your limits and strengths. You need to have self-confidence, which is the ability to be sure of one's capabilities and self-worth.

2. Self-Regulation

Self-regulation is all about being able to manage your emotions and how they affect you. For you to manage your emotions the right way, you need to maintain high levels of integrity and honesty, as well as take full responsibility for your performance. You also need to be flexible in handling change that comes both professionally and personally. You also need to be innovative, so that you are comfortable with and open to new information and novel ideas that come your way.

3. Self-Motivation

As the name suggests, emotional intelligence requires you to have the drive to meet standards. You have to try and improve so that you meet a certain standard of excellence. You also need to be committed to what you do. The commitment that you have needs to be aligned with the goals of the organization and the group. You also need to be ready to grab any opportunities that come your way. Self-motivation needs a lot of optimism, as well. You need to be persistent when pursuing goals despite the setbacks and obstacles.

4. Empathy

When you are empathetic, you can place yourself in another person's situation and understand it. You can sense what the other person is going through, see their perspective, and take an active concern in what they are going through.

As business owners, we are tasked with the responsibility of understanding our customers the right way. When it comes to being empathetic, we can recognize, anticipate, and meet our customers' needs the right way.

Empathy doesn’t stop at knowing what other people are going through and understanding them; rather, it also begs us to sense what other people need so that we can develop and improve their abilities. To do this, we need to understand what diversity all is about then cultivate the various opportunities through the people that we meet.

5. Social Skills

Social skills beg us to have influence, which refers to the use of effective tactics to be persuasive. We also need to be able to communicate clearly and in a convincing way. It also encompasses being a leader, being agents of change, and managing conflict the right way. We also get to build bonds and collaborate with other people.

The Dimensions of Emotional Intelligence

According to the theorists Mayer and Salovey, four unique branches of emotional intelligence guide us in knowing our emotional abilities and skills. These include:

1. Perceiving Emotion

Perceiving emotions is all about being able to identify and label the emotions that you come from other people. For instance, if I am in the office and call someone that needs to get disciplined, I need to read their emotions to understand what they are going through. At times you have to look beyond the mistakes and read your emotions before you get to know what to do.

You also need to express your own emotions the right way. When you express the emotions, you will be able to label them then distinguish between the ones that are honest and dishonest.

2. Utilize the Emotions

Once you perceive the various emotions, the following step is for you to use them in making decisions. Most of the time, we fail to utilize emotions because we don't know that they are vital to our survival. Instead, we experience them and identify them.

For you to utilize emotions, you need to prioritize your thoughts based on the emotions that are associated with different thoughts. You have to learn about and come up with thoughts that will allow you to make better judgments later on. You also need to capitalize on the mood changes so that you appreciate the different points of view, and then use the different emotional states so that you can make better decisions when faced with problems.

3. Understanding Emotions

You also need to understand emotions the right way. To do this, you need to make sure you identify the emotions and see the connection between all the emotions. You also have to look at the various causes and consequences of the emotions and then understand the complexity surrounding them. You need to look at how the various emotions change from one state to another.

4. Managing Emotions

This is the final dimension of emotional intelligence. Here, you have to manage both the pleasant as well as the unpleasant emotions, as well as to monitor them then reflect on them. You need to understand how to prolong your attachment or detach yourself from the emotional state. You must learn to manage your emotions both within you and in other people.

Examples of Emotional Intelligence in Daily Life

For you to understand what emotional intelligence entails, let us look at the different examples of emotional intelligence in your daily life:

Managing Your Emotions

Say you are deep in a conversation with someone, then it suddenly turns from friendly banter to an argument. As you realize that the situation has gone from being a casual conversation to being emotionally charged, you try to work hard to bring the situation under control by controlling how you react to the situation. You can decide to pull back, or you can take leave so that you prevent yourself from saying something that you will regret.

Managing Other People's Emotions

Once you take your leave, you realize that the other person is still talking about what happened more than necessary. You realize that the person is in an emotional state that makes them furious even when you are calm.

The following step is for you to try and diffuse the situation the right way. You can make efforts to defuse the situation by calling in a few mutual friends to handle the situation or try to change the subject.

If it is necessary that you have to see the conversation till the end, the only logical thing to do is to set aside your argument and wait until the person cools down before you can start the subject again. Some people need time to reduce their anger, and this is why you need to allow them enough time to change their frame of mind.

Why You Need to Improve Your Emotional Intelligence

When you hear about emotional intelligence, you need to have a high level, which is why you need to improve on it. Before we look at the various ways of improving your emotional intelligence, we need to look at the various benefits.

- **It Creates Better Teamwork**

Teams that have emotionally intelligent members form a good working relationship because they can understand each other. They also have good communication and value what every team member contributes to the group. Whenever someone suggests something to the group, all the members get to respond productively and positively.

• You Can Deal with Change

Many people don't like change, and they struggle to make sure they don't change their beliefs. The good thing is that if you become emotionally intelligent, you get the tools that will help you to deal with the change that comes your way both in personal life and at the workplace.

Others don't resist change, but they regard it with negativity and fail to handle it the right way. When you are emotionally intelligent, you can be more positive and inspire your team members to feel that they can accept change.

• You Handle Tough Conversations

Whether you are dealing with an angry employee or a customer that is shouting at the top of their voice, difficult conversations usually give rise to a host of emotions.

With the right skills, you can handle the conversations emotionally because you can connect with the other person. When you connect with others, you get to find a resolution to issues faster than ever.

Maintaining a conversation, especially in the face of conflict, requires a high level of emotional intelligence. Conflict resolution usually relies on one of the people in the conversation being more emotionally intelligent than the other person.

Another benefit of being emotionally intelligent is that you make decisions much easier than before. You will be able to struggle less when looking for both sides of the argument.

• Helps You to Connect

If you are poor at meeting and talking to people, the essential ingredient of making things work for you is to be emotionally intelligent. When you are emotionally intelligent, you can build trust with other people. Making rapport is also quick and east. When you meet someone for the first time, you can understand what they feel and empathize with them to a greater level. This makes you a valuable part of any team.

Practical Test

1. What is emotional intelligence?
2. How do you improve emotional intelligence?
3. Do you think increasing your emotional intelligence help you become a better person?

CHAPTER 45:

Stress and Anger

Relationship Between Anger and Stress

This anecdotal relationship is paradoxically about the differences between anger and stress. When you are considering rage and anxiety, it is particularly interesting to note how often people do not treat these two terms as mutually exclusive when speaking. In your everyday language, you find others applying these two terms interchangeably in a sentence or within the course of your communication at large.

However, you will notice that this relationship has tiny, albeit negligible differences in proper grammar. You will find out that anger and stress are different, but these differences blur entirely except under particular circumstances. To convey your specific message, you will have to pay special attention to the difference between anger and stress. You can apply the following actions to highlight the usually blurred or negligible differences in our everyday communication.

1. Anger can lead to stress - Both anger and stress can result from or lead to either one or the other. For instance, whenever things do not go your way or as you expected, you will be frustrated. Now, since this occurrence is unfolding at a particular instant in time, you get angry.

Anger may cause you to lash out in frustration. However, when the rage persists over an extended period, the resultant emotion will be stress. In this case, your anxiety is borne out of a continuous series of angry instances. In this case, repeated anger leads to stress.

2. Stress can lead to anger - As you know, stress is an emotional state of anxiety accompanied by physical symptoms such as a pounding heart, restlessness, sweating, and a lack of focus. Tension had built up over time. However, from time to time during this stressful period, you may engage in an angry outburst.

Such a passionate outburst is often due to the hopelessness experienced during stress. Desperation leads to frustration, which in turn results in sudden outbursts of anger. You will notice that although the tension persists over an extended period, passionate passion comes out in instantaneous outbursts. In this case, stress leads to outbursts of anger.

3. Identify the onset of timescales - Anger is instantaneous, while stress spreads out over time. When you look into the relationship between the two, your viewpoint of rage as an irritated state of mind at a specific instant in time will contrast your perspective of stress. You notice that pressure is the emotional state of anxiety over a given length of time. Anger is sudden or immediate in occurrence, while tension progressively builds up over time.

4. Anger is a reaction, while stress is an emotion - Consider being involved in a work project from which you expect a particular result. This result is the overall objective. You can also set sequential targets at various stages within the project, which eventually lead towards the overall goal. These small and staged targets are micro objectives. As expected, while executing your plan, you will have trouble at various stages.

Your response to potential upsets is of vital importance when differentiating anger from stress. For instance, whenever you run into a set back at the sequential stage affecting your micro objective, you are bound to get frustrated. Your initial reaction may be to lash out in anger.

However, since the setback may be fixable, your passion becomes a reaction to an unfavorable minor hiccup.

On the other hand, in case your completed project fails to meet its overall objective, then you or others may consider it a failure. Since this situation becomes a reflection of you as an individual, your sense of worth will suffer, leading to a stressful state of mind. Your deflated state of mind causes a depressed mood. As you can see, all these final situations describe an emotional state; hence, stress is also an emotion.

5. Anger is short term, while stress is comparatively longer in duration - This trait of distinguishing the two terms is different from the earlier described times of onset. This characteristic will tackle differences in the overall duration as opposed to the nature of the beginning between anger and stress. Typically, you do not stay angry over long periods. Your irritation would often result from identifiable triggers, which are usually fixable. As a result, your state of anger is relatively easy to reverse.

Besides, outbursts would often characterize your rage. Such passionate outbreaks are relatively short-term events and do not last over long periods. You are unlikely to stay angry for long unless under exceptional circumstances such as holding grudges. However, when you hold grudges, you are expressing your disagreeable state of mind rather than giving a reaction to the other person or his view. Anger follows the cause and effect convention, i.e., without an aggravating cause, you will have no rage.

On the other hand, stress is comparatively long-lasting. Given the fact that it affects your emotional state of mind, a reversal takes a considerable period. The long-term duration of stress is also a reason why therapists may be involved in management as opposed to anger, where you will have the opportunity to cool off as a remedy.

6. Anger is physical, while stress is psychological - Whenever you are angry, your initial reaction is out of pure reflex. You get frustrated, become inflamed, and physically lash out at targets within your vicinity. You may bang the desk, smash a window, or even hurl an object across the room. This physical reaction is a means of releasing the tension associated with the anger. Since anger usually has a specific cause, reversing this cause will most often get rid of the violence. You become rational once again and apologize to your colleagues for your apparent irrational reactions.

However, a stressful person will be psychologically impaired. As an emotional event, stress usually causes a cycle of panic attacks and depression. Panic may lead to irritability, paranoia, and irrational fear of impending doom. During depressive moods, you withdraw from society, avoid interactions with others, and possess a feeling of worthlessness. While anger is easily reversible, stress may need professional intervention in extreme circumstances.

Stress Reduction Techniques

1. Have regular exercise or yoga in places where available

You should know that a good cardio workout improves your blood flow. The increased blood flow will result in proper perfusion of your brain. Typically, your brain tissue usually accumulates toxins throughout your stressful period. With improved blood circulation, fresh oxygen can get directly into the neurons.

At the same time, your brain cells effectively flush out the accumulated toxins, such as cortisol. In addition to this improved blood flow, regular exercise causes your endocrine system to release endorphins into your circulation. These endorphins are the hormones responsible for your feel-good factor. Your unwanted toxins have to exit, and these feel-good hormones will replace them. As a result, you will experience a reversal in your state of mind for the better.

Your overall mood will change from a gloomy, depressed feeling into an upbeat state within a relatively short time. Your endocrine system releases and, therefore, your overall mood for the better. In addition, your endocrine system is responsible for releasing prostaglandins. Your prostaglandins act as natural pain relievers that relieve the headaches and muscular aches.

2. Add dietary supplements

Supplements are helpful in case you are the type of person who detests pharmacologic drugs, but you would still prefer to combat your stress by ingesting something. You should know that such supplements act only as aids to stress relief, and you should use them in combination with other appropriate techniques.

You should not expect supplements to give you instant stress relief as you would expect of most drugs. Once you understand how supplements work, then you could try them. Examples of supplements include green tea, omega three fatty acids, kava-kava extract, ashwagandha herbs, valerian root, and various mint sources.

3. Use essential oils, soothing music, and light scented candles

When you burn scented candles or use essential oils, your olfactory nervous system will significantly appreciate this simple act. These two items give off a soothing aroma. This aroma has the effect of calming down your mood through olfactory stimulation. You will have to depend on your sense of smell to appreciate this reward. Your nostrils will transport the soothing aroma into your brain neurons.

As a result, these basal neurons face stimulation and in turn, release a calming effect. Your neurons will release stabilizing signals, which will spread throughout your body resulting in a calm mood. To achieve the most out of your aromatherapy session, you can include some soothing music in the background. This combination of sensual music with scented candles and essential oils will maximize the benefits from your lowered levels of stress.

4. Reduce your caffeine intake

You should know that caffeine and stress or anxiety do not go hand in hand. Remember, caffeine is a stimulant. Therefore, during stressful periods, it is imperative to have this fact at the back of your mind. Readily available sources of caffeine in your daily life include casual drinks such as coffee, Coca-Cola soft drinks, and specific energy drinks.

These drinks are counterproductive when you are trying to calm yourself down following a stressful trigger. When under stress, you might be tempted to have a cup of coffee to relax, but these drinks will instead worsen your anxiety and increase your pressure. Here is how: coffee stimulates the nervous system. Caffeine causes the release of high amounts of excitatory transmitters from the brain. Neurotransmitters are signals produced by brain cells.

As expected from their description, these excitatory signals will increase the rate of activity of your heart muscles, i.e., excite the heart. As a circulatory pump, your restless heart will start pumping faster in frequency and duration. In turn, your increased heart rate will in no way contribute to a state of calm. You will spiral into further anxiety. Therefore, if you want to have at relieving your stress, then avoid caffeine.

5. Monitor your progress by writing things down

Turning yourself from a stressed individual to a stress-free person is a journey. The habit of writing down your experiences at various stages in this journey is crucial. This technique allows you to visualize your progress at those stages during stress relief.

You are encouraged to jot down your targets and achievements since this action will give you focus. Staying organized will provide you with a higher shot at success as opposed to haphazardly mixing different strategies and tactics. For instance, you can practice answering the following self-queries: What irks you? Why does it anger you? Is there anything you can do about it? If so, then how do you go about that?

You have to provide answers to each query to the best of your satisfaction.

Along the way, you could check off what you have managed to complete. Once you accomplish everything, you could revisit the various stages and adequately tackle all pending issues. In this way, you will end up being adept at personal stress relief. In addition, you may as well share this skill with other people going through similar stressful situations.

Practical Test

1. What is stress?
2. What is anger?
3. How do both correlate?

CHAPTER 46:

Turning Emotions To Emotional Intelligence

One of the most fundamental parts of emotional intelligence is self-regulation. This is your ability to regulate yourself, allowing you to essentially use, control, or transform your emotions using your emotional intelligence. When you can do this, you are able to keep yourself happier and healthier. You will find that managing your own emotions gets easier the more you do it, and the more you manage your emotions, the more effective it becomes. People around you will be happier as you are able to regulate yourself. You will find that your relationships with people are easier to maintain. It is absolutely essential to understand how to transform your emotions.

Observing Feelings

Before you are able to begin regulating your emotions, you must first be aware of them. Remember, the foundation of emotional intelligence is self-awareness. This is for a reason—if you do not understand your own feelings, how are you supposed to control them or understand and influence the feelings of others? The answer is you cannot hope to do so. The first step, then, to be able to regulate and transform your own emotions is to develop a deeper understanding of your own self-awareness.

When you want to learn how to be self-aware, you must begin by understanding your own emotions. The simplest way possible to do this is to make sure you are regularly taking the time necessary to reflect on the emotions you are feeling. If you ever notice that you are particularly flustered or upset, stopping to check in with yourself is a great idea. You need to be able to recognize exactly what you are feeling as well as identify why you are feeling it.

If you notice that you are feeling bad, for example, you should stop, take a deep breath, and try to name the feeling. Be as specific as possible and make sure you reserve judgment. You should name the feeling without stressing about what that name is, and then try to identify what happened to make you feel that way. Look at what had just happened—were you hungry and therefore quicker to anger? Did someone say something that made you feel sensitive or threatened? Did something go wrong? Whatever the reason, you should try to make that connection. You cannot start transforming your feelings if you do not understand what caused them. Try keeping a journal to keep track of these feelings, both good and bad. While the negative emotions are probably easier to identify for you, positive ones are important to understand and analyze as well. When you do, you will find that there are likely patterns to your moods. You may be particularly easy to anger when you have not eaten in a while, or when you are stressed out over bills or your job.

If you do not know where to start with your feelings or you struggle to identify feelings beyond labeling them as good or bad, that is okay. You can start with a feelings chart. There are several designed primarily for writers that you can find online. Try searching for a feelings wheel, where the center is a basic emotion, and then you make them more complex as you move further down the wheel. This may aid you in identifying whatever the emotion you are aware of is. Practice using this chart regularly to make your emotions as specific as possible.

As you continue trying to identify your own emotions, make sure you are allowing your feelings to pass without judgment. It can be easy to try to dissuade yourself from a feeling because you feel as though it is inappropriate or unwarranted. The fact that you are feeling whatever it is you are feeling is enough justification for it. If you feel sad over dropping your ice cream, do not try to discourage that—it is okay to feel any way you do. These feelings are just that—feelings. They come and go in response to the environment around you and they deserve to be valued and respected. Just keep moving on with your life after acknowledging the feeling. When you tell yourself that getting upset about ice cream is irrational and too much of a "first world problem," all you are doing is teaching yourself to invalidate your own emotions, which is counterproductive to everything you are trying to do. Let your emotions stand however they are and trust them. There is a reason for feeling them, and even if you decide not to act upon them, understanding them is relevant to everyone.

Changing Interpretations

The following step to transforming your emotions is to change your interpretations. Oftentimes, your interpretations of what is happening around you can be entirely skewed by the emotions you are feeling in the moment. While emotions are important to recognize and acknowledge, they can also cloud judgment. This is why self-regulation is so important in the first place! You do not want your emotions to be controlling everything you say, do, and think, and that goes for interpretations of what is going on around you as well.

Think about a time you were angry and then said something you regret. The cause of anger is not so important here. When you were angry, did you misinterpret something the other person had said? For example, imagine you were already really angry about something that happened. You then did something wrong. It does not have to be some huge, egregious mistake, but could be something as simple as you put the garbage into the recycling bin accidentally, and your spouse called you out. He did not say anything mean or use a rude tone or anything. He simply said, "You mixed up the trash and recycling."

That was enough to set you off. Already angry, you went into a tirade about why he has to say that you are too stupid to take out the garbage correctly, ranting and raving about how awful he is to you and that if you cannot do it right, maybe he should do it instead. After the fact, you may be confused about what possibly could have caused you to think that way, especially when your spouse simply pointed out a mistake without any sort of judgment or harm meant.

The answer is that you were interpreting undertones that were not there due to your state of being angry at that moment. You were already upset about something else, and when your spouse challenged you, or you felt as though you were being challenged, you lost it. It was the final straw that broke the camel's back, and it was a gross misinterpretation.

Frustrated, you thought what he said was a dig, and you filled in the blanks. Clearly, he was implying you were dumb, you told yourself at that moment, and you went off on him.

This kind of reaction is all too common with people who struggle with self-regulation. You may struggle to interpret things accurately when emotions are coloring your perspective on everything. Instead, you should focus on changing your interpretations at the moment. This will help you drastically as you attempt to learn to control yourself.

This can be done through repetition. If you must, come up with some sort of mantra or affirmation to trigger you to stop and look at the situation objectively. Remember how you were suggested to use a hair tie around your wrist to trigger yourself to quiet yourself? You want something like that—some sort of reminder for your brain to stop the path it is on and reanalyze the situation. Let's use the hair tie example again here.

Whenever you feel as though you are going to react negatively in an already charged environment, snap your wrist with the hair tie. Take a moment to stop, take a deep breath, and run your interpretation of what was said by yourself one more time. Ask yourself if it is really an accurate interpretation or if you are reading into it too much. It is entirely possible and plausible that you added an undertone that was not there nor intended to be there, especially if what was said was innocuous.

Let's play the scene between you and your spouse again but using the trigger to reinterpret what happened.

You get home from work, angry about what had happened at the end of your day. You go inside, grab the trash and recycling, and take it out. Your spouse came to greet you and sees you as you accidentally mix up both bags, putting the garbage into the recycling bin and the recycling into the garbage. As you go back inside, your spouse points out the mistake with the same direct phrasing: "You mixed up the trash and recycling."

You immediately feel the anger at the accusation, and as you open your mouth to retaliate, you stop, snap your wrist with the hair tie a couple of times, and think for a moment. Your spouse did not say anything cruel, nor frustrated, nor demeaning. Your spouse pointed out a simple mistake with no judgment. Your spouse was not implying you were stupid, although you may have felt dumb at the moment for making such a simple mistake. You realize that, between already being frustrated and then feeling dumb from the mistake, you were putting words into your spouse's mouth instead of saying thank you and fixing things.

This sort of stop and reanalyze can be repeated with any sort of negative reaction. It is an essential skill to have and is the first step toward managing your own emotions. When you can stop yourself from responding inappropriately, you will be far more likely to manage things in an appropriate manner. You will not yell at someone out of frustration. You will not damage relationships with other people. You will instead be able to get through your life managing yourself appropriately.

Practical Test

1. How do you turn your emotions into emotional intelligence?
2. Why do you think it is helpful?
3. Which tip is most helpful for you?

CHAPTER 47:

Master Of Control

People have specific ways of processing and dealing with the negative emotions they feel. Some choose to avoid them; others choose to deny them. Some people choose to play the victim card by trying to make their misery seem bigger than anyone else's. It's not uncommon for the latter group to say something like this: "You think your life is miserable? You don't even know half of what I've been through." There is, however, one group of individuals who succeed. They are the ones who choose to learn from their emotions and find better-coping strategies. They are the ones who successfully overcome their unhappiness because they choose to learn from their emotions. They have realized that only they have the power to change the way they feel.

No emotion is going to be stronger than your desire for change. The moment you decide to change is the moment change happens. You start to bring about a shift in your emotions when you decide you want to turn things around. Let's go back to emotional intelligence again really quick and see how the core pillars are going to help you as you learn to masterfully control your anger, depression, and anxiety. To recap, the five core pillars of emotional intelligence are:

- Self-awareness
- Self-regulation
- Empathy
- Motivation

- Social skills.

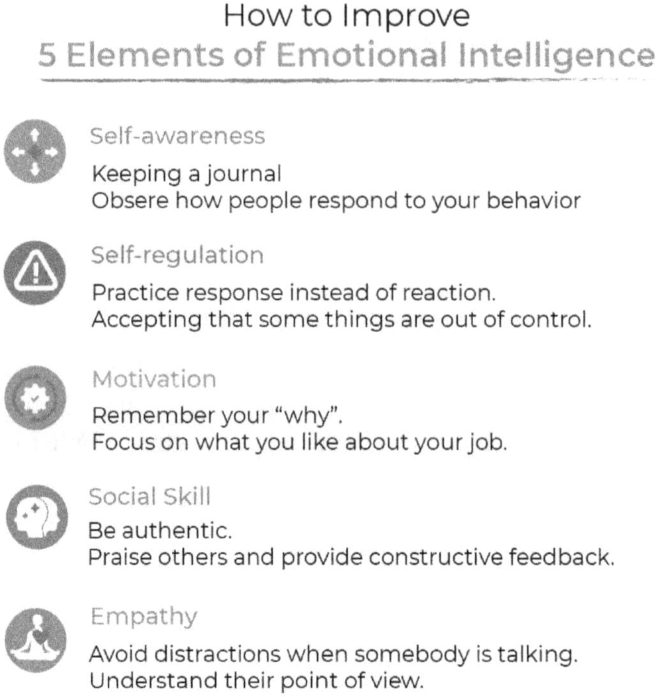

Each pillar now plays a specific role that is essential in changing your perception and the way you view and handle things that happen in your life. Masterful control through emotional intelligence happens when:

- **You Develop a Greater Sense of Self-Awareness -** By far the most important pillar out of the entire five, self-awareness is the foundation that sets the standard for the other four pillars. Particularly when it comes to conquering your emotions. To be so aware of your emotions and the way that it affects you as well as the people around you is a skill that not a lot of people have mastered because it's not as easy as it sounds. On paper, it does but put it into practice, and you'll see what a challenge it can be to shift your emotions if you don't understand what it is that you're feeling.

- **You Learn to Be Assertive -** Anxiety and depression, for example, can cause many people to be wary of or afraid of their emotions. As such, they have difficulty expressing and asserting the way they feel. Emotional intelligence encourages awareness about the way you feel, and to regulate your emotions enough, so they don't have to feel more powerful than you are. You are stronger than any emotion that you feel.
- **You Respond More Than You React -** Responding negatively results in subsequent negative reactions, leading to anxiety, negativity, chronic worry, and of course, depression. Emotional intelligence is the necessary skill needed to stay calm in any stressful situation. By being aware of your emotions and regulating them in the way that is needed, you're able to mitigate your reactions by refraining from impulsive decisions. Before you respond to anything that you go through with immediate anxiety and negativity as your default reaction, think about the situation rationally. Is it really as bad as it seems? 90% of the time, things feel a lot worse than they really are because of the way we choose to respond. By learning to respond without reacting, you're assessing the situation internally and acknowledging the way you feel, but on the outside, you try to maintain and calm and cool composure without giving away how you feel. This gets easier to do with emotional intelligence, which gives you the capacity to (even in your highly emotional state) to understand the consequences of your actions.

- **How to Master and Control Anger**

You can hold a grudge for years because of your anger. You know people whom you have not spoken to for a very long time because you still feel anger towards them. You find yourself having dangerous suicidal thoughts, perhaps even have tendencies of violence. You are unable to express your anger appropriately, choosing instead to keep it buried inside. Your anger is preventing you from living a meaningful, happy life. You constantly find yourself feeling disgruntled, irritated, and frustrated more than you are happy, and even the smallest of instances could set you off because of it. You're verbally, emotionally (sometimes even physically) abusive towards others around you. You find that it spills over not just into your personal life, but professional life as well. Any of these scenarios sound familiar to you? If yes, then it's entirely possible you've got an anger problem that you need to now learn how to control.

If you think anger is only a problem when it's violent temper tantrums and shouting matches, think again. Repressed anger can be just as much of a problem. This unexpressed anger works the same way as a volcano does. It bubbles and boils under the surface until one day when something sets you off, all that repressed anger just comes shooting out with catastrophic consequences. Anger, which is not expressed or shown, is just as bad as anger, which is blatantly displayed. Either way you spin it, anger is a very real problem that can't be ignored any longer. Not if you want to become a true master of your emotions, at least.

Controlling your anger is not about suppression. Suppression is not the goal. The goal here is to learn how to control that anger, to understand why you are reacting the way that you are. To learn how to respond better without jumping to anger as your first immediate reaction. To be able to effectively handle situations that would have normally aggravated you without losing control. That is the goal of learning how to control your anger. Denying your anger issues is one of the WORST things you could do. More importantly, it will not help you learn to control it.

Facing your less than desirable qualities may not be something that you want to do but living in denial and ignoring it never solved anything either. The more you deny your emotions and anger issues, the worst it will be for you when it comes to managing it. A more likely scenario is you find yourself feeling angrier and losing your temper even more because you feel helpless and unable to control the situation.

Mastering your angry emotions, like everything else, comes down to the right coping techniques and skills to get the situation (your emotions) under control. To effectively do that, you need to:

- **Look At The Root Reason -** Anger always stems from something. There is always a cause and a trigger. Your childhood, a last traumatic experience, your role models growing up, your stress levels. All these things add up and could build towards anger problems. To begin learning how to control your anger, you must first explore and connect with the core reason anger is your first line of response is how you to control it. Did you know that your anger is very often a response that is meant to cover-up other feelings that you may have? That is why exploring the root reason is the only way to treat the problem at its core. What are those feelings? Jealousy? Embarrassment? Hurt? Shame? Insecurity? These are some of the reason you need to think about. When was the last time you asked yourself: "Why am I REALLY angry?"
- **Distract, Don't React -** Anger is such a disruptive emotion. It causes a lot of hurt, pain, trauma, and worse, physical hurt at times. All common sense just seems to go out the window in the heat of the moment. Distract instead of reacting is not always easy, but it does get better with practice. Instead of choosing to act on your emotions, deflect your attention elsewhere until you've forgotten about what it was that was threatening your temper. You

need to distance yourself from your emotions for as long as it takes until you are properly distracted enough to forget what it was you were about to feel angry about.

- **Think Happy Thoughts, Do Happy Things -** Peter Pan may have got it right when he said: "Think happy thoughts." People who struggle with anger issues have a lot of misery and unhappiness inside them. How can you learn to control your anger if you're still harboring all that negativity inside you? There's nothing better at getting rid of all those unhappy, miserable feelings than to very simply think about and do something that makes you happy. Indulge in a passion or a hobby, throw yourself into an activity that you love. A happier state of mind makes it easy to think with a clearer head, you don't get as worked up so easily anymore, and it becomes much easier to learn how to control your anger issues.

- **Emotional Journaling -** It may not be for everyone, but when it comes to controlling your anger issues, it can be very therapeutic. One of the challenges when it comes to anger is that you're so overwhelmed with all sorts of emotion (anger, frustration, irritation) that it all comes out all at once. A lot of people tend to strike out or lash out in anger because they don't have proper channels or outlets to release that anger unto. This is where a journal comes in handy. It gives you a safe and private place where you can express every feeling and emotion you have without the fear of being ridiculed or judged. Even better, it is possible the safest outlet for you to release your feelings of anger with repercussions, without hurting anyone or yourself in the process.

Practice 4 steps of meditation for easy anger management

Meditation helps you control your emotions both in the moment of anger and in the long term. To meditate in the moment of anger, first remove yourself from the situation causing the anger.

1. Take slow, deep breaths to bring down your elevated heart rate.
2. Breathe deep enough that your belly extends on the "in" breath.
3. Visualize a golden-white light filling your body as you breathe in.
4. When you breathe out, visualize muddy or dark colors leaving your body.
5. Once calm, think about your emotions.
6. Practice daily meditation.
7. Decide how to deal with the situation that angered you.

Practical Test

1.Why is it important to master your emotions?

2. Do you think that when you are in control of your emotions you are already mastering it as well?

3. What emotion is the hardest for you to control and master?

CHAPTER 48:

How to Be Mentally Strong

If you wish to live your best life at every point of your life, you must find ways to build your mental strength, as it is essential to helping you live a good life. Just the way you work out to stay fit and develop your physical muscles, you have to also pay attention to your mental health by employing the use of mental tools and techniques.

Reaching the highest level of mental health will enable you to keep doing the things you love and build meaningful relationships with others. It will also help you to work on your self-esteem. A mentally strong person will not be afraid of taking risks, trying out new things, or coping with any type of tough situation that he/she comes across in life.

To have a healthy mind, you will first have to work on your mental strength. This is something that you can easily work on as an individual over a period of time by making a conscious effort to make your personal development your priority.

In the same way, you will notice physical results from going to the gym and staying on a healthy diet, and you also have to cultivate good mental habits like being more appreciative if you must reap the fruits of mental health. To begin to reap these physical gains, you must also abandon your bad habits like feeling sorry for yourself and the likes.

Everyone can become mentally stronger, and this is a very important part of the continuous exercise of your mental muscles. This is the same thing that happens when you work out to build your physical muscles.

To successfully set goals and achieve them, you have to first work on your mental strength because it is never easy to achieve your goals.

Hence when things become difficult, you will have the necessary discipline to keep going. Mental strength will also boost your ability to continue to make the best choices to achieve your goals. You should always be aware of the fact that you cannot sacrifice the things you want for momentary pleasures.

The fact that you are mentally strong does not mean that you have to live a difficult life or face difficult situations. You are going to learn a few tips on building your mental strength by engaging in some physical exercises to help you uphold those beliefs and habits.

In order to build your mental strength, one of the best things you can do is to find habits and little tips that you can practice throughout your day to maintain a high level of energy. This will help you to maintain a positive mindset and arm you with skills that will help you to forge ahead and help you maintain a good feeling about your daily activities while you are still improving on your mental strength in a way that will not become drained or overwhelmed.

With the following tips, you will be able to improve your mental strength and ultimately, achieve your goals:

- **Find Healthy Ways of Dealing with the Emotions You Are Not Comfortable with**

Attaching names to your emotions is only the beginning of the battle, as you will also require healthy skills that will enable you to control your emotions. Consider your present coping machinery and ask yourself some valid questions.

Do you sweat when you get nervous? Do you drink water to calm your nerves? Do you throw anger tantrums when you are angered—or do you simply curl up to your bed when you get anxious? Though these reactions can make you feel better for a moment, you will feel worse after some time. By finding ways of dealing with these habits, you will be able to relieve yourself of the tension that comes with these emotions.

Find the best ways to cope with these emotions in the long term. They should be ways in which you can manage these emotions without causing any harm to your health, relationships, or goals in the long run. Always remember that things work for different people differently. What works for your friend may not always work for you, so you have to find the one that works for you.

Try out different coping mechanisms and figure out the one that works for you. You can try mindfulness, deep breathing, reading, singing, taking time out to retreat, or just taking a walk. There are different strategies that you may find useful.

- **Find Out Your Unhealthy Thought Patterns, and Replace Them with Healthy Ones**

As you already know, your thoughts have a tremendous effect on your actions. If you occupy your mind with negativity, you are going to act accordingly, and it will reflect on your mental strength.

Be attentive to the way you think. You are going to observe that there's a common theme in your thought patterns. It may be that you usually talk yourself into shying away from doing scary things, or you manage to convince yourself that someone else, like your spouse or parents, are in control of your life.

You should meet those unproductive or unreasonable thoughts with things that will help you more. Instead of thinking that you are not going to succeed, think about it as your time to show the world what you are capable of, so you are going to put in your best. By switching the kind of conversations, you have with yourself, you will arm yourself with the most important things you need to become successful.

- **Take a More Positive Stance or Action**

Changing your attitude is your best bet to training your mind to see things differently and think differently. Try your hands out on difficult things and continue to do them even when it may look like you can't.

This will prove, first to yourself that you are stronger than you think and will also show the world that you are strong.

Form daily healthy habits that will boost your productivity. Be more grateful, do more exercise, and sleep well. Eating healthy will also do your brain and body a lot of good. All of these will optimize your body to be at its best.

You should also reach out to people that will motivate you to be the best version of yourself and find or create an environment that will contribute to your efforts in building a healthy lifestyle.

- **Give Up the Bad Things That Kill Your Mental Muscle**

Though you may have several good habits, they are not going to help you if you are still holding on to some other bad and unhealthy habits. It is like stocking up on calories when you are trying to lose weight.

You should focus on those bad habits that are hurting your mental strength. You can trust that everyone has those habits. It may either be that you are always feeling sorry for yourself, or you are never happy about the successes of others, or you are easily stuck at one point in your life.

As soon as you have been able to note these bad habits of yours, you can then focus all of your energy on replacing them with some other healthy options. By so doing, you will be able to get out of the recurrent circle and move further towards your goals.

- **Reflect on the Past, Live and Enjoy the Moment, and Make Plans for the Future**

People who are mentally strong do look back at the things that have happened in the past and learn from the experiences or let me say, honor the experiences. While they do this, they ensure that they don't get mentally stuck in the past, even if those times were their best. This is because they are well aware of the fact that the heavyweight of the past is capable of making the soul age.

Those who are mentally strong understand the importance of the moment because they know that there is no more precious time than the present as it is all they have. This is one of the reasons why they practice mindfulness.

- **Take Calculated Risks**

To be mentally strong, you have to be prudent. Always have a plan for everything and all your days. You should make an estimate of your options and point out the possible consequences of your actions. This is the only way you can make intelligent choices.

This doesn't mean that you cannot have big dreams; neither does it mean that you have to give up on difficult worthy endeavors. Rather, what it means is that you have to prepare your mind to go high and beyond because you have built your mind to overcome obstacles and achieve the much-needed goals. You should take risks but try not to be reckless in taking those risks. Be aware of the fact that everything that you do has consequences, so you should be conscious of your actions.

- **Note the Positive Parts of Every Challenge**

Your success in life depends largely on your perspective. If you can change your perspective, you will be able to change your life also. Rather than brooding over your losses and getting angry over them or being disappointed and having negative self-talk about your challenges or the ones ahead, you should come up with positive mental energy.

This can be done by simply jotting down the good part of your tasks, which are the things you should be grateful for. They are also the lessons you can take from the challenges. Also, find out if there are things that you should be grateful for daily.

Engage in Mindful Happiness

Always try to live in the moment by being comfortable with your happiness. This can be done by practicing mindful happiness. Simply think about those times when you felt fulfilled, or when you felt good about yourself and at peace with yourself. Hold on to that feeling and savor it all the time.

Try to take note of the way your body reacts to this feeling and how your thoughts suddenly change with the feeling. Your body will also change with this feeling. Now, ponder on the general feeling that comes with it. You should always spend time with this happy mood and carry it along with you.

You should keep in mind that this feeling of joy and happiness emanates from you, which means that it is always lurking within you, and it can always rear its head when you want it to. The only thing you need to do is to stay mindful at the moment.

Practical Test:

1. Why is being mentally strong important?
2. Do you think being positive at all times is a sign that you are mentally strong?
3. What is the most positive part of being mentally strong?

CHAPTER 49:

Changing Emotions with Behavior

Remember how your thoughts impact feelings, which impact behavior? In this step, you will be focusing on how to change your emotions by changing your behavior. Behaviors can be tricky to overcome, especially if you have become habituated into them, but it is possible. You can learn how to control your behaviors in order to manage your emotions if you take a little bit of time to do so.

Have you ever heard of the Stanford prison experiment? It was done with two groups of undergraduate students that were selected at random for an experiment. Some were chosen to be prison guards and others were chosen to be prisoners. They were all placed into a basement of a building that was turned into a pretend prison and watched to see what would happen naturally when some people were given the false idea of authority and others were told that they had none. It was entirely voluntary, and people did not have to participate. They could leave if they desired to do so. They could discontinue if they desired to do so.

It is important to note that of these prisoners and prison guards, none had actually done anything wrong, nor had any of them ever earned a job as a prison guard. There was no real authority or revocation of rights that comes with incarceration. Despite the fact that there was no real power holding anyone there, within days, the prison guards were acting aggressively, humiliating some of the prisoners simply because they could whereas prisoners were becoming depressed and were quite passive, obeying whatever they were told with no regard to the fact that there was nothing keeping them locked up there. They did not exercise their freedom to leave. The prison guards grew increasingly cruel, enjoying their perceived authority that allowed them to demean their prisoners, even though just days prior, they had been peers and the only thing that had changed was that they were placed in a room together on different sides of the bars while some scientists told one group they were prisoners and the other that they were guards. The experiment was never finished—it had to be ended early because of how extreme it was becoming. Their environments were literally changing their emotions.

A toxic environment can leave you feeling negative and depressed. Conversely, a positive environment can leave you happy and relaxed. You can directly influence your emotions by changing your environment or behaviors. You can trick yourself into feeling certain ways. You can change your emotional state by forcing yourself into a calming one. You can agitate yourself by completing other behaviors. Ultimately, your behaviors are quite indicative of the emotional state that will follow.

One specific theory of emotions, the James-Lange theory, posits that emotions are the last in a sequence of events. First, there must be a stimulus, then a physical response, followed by a mental interpretation, and ultimately, those three things combine to create the emotion. Using this theory of emotion, then, you should be able to see how you can influence your own emotions.

If you want to behave in a relaxed manner, take deep, calming breaths, no matter what the stimulus you are faced with is. If you physically go through the actions of feeling calm, you can essentially fool your mind into feeling as though you are relaxed.

You can see the effects of this frequently with treatment of anxiety—people going through anxiety attacks are given medication to take if necessary, but they are also given tools and tasks, such as taking deep breaths, reminding themselves that they are okay, and relaxing their bodies to stop the feelings of anxiety that were lastly overwhelming them. The ways in which we act can be incredibly powerful.

Changing Emotion with Behavior

Consider the James-Lange theory provided, and you are left with the following sort of equation that equals emotions:

Stimulus + Physical Response + Interpretation = Emotion

This can be manipulated to your benefit. You could use this to break some sort of negative emotional habits, such as growing angry and yelling, which only makes you grow angrier or to end a phobia through exposure and reminders that you are safe and okay along with deep breaths and plenty of patience. The potential is nearly limitless; you can use your actions to change your emotions. All you have to do is change the physical response and the interpretation of that physical response in relation to whatever stimulus you are trying to alter your feelings about.

For example, imagine that you have gone through a divorce. The very sight of your ex-spouse during custody exchanges is enough to make your blood boil, and no matter what you do or what the context of seeing your ex-spouse is, you cannot help but be immediately enraged. Maybe he cheated on you or did something else that left such a significant impression on you that you feel the emotion immediately and overwhelmingly at the mere sight of him.

The following time you are to see your ex-spouse, you should prepare yourself. When you see him, you will take a deep breath. You will stand up tall and straight. You will loosen your shoulders. You will calmly look him in the eyes. You will not raise your voice. You will not tense up. You will keep your breathing even, deep and slow, counting to four between breaths if you have to. Prepare yourself with a list of what it is that you will do the following time you have to exchange custody. After all, you know that your children seeing you hating their father is unhealthy and you do not want to do that to them.

The following time you are there, then, you should attempt to do all of the above. It will be difficult. You will absolutely be fighting against your gut reactions linked to your hatred for the man that betrayed you, but as you do so, you will find yourself gaining control of the situation and yourself. You will be able to guide yourself into a calm state in which you can control yourself.

You can tweak your emotions other ways as well, though the most frequent one is typically a state of agitation, fear, or sadness into a state of relaxation and levelheadedness that allows you to further analyze your situation and setting in order to act appropriately. You can trigger states of joy or happiness through exercise, utilizing the endorphins. Or you can trigger patience through breathing and body language.

Changing Emotion with Environment

Your environment has a huge impact on your mood as well, particularly if you are empathetic. You draw on the mood around you and feed off of it—if the mood is tense and apprehensive, you are bound to absorb that apprehension as well. You will be afraid of the environment if you feel that it is dangerous. You will be sad in an environment filled with others that are sad.

This is why it is so incredibly important to be mindful of the kinds of company you keep. You need to keep good company that is kind to you and respectful if you want to keep a happy mood. If you want to be calm and relaxed, feeling confident in your surroundings, you need to be in an environment that is conducive to exactly that—calm and relaxation. Your body will be clued in on how to behave based on how others are behaving. You will calm down when the body language of others says that there is nothing to be afraid of. You will feel energized if those around you appear to be energized as well.

If you want to change your emotions, you should stop to look at your environment. Is it strict? Is it harsh and uncomforting? Do you feel loved or safe? If you cannot answer that you are happy and comfortable in your relationship, it is time to consider removing yourself from the toxic environment.

Toxic environments only breed more toxicity. Negative environments only breed negativity. It is okay to cut that negativity and toxicity out of your life, no matter how familiar or comfortable it is. Your mental health will thank you for it if you do so.

Further, if you want to influence your mood to be happier and energized, you should surround yourself with good energy. Surround yourself with good friends. Put on some energetic music that gets you in the mood to move. You are far more likely to enjoy yourself if the environment around you is conducive to enjoying it.

Ultimately, you will have to recognize that your emotions are linked to your environment. Your emotions will almost always reflect whatever environment you have surrounded yourself with, and that is okay. However, if you are in a toxic environment, you owe it to yourself and your loved ones to fix that. You do not have to put up with toxic individuals, even if they are family. You are well within your rights to end a relationship from someone, familial, romantic, or platonic if you feel as though it is a toxic environment that needs to be left.

Remember, just as you can grow a plant virtually anywhere, you will likely survive virtually anywhere. You will be able to get by while surrounded by toxicity. But you will not thrive. Just as some plants will grow but not thrive out of their elements, you will get through life alive, but not the best you can be. The best way to be the best you is to find the environment in which you belong. It is out there somewhere, although it may take some persistence to locate.

While on the topic of environments, if you are being abused in any way or feel unsafe at home, there are resources for you that can help you escape. Please look up your local domestic violence hotline if you do not feel safe and ask for help. No matter how difficult it may feel for you, you can get out alive and flourish somewhere you are meant to grow instead of being stunted and barely surviving somewhere toxic.

Practical Test:

1. How does your thoughts impact your emotions?

2. How does your emotions impact your behavior?

3.How do you balance the three of them?

CHAPTER 50:

You Can Deny Your Feelings but You Can't Eliminate Them

Emotional intelligence shapes your thoughts and actions to enable you to have control over your behavior as well as develop to handle it more effectively. With good levels of emotional intelligence, you will increase the way you identify and handle your emotions as well as how you react to the feelings of others. By becoming more emotionally stable, it allows us to grow and gain a comprehensive understanding of which we are, and this allows us to communicate better with others and sustain stronger relationships. The following steps will give a good beginning point to discover the pillars of your emotional intelligence.

- **Practice noting how you feel**

Let us take an example where you have a loan to service and the business you invested the loan is not doing well.

You are now working more than 15 hours a day to make extra income to sustain your lifestyle and also save some to service the loan. Due to frequent burnouts, you sometimes scream at your children when they play music at full volume. At the grocery store, you are easily irritated when the seller mixes up the groceries you selected. When driving home, you tend to experience road rage wondering how some drivers got their driving license. In essence, your lifestyle is taking a toll on your emotional intelligence.

Under these circumstances, it is important that your busy lifestyle makes it easy for you to lose touch with emotions. For you to reconnect, you should set a timer for different points during the day. As soon as the timer goes off, take a few deep breaths and observe how you feel emotionally. Then, focus on what emotion manifests as a physical feeling in your body and what the perception of the feeling is. You will note that the more you practice, the more the feeling becomes second nature. One can also use other ways to reconnect with your feelings such as keeping a journal of how you feel at various times of the day.

- **Interrogate your opinions**

Still, on our example, you have formed an opinion of your workers as impatient because of the conversations you have had with fellow businesspersons on how new employees have unrealistic expectations. Your opinion on your employees has been reinforced by a Facebook post that you did and most of the commentators agreed that new employees are highly impatient individuals. The advisable way to be emotionally intelligent in these scenarios is to question your opinions, especially how objective your opinions are. Another way to help you question your opinions is to practice empathy as it requires you to temporarily drop your premise of argument and conclusion.

- **Become accountable to your feelings**

Assume that you tend to justify why you scream to your employees because they do not understand how costly it is to run the business. You also justify your road rage by arguing that some drivers never seem to adhere to all traffic rules. At home, you qualify your behavior to your children by arguing that they invited that reprimand for not being productive. In essence, you are avoiding being accountable for your feelings. You should be responsible for your feelings and state that you screamed because you are feeling overwhelmed by fears and demands due to the struggling business. Similarly, your other feelings are occasioned due to the demanding expectations from your creditors and unforgiving external factors that you feel hopeless about.

• Celebrate the positive emotions

Let us imagine that you have now started experiencing an increase in income and your relationship with your employees is improving. However, you are to celebrate these small improvements even though you feel relieved. Your excitement is held back by the worry that things may return to an earlier challenging state. In applying emotional intelligence, it is advisable to set time aside to celebrate positive emotions. Positive emotions are the desired emotions and you should allow them to manifest for the longest possible. Individuals that experience positive emotions tend to be more resilient and have more satisfying relationships in life.

• Do not overlook the negative

We now assume that you are now focusing on the positive emotions by looking for happiness and hope within your challenging situations. Even though you feel anger and get worried when things stagnate, you quickly find a way to overlook the negative emotions. In line with emotional intelligence, what you are doing constitutes suppressing negative emotions, since they are undesired. Emotional intelligence requires that all emotions are acknowledged and expressed. Remember the argument that emotions are a form of energy and holding them up is counterproductive as you might get emotional outbursts or get overwhelmed by the emotions and act irrationally endangering yourself and the lives of others around you.

• Emotional intelligence is a lifetime process

Again, using our earlier illustration, one of your employees has asked you to consider seeking emotional intelligence training. Initially, you felt you are okay, but you welcome the idea and approach a psychotherapist to assist you in building your emotional intelligence. Unfortunately, you feel that what you are being taken through can be hurried because it appears obvious. You also want immediate improvement because time is of the essence. When you get home, you go online and try to combine as many lessons on emotional intelligence as you can to acquire most of the emotional intelligence. All your actions are well-intentioned but counterproductive. Emotional intelligence happens over time and it is a lifetime process. You should start by analyzing your weaknesses and focusing on the shortcomings fast. While addressing your weaknesses, start with few measures to rectify your weaknesses and expand gradually to attain an all-around improvement.

Look at yourself objectively

A common mistake that we make is to assume that we know ourselves when in essence, we do not. Using our series of one illustration, assume that you think that you are simply ambitious and there is no major weakness you have. By not welcoming the interrogation of yourself, especially your strengths and weaknesses, you are not helping matters as you cannot completely understand yourself. Understanding yourself means that you are evaluating and scoring yourself. Therefore, you need a comprehensive score guide to help you assess your strengths and weaknesses. One of the components of evaluating yourself is to seek feedback from those people that you frequently interact with. From the feedback given, examine the presence of any pattern and note them. Feedback is not condemnation or profiling; it is the impression you create through your behavior and actions.

- **Maintain a diary of your emotions and corresponding reactions**

Even though emotional reactions and behavior are diverse, they tend to occur within a predictable pattern. Now that you know yourself, start noting how you felt within specific situations and how you reacted. Ensure that writing down your emotions and subsequent reactions are consistent to help you develop a comprehensive view of your emotional intelligence. Where possible, you can request a partner or an employee or colleague to enable what they think were your emotions and matching reactions. Using these two diaries of your emotions, you will adequately classify your intelligence levels. Maintaining a diary is a way of generating self-feedback and also increasing self-awareness. Like any condition, understanding yourself is critical for an effective fix.

• Take time to understand what motivates you

Using our earlier series of one illustration, assume that you sometimes feel energized, and at other times, feel demotivated. Even though you sometimes feel energized, you cannot correctly pinpoint what motivates you. It could be several things or situations that cumulatively excite you. Understanding what motivates you will help you sustain the positive energy. For instance, accomplishing a project can be a source of motivation. In this case, you can increase motivation by splitting the project into modules that enable you to complete them successfully rather than having one entire undertaking. Losing motivation can lead to a cascade of frustrations. It is important that you identify what motivates you and seek to optimize motivation.

hours just to sit and do nothing other than assuring yourself that all is well.

• Learn to predict how you will feel

One effective way of handling your emotions is to learn to anticipate them and deploy all your mental strategies against them. The ability to anticipate your emotions should not imply that you try to block them. For instance, learn to think about a situation and predict how you will react if the outcome goes contrary to your expectations. With this knowledge, deploy your coping mechanism but remember to let the emotions manifest. The continued emphasis on letting all emotions express stems from our argument that emotions are a form of energy and should be allowed to dissipate to help restore mental status balance prior to the emotion.

• Remember you have a choice

At the end of everything, you have a choice on how you react to different situations. Even though it may appear beyond your control, you still have a choice in the manner that you are reacting. By recognizing that you have a choice, you will commit to internalizing and applying desirable choices. In other words, acknowledging that you have control over your emotional reactions, you will seek help on how to better handle them. For example, your reaction to an irritating situation is completely manageable if you seek ways to control your feelings. By learning to anticipate and manage the temper, you will completely control your reaction to irritating situations.

• Seek help

One of the most ignored areas of acquiring requisite emotional intelligence levels is to seek help. Becoming emotionally competent requires some reflection and adjustments, and external help is critical. Most individuals wrongly assume that on their account, they can manage personal challenges, which in essence, are emotional in nature. There are individuals that are better experienced than you are and may possess more skills than you are in managing temper. For this reason, you should actively seek help than suffering in solitude. It is through interaction with others that you will discover that you may not have known your strengths and weaknesses.

- **Walk your mind to the solution**

When facing a volatile emotion, ask yourself and write down what you are feeling, the options you have and what you truly want. Sometimes, learning of the outcome of your pending action can slow you down and help you manage the emotion better. For instance, you might be feeling angry and the options you have are to shout at the other person or tell the person that you are angry, and disappointment and you will engage them when you have calmed down.

Practical Test

1. What are the reasons why sometimes you deny your feelings?
2. How do you deal with your emotions?
3. What is the best way to see the positive side of every emotion?

CHAPTER 51:

Improving Conflict Resolution Skills

We all want to be able to manage a situation without any adverse outcome, or at least, with minimal negative consequences. But how many of us really can do that? How many times have you intervened at a situation and arrived at an amicable conclusion?

Conflicts trigger strong emotions in us, which, when we do not resolve correctly, results in hurt and disappointment, and this could lead to breaking relationships.

Conflicts are often a sign of healthy relationships. When you can share your view with another person even when they do not agree with you, it shows that the relationship is open, and the parties are open with each other. However, it is during conflicts that a lot of negative emotions arise. In battle, you become stressed, angry, fearful. Because of the high-voltage emotions, the chances of acting irrationally and in a way that damages the relationship are high. How, then, do you manage this delicate situation? How do you and the other party/parties get through this situation by maintaining the core of the relationship yet without being dishonest with each other just for civility?

So, how do you improve your conflict resolution skills?

Understand the conflict

During the conflict, it goes beyond just a disagreement. A battle stresses the body to see to it that there is a threat, even when there is none. So, to understand the conflict, be able to realize that the other person, just like you, are fearful and therefore, know that they do not have an issue with you.

So, take the time to know what caused the conflict? Were you on the wrong? If so, make a sincere apology? If your partner was on the wrong, you could bring them round in a respectful, non-condescending manner to their fault.

Throughout this process, it is essential to keep in mind that your problem is not with the other person, but rather, with an issue. So, avoid making remarks about the other person and instead, always ensure that you are speaking on the subject. So, rather than say "you are always hurting me', say instead "whatever you say always hurts me.' the second part brings attention to the person's utterances, rather than accuse them as a whole as is the first statement.

Understand the Needs of The Other Person

A second part of resolving a conflict is always to keep the other person in mind. With each back and forth, try to see their point of view. We all deserve to be respected and have our opinions considered. Therefore, to manage conflict better, always keep in mind the humanity of the other person. The understanding of other people is our role to humankind - to acknowledge the other person and their feelings, their needs, and their views. To see where they are coming from and why they see the world as they do, even when we do not agree with it.

Be Willing to Compromise

We all get the feeling of wanting to be right in a conflict. Thus, when the other person says something, you counter them with your hottake, the result then being that throughout the battle, none of you listens to the other. This emotive back and forth will most often result in resentment and will lead to further breakdown in communication.

To manage conflict better, is necessary that you listen to the other person, and they then listen to you, and the two of you come to a compromise that will take into account the views of the other person.

Compromising doesn't mean that you waver on your principles. Instead, it shows that you value the relationship and the needs of the other person.

However, also note when you become the only one compromising, or the one making the most significant compromises after a conflict. This one-sided compromise is a symptom of a toxic relationship. While it is challenging to split settlement down the middle in a way that satisfies both parties, you can make it better by making sure that none of you holds the heavy side of things during every conflict.

When you make winning an argument or being right a priority, you will then not be willing to listen to the other person, and this will break down the communication further.

Focus on the Conflict In Front of You

It is often tempting to throw in last encounters into a new conflict. You and the other person are arguing about whether or not to buy a new item, and then suddenly, you get a boost. "Remember that time you didn't (insert unrelated issue here)' you say. Suddenly, it devolves into the two of you just going on and on about an issue that wasn't part of the day's argument.

When we hold on to what was past, we become less able to make rational decisions. Rather than look to resolve the present conflict, we begin to dig deep into the past, trying to dig up something that will help you to win the argument or shut the other person up.

Be Willing to Let Go

Letting go can be a very delicate thing to do since you will often be conflicted as to whether you are making go or if you are sweeping the issue under the carpet.

But it is important to note that you should make a point of resolving the issue before you consider letting it go. You need to get to a situation where you can confidently answer "no' if you ask yourself if the problem still bothers you.

When you sweep things under the carpet, you will often still be bothered by them and would just be postponing them. So, to decide to let go, do so at a time when you are less angry or stressed and volatile. That will allow you to weigh the outcome of your decision rationally. If you still find yourself unable to let go, then you may not have resolved the issue.

Pick Your Battles

Not every potential conflict will need your input. When you become more in touch with your emotions, you will be able to know what is worth your effort and what is not.

Conflicts are high-stress situations and will drain you of your strength. So, it is key to then, engage in only those conflicts that will result in an improvement of your perspective, well-being, and better understanding.

A lot of the time, most of the conflict we may find ourselves getting into will not be worth it. In economics, there is a principle called the Pareto Principle. From this, came the belief that 20% of our actions shape 80% of the consequences. Using this rule, you will then realize that you should focus your efforts on conflicts and relationships that give you the best state of mind, the best instances for growth.

This rule will give you a peaceful state of mind as it will force you to sit down and try to identify what gives you great satisfaction as such, what requires your attention.

Relationship/Social Awareness

How do you tell if someone is saying what they mean when they aren't straightforward? How do you pry someone open when they aren't willing to be opened up?

In order to become emotionally intelligent and grow from the situations that you have faced; it is essential that you then channel your understanding of your emotional state also to understand the emotional being of the other person.

Social awareness is what allows us to develop relationships and maintain them.

When you make it a priority to understand the other person beyond the words that they speak, you will be able to gain a better understanding of them. So, how then, do you build social awareness?

Listen Keenly

Listening is one of those skills that, while important, is one that has hardly mastered. It is tough to listen, especially when you also have issues of your own going on. To relate well, or better with others, you must listen.

Listening allows you to hear, and the process then understands where the other person is coming from, how they see the world. Actively listening, which means repeating to the person what they say after they have said it, allows you to build a connection with the other person.

When you listen, you can put yourself in the other person's shoes, thus, understanding them better.

Be Aware of Non-verbal Cues

Psychologists say that we say a lot without speaking than we do speaking. But let us not dwell too much on whether this is true or not and instead, put ourselves in the situation where we do not feel comfortable expressing ourselves verbally. What do you often do?

If you are waiting for someone at a place where there are many other people, you may find yourself tapping impatiently at something, perhaps a table or the armrest of your chair. Or you may begin fiddling with something in your hands when you become anxious and restless.

We often send out these signals without our knowledge sometimes. Therefore, even when we say something that is in dissonance with our emotional state, our body language may betray us.

Thus, to build on your social awareness, be keen on what people are not saying. Look at how they carry themselves when they aren't speaking. Look at how they act when they cannot talk. Learning how to read these signals will help you become better at tailoring your message to match their state of being at the moment. So, you will try to make the anxious person relax by, say, cracking a joke before you proceed with your point.

When you show high awareness of people's actions during interactions, you will come across as someone who value them and what they say. This awareness will help you build a rapport faster with them. However, it is essential to note that you should do this expertly as you will come off as creepy if you are not careful. The key is to notice their non-verbal cues and interact with them in ways that make them feel the opposite of their reaction, all without making them feel watched.

Practical Test

1. Why does conflict arise?
2. How do you handle it?
3. Should you confront it directly or still pass time to think?

CHAPTER 52:

Healing Emotional Past

Each and every one of us has a past that is full of different experiences, many of which trigger various emotional responses. While some people seem to have an easy time navigating their memories without feeling triggered, others tend to find that their memories can create a huge amount of emotional turmoil for them. Others still find that their past creates emotional turmoil for them, but that they cannot always fully understand why or where their emotional turmoil is specifically rooted into. Learning how to heal your emotional past means that you can heal any painful memories that may be triggering certain emotional responses out of you every time you find yourself in a similar situation or recalling those memories. This way, you can stop experiencing intense emotional responses to your past experiences.

Dealing with your past and healing emotional experiences you have that are entangled with your past, can be a particularly challenging situation. Depending on what specifically you are healing, you might find yourself experiencing quite a bit of emotional distress in dealing with those particular memories. If you find yourself feeling especially triggered or experiencing true emotional distress as a result of your memories, it could be helpful for you to work with a therapist. Working with a therapist can help you sort through those memories in a safe, structured way that allows you to tap into them and heal them without creating more, or unnecessary distress for yourself.

While there are many ways for you to heal from your past, the biggest methods for healing your past include perspective, closure, and emotional release. These are the most important components of healing from your past so that those emotions are no longer so triggering for you. Let me show you how!

Recognize How the Past Is Affecting Your Present

When you really think about it, the past is not about the past at all. Although you may believe you are thinking about the past, and that your thoughts are rooted in the past, the truth is, your thoughts are happening in the present. This means that the problem is not with something that happened in the past, but with what is happening now, in the present. Any anger, hurt, or fear you are feeling as a result of your past are occurring right now, and it is your present moment experience that is keeping the past alive. This means that the problem is not in the past; it is in the present.

By removing your problem from the past and bringing it into the present, you release some of the powerlessness you may feel by believing that the problem is somehow far away from you. The truth is, the thought is very close to you, and it is affecting you right here and right now. You must bring your realization into the present problem, rather than the past problem, if you are going to be able to take back the power that you have over the situation to be able to heal from it.

Realize That Your Memories Are Not the Problem

Like the past is in the past and the problem is in the present, it is also important to realize that your memories themselves are not the problem. It is no longer the memory of what happened that is causing you pain, but it is the continuous remembering of that memory that is causing you pain. The sooner you can realize that the memory itself has no power or meaning, but the behaviors you are engaging in surrounding the memory do, the sooner you can reclaim your power surrounding the troubles you are dealing with from your past.

In realizing that your memories are not the problem, you realize that the goal is not to erase the memory, but to erase the behaviors you have around those memories. For example, the sticky thoughts you have that keep bringing that memory forward for you and causing you to relive it or find new reasons to be angry or hurt over it. The sooner you can release those sticky thoughts, the sooner you can stop giving those past memories any power. The best way to release the power the sticky thoughts have is to lose interest in them. Stop feeling like they mean anything, or like they are worth your time or attention. Instead, let them go.

Let Yourself Grow Tired of the Past Affecting Your Present

One particularly powerful way that you can release the impact that your past has on your presence is to grow fed up with how your past is affecting you. Getting annoyed by how your past continues to hold you back can motivate you to find ways to let it go because, quite frankly, you are done with it! You are no longer attached to the feelings of sadness, anger, pain, or anything else. Instead, you are tired of feeling those emotions, and you are ready to be rid of them altogether.

The best way to let yourself grow tired of the past affecting you anymore is to become as willing as possible to get annoyed with the past affecting your present. Become willing to see through the memories and to see them being released, because you are tired of how they are holding you back. Then, watch how this willingness transforms into a mental and emotional capacity to truly release your feelings so that you can begin to feel free from your past experiences.

Take Full Responsibility for Yourself and Your Life Now

Experiences that happened in your past might have not been your fault, but healing is certainly your responsibility. What this means is that you need to recognize that you are the one who is continuing to think the thoughts that are hurting you, and you are the one that is continuing to engage in behaviors that may be causing you to relive the pain from the past. This does not mean that you should become angry with yourself, or that you should try to simply "turn off" the thoughts and feelings, but it does mean that you should take responsibility for finding ways to release those thoughts and feelings.

For many people, realizing that their inner landscape is their responsibility, and that they need to be the ones to fix that landscape if they do not like what they see, is incredibly empowering. You will likely find that you feel a greater sense of freedom and emotional release in realizing that you have the power to shift how you are feeling and what those feelings are creating. You can choose to get into the root of what is causing your problems, to resolve those root problems, and to begin experiencing greater happiness inside of yourself.

Change Your Beliefs About Healing

If you have specific beliefs about healing that are not serving your ability to heal, it may be time for you to change those beliefs. Beliefs about healing often revolve around the idea that certain things need to happen in order for healing to happen, or that healing has to look a certain way in order to count. This, however, is not true. If you believe that you are justified in staying stuck because you were wronged, that it is someone else's responsibility to make you feel better, that letting go approves that person's behavior, that you require an apology to heal, or that it is impossible for you to heal, you are holding yourself back. Likewise, if you believe that healing looks like you go back to the way you were before the hurt happened, or that you can simply forget about that hurt and move on, you are holding yourself back.

Focus on shifting your beliefs so that you can believe in your capacity to heal, and so that you can develop an idea of what healing looks like that will be more attainable for you. For example, believe that you can choose to begin healing right now, no matter what has happened or has not happened, and that in order to truly heal, all you need to do is find peace with the past, and with the experiences you are having because of the past. By shifting your beliefs to this, it becomes easier for you to achieve healing because you open up the path for you to pursue it, and you allow healing itself to become an achievable goal.

Find Peace, Not Happiness

Dwelling on what happened in the past is sure to cause more pain in your present. Likewise, stuffing the past down and trying to pretend it never existed is going to cause more pain in your present. Both of these forms of "dealing with" the past is incomplete and will lead to you having negative experiences as a result of your past. Rather than dwelling or denying the past, you need to be willing to find peace with the past. This means that you do not sit and stew on it, but you also do not shove it away or try to stuff it down if topics from your past come up. Instead, you find a position where you think about it only when it is necessary and thinking about it does not bring up any pain or discomfort for you.

In order to allow yourself to find this middle way of being able to release the pain of the past without dwelling on it or denying it, you need to be willing to start working with your thoughts around the subject of your past. CBT would be a great modality to use here, as it will allow you to redirect your thoughts as needed, while still allowing you the capacity to tap into them if you find it is necessary at any given point.

Use the Past as a Self-Discovery Tool

While the past is something that you do not want to dwell on, spending time reflecting on the past can be an incredibly helpful activity for you to engage in. Regularly reflecting on the past allows you to recognize who you are, including your patterns, your strengths and weaknesses, your stories, and more. This way, you allow yourself the opportunity to understand who you are, have compassion for yourself, and work with yourself, rather than against yourself, when it comes to achieving growth in your life.

People who refrain from digging into the past to understand who they are in the present often find themselves experiencing confusion around who they truly are. It can be easy to deny parts of yourself or pretend certain aspects don't exist or are unexplainable if you are unwilling to acknowledge the past and use it to your benefit. Allowing yourself to indulge in understanding how the past has affected who you are today, and how you can use that to identify probable healing routes, is a powerful way to transform your experience with the past. It can also transform the way you approach problems in the future, giving you the chance to approach them in a far more meaningful and fulfilling manner.

Practical Test

1. Why do you think the past have a big impact on the present?
2. How do you handle things that triggers you from your emotional past experiences?
3. Why should you find peace at all times?

Conclusion

Take a deep breath. How are you feeling? We have done a lot of work, and you should have quite a garden after mastering your emotions through all this. What are you going to do when you are finished reading this? I hope you practice and continue the process. What are you going to do every morning you get up? You're going to water your flowers. Look in the mirror and tell yourself, "I am worth it." You aren't going to spend any more of your life in the dark – you are going to keep that light on. When you start to feel tension in your neck and body, caused by stress, it's your body telling you it's time to take a break – from work or stress. Play some music. Go outside. Pet a dog.

What else can you do when you begin to feel anxious and scared? Here are some suggestions. Look for a stress ball; squeeze it and count how many times you need to squeeze it to bring you outside your head. And what do we do when we encounter barriers while climbing our mountains? We're going to throw the rocks impeding our access, sending them down the slope behind us. We are going to listen to our internal mediator, calm our instigator, and say balanced. We are going to write down our worries and put them away for another day; because by then they'll probably have disappeared. And we're going to spend more time outside or face-to-face with friends and less time on our phones.

You have already taken the first step – you chose to read this because you want to succeed – you want to be balanced and calm. Because of the way our brains work, emotions happen so suddenly you can't possibly stop them, or even delay them. But we can notice them and identify what exactly we are feeling and how often we feel this way. We might not always get it right, because sometimes processing emotions and trauma can take years after an event, but just because you can't do it always doesn't mean you shouldn't try. And if you can do it without medication, so much the better.

When you feel like all is lost and you just want to clock out of this life, I want you to look around. I want you to observe, to see if there is anything at all that is bright or warm -- maybe a light, book cover, a chair, wall design, car, art on the wall, or even just look outside for anything green. The blue sky. You're not alone and I am trying to get your mind to find something that will take your mind off this negativity, which is dark. You can hold on to something besides your phone -- a blanket, a pillow, or maybe you have a favorite pen or journal that helps. Once you do this, close your eyes after observing whatever it was that was bright or warm and think of that color and only that color. Not what the object is, just its color. Breathe slowly in through your nose, out through your mouth and count in your head to five but don't stop breathing slow breaths. Imagine where you would love to be after you're done counting.

Don't think of where you are but where you want to be. Keep your eyes closed for a bit, then open them slowly. Keep breathing. After you open your eyes, go for a walk outside, even if it's cold -- grab a jacket and think about where you were mentally; don't think about when, but how you're going to get there. Try this the following time you experience this feeling of wanting to end it; write down the outcome and if it worked you can refer to it. Not knowing what is going to happen can be scary, especially when you are one who wants to be in control of situations around you and that involve you but knowing leaves no room for surprise. Surprises bring happiness. You don't want to feel vulnerable; you don't want to lose -- who does? But that's when you learn balance, which is what we have been chasing throughout this.

Enough of the negative. Let's look at the happy list. For all the items on your list, find bright, colorful, joyful pictures of those things; print them out or cut them from magazines – above each picture, write the item from your happy list. Make it big and bold letters, so you can see it even from across the room. Underneath or on the back, write down why these particular things make you happy – what are the emotions or feelings each of these things bring to your life? Staple them together into a book.

Take the sad, angry and stressful lists and crumple them up, but don't tear them – they should still be readable. On the stress list, take a black Sharpie□ and scribble all over it. Take the angry list and tear it to shreds, although the pieces should be big enough to put back together. With tape, put the angry list back together.

Take these pieces of crumpled, torn and scribbled-on paper and add them to your book. The crumbled pieces are your sad times – the wrinkles reflect how worn-down sadness can make you.

If this doesn't work, try to picture your happy place in your mind and put yourself in it. Or take out your happy thoughts book and page through those colorful pictures of the things that make you happy. read the captions that remind you why they make you happy.

If you can't chase the negative away, try distracting it. When you feel sad or angry, and none of these actions works to make you feel better, start naming as many states and capital cities as you can, rapidly. By the time you have names about a dozen, you should have sent those negative thoughts back to the dark where they belong.

Let's practice. Close your eyes and clench your fists. Count to three and clench those fists harder. Visualize something that makes you angry: maybe a friend betrayed you, or you were passed over for a promotion you deserved, did someone say something hurtful about your family? Or did your car get dinged in the parking lot, and the jerk who hit you didn't even leave a note? Whatever it is, form a clear mental picture and remember the anger. You should feel yourself getting angry again just remembering it. Your fists are clenched very tightly now, and perhaps your blood pressure is rising. Open your eyes and start naming states – it helps even more if you do it alphabetically – Alabama, Alaska,

Arkansas ... This is putting your focus someplace other than your anger, distracting it.

These practices come from a young lady named Lisa Aragon, who figured these things out to better her own life. They worked for her, so now she wants to help others better their lives, too. Many of the things she preaches are low- or no-cost, although she also likes yoga and working out at the gym.

What do you need in your life? What would you say if you woke up and you had won the Publisher's Clearing House drawing, winning thousands of dollars? Money is important, but we let it consume us and base our happiness on it. But how much does it cost to enjoy the sunshine or go on a run? Many of the gifts we receive daily have no cost – sunshine, blue skies, clean air, loving family, good friends. We have free will – just because someone wants us to do something doesn't mean we have to do it. You make the decisions about your life. Only you can decide if you want to be happy and successful, and only you can get yourself there. Myself -- all I want is a smile and respect for myself on my worst days; practicing what I've been sharing with you has brought me to where I am very happy. The day you look in the mirror and don't have to convince yourself of your worth will be a good day. The day you quit the job you dread so much is a good day, because there will be plenty of opportunities.

I want to end by revisiting some of the exercises I've shared with you.

Sit down and put your feet straight out in front of you; try to touch your fingers to your toes. Don't strain or hurt yourself – it's okay if you can't quite reach. But stretch until you feel a bit of a sting.

You can do this same thing with most of your other chores. For example, you can text your friend and vacuum while waiting for a response. Start the laundry after you vacuum while you are texting your friend back. Don't be absorbed in just one task. Stay busy. Don't sit down and text your friend, because it might take your mind off what needs to be done. When you can balance keeping the mind busy when starting a task, and not think about the emotions behind it or the way it makes you feel, you can envision the reward for getting it out the way. Make a list of all the things you're putting off; see which ones can be done in tandem; this will take two chores off your list at one time, making things go much faster. Leave the list where you can see it, where it will taunt you if you try to ignore it.

Stay healthy. Eat three meals a day and get eight hours of sleep. Our physical health very much impacts our emotional health. It's all about balance.

There are twenty-four hours in a day and hypothetically speaking, you sleep for eight, work for eight, relax for two and do chores for the same amount of time. As for eating, you eat three meals and have two snacks, about one hour spread out through your day. Let's say it takes you fifteen minutes to eat each meal and about seven and a half minutes for each snack; a total of twenty-one hours, leaving you with three hours to spare and do as you please till your day is over.

When someone yells at you and you yell back, it doesn't get anyone anywhere – it's like throwing a basketball against a wall only to have it come back and hit you in the face. Why do that? It doesn't feel good. Neither does yelling back – and it's unproductive as well.

Pay attention to your environment, Make your lists and practice. Practice what works for you. I have been typing for the last six hours -- putting all my emotion in this. I want you to know one last time you are worth every minute of practice and every word of this. You are worth every smile and every chance. You can be someone else's inspiration without knowing it and make an impact on someone else. Look at the sky and feel the breeze. Change your life for yourself -- when you stop caring about what everyone else wants or expects from you and you are confident, staring your fears in the face, then you have conquered them. And people will notice.

CPSIA information can be obtained
at www.ICGtesting.com
Printed in the USA
BVHW092102180321
602886BV00004B/1004

9 781801 231282